THE
INTELLIGENT
OPTION
INVESTOR

THE INTELLIGENT OPTION INVESTOR

Applying Value Investing to the World of Options

ERIK KOBAYASHI-SOLOMON

Mc Graw Hill Education

New York   Chicago   San Francisco   Athens   London   Madrid   Mexico City
Milan   New Delhi   Singapore   Sydney   Toronto

1 2 3 4 5 6 7 8 9 0 DOC/DOC 1 2 0 9 8 7 6 5 4

ISBN: 978-0-07-183365-3
MHID: 0-07-183365-X

e-ISBN: 978-0-07-183366-0
e-MHID: 0-07-183366-8

Library of Congress Cataloging-in-Publication Data
Kobayashi-Solomon, Erik.
   The intelligent option investor : applying value investing to the world of options/ Erik Kobayashi-Solomon.
       pages cm
   ISBN 978-0-07-183365-3 (hardback)—ISBN 0-07-183365-X (hardback) 1. Options (Finance) 2. Investments. I. Title.
   HG6024.A3K63 2015
   332.64'53—dc23   2014016715

McGraw-Hill Education books are available at special quantity discounts to use as premiums and sales promotions or for use in corporate training programs. To contact a representative, please visit the Contact Us pages at www.mhprofessional.com.

To Fred Solomon

(1930–2013)

To my family and my "tribe"

CONTENTS

ACKNOWLEDGMENTS

Many thanks to all the people who have been part of the process during the writing of this book. I am indebted to three people in particular, Mr. Brent Farler, Mr. Ben Louviere, and Mr. Neil Kozarsky, who have graciously offered their time, help, and business expertise in bringing this project to fruition. Certainly this book would be much different and of not nearly the quality without Brent's guidance, thorough reading, and insightful, helpful suggestions, starting with the very first draft in late 2012.

In the literary world, I cannot say enough good things about Mr. Sam Fleishman, of Literary Arts Representatives, and Mr. Knox Huston and Ms. Daina Penikas, my editors at McGraw-Hill, all of whom have allowed this work to move from conception to completion and whose advice and support have made all the hard work worthwhile.

In the investment-management world, I am indebted to Mr. Steve Silverman, owner and portfolio manager of Ironbound Capital Management, who taught me important lessons about the business of investing and about how to critically assess the value of a company, and to Mr. Deepinder Bhatia, Founding Partner of Bayard Asset Management LLC, a true expert in the art and science of equity research and analysis.

In addition, I thank Mr. Rafael Garcia, of the International Financial Corporation; Mr. Joe Miramonti, of Fedora Investment Partners; Mr. Franco Dal Pont, of Batalha Capital Management; and Mr. Paul Neff, of the Federal Reserve Bank of Chicago, for the excellent discussions about valuation, option theory, and bringing the touchstone of valuation into the realm of option investments.

When I began work on this book, I did not realize just what an enormous process it would be. Truly, without the help and support of all the people mentioned here and all my friends and family around the world, I would have had a much more difficult time completing this work.

INTRODUCTION

You have a tremendous advantage over algorithmic trading models, investment bank trading desks, hedge funds, and anyone who appears on or pays attention to cable business news shows. This book is written to show where that advantage lies and how to exploit it to make confident and successful investment choices. In doing so, it explains how options work and what they can tell you about the market's estimation of the value of stocks.

Even if, after reading it, you decide to stick with straight stock investing and never make an option transaction, understanding how options work will give you a tremendous advantage as an investor. The reason for this is simple: by understanding options, you can understand what the rest of the market is expecting the future price of a stock to be. Understanding what future stock prices are implied by the market is like playing cards with an opponent who always leaves his or her hand face up on the table. You can look at the cards you are dealt, compare them with your opponent's, and play the round only when you are sure that you have the winning hand.

By incorporating options into your portfolio, you will enjoy an even greater advantage because of a peculiarity about how option prices are determined. Option prices are set by market participants making transactions, but those market participants all base their sale and purchase decisions on the same statistical models. These models are like sausage grinders. They contain no intelligence or insight but rather take in a few simple inputs, grind them up in a mechanical way, and spit out an option price of a specific form.

An option model does not, for instance, care about the operational details of a company. This oversight can lead to situations that seem to be too good to be true. For instance, I have seen a case in which an investor could commit to buy a strong, profitable company for less than the amount of cash it held—in effect, allowing the investor to pay $0.90 to receive a dollar plus a share of the company's future profits! Although it is true that these kinds of opportunities do not come along every day, they do indeed come along for patient, insightful investors.

This example lies at the heart of intelligent option investing, the essence of which can be expressed as a three-step process:

1. Understanding the value of a stock
2. Comparing that intelligently estimated value with the mechanically derived one implied by the option market
3. Tilting the risk-reward balance in one's favor by investing in the best opportunities using a combination of stocks and options

The goal of this book is to provide you with the knowledge you need to be an intelligent option investor from the standpoint of these three steps.

There is a lot of information contained within this book but also a lot of information left out. This is not meant to be an encyclopedia of option equations, a handbook of colorfully named option strategies, or a treatise on financial statement analysis. Unlike academic books covering options, such as Hull's excellent book,[1] not a single integration symbol or mathematical proof is found between this book's covers. Understanding how options are priced is an important step in being an intelligent option investor; doing differential partial equations or working out mathematical proofs is not.

Unlike option books written for professional practitioners, such as Natenberg's book,[2] you will not find explanations about complex strategies or graphs about how "the Greeks"[3] vary under different conditions. Floor traders need to know these things, but intelligent option investors—those making considered long-term investments in the financial outcomes of companies—have very different motivations, resources, and time horizons from floor traders. Intelligent option investors, it turns out, do better not even worrying about the great majority of things that floor traders must consider every day.

Unlike how-to books about day trading options, this book does not have one word to say about chart patterns, market timing, get-rich-quick schemes, or any of the many other delusions popular among people who will soon be paupers. Making good decisions is a vital part of being an intelligent option investor; frenetic, haphazard, and unconsidered trading is most certainly not.

Unlike books about securities analysis, you will not find detailed discussions about every line item on a financial statement. Understanding how a company creates value for its owners and how to measure that value is an important step in being an intelligent option investor; being able to rattle off information about arcane accounting conventions is not.

To paraphrase Warren Buffett,[4] this book aims to provide you with a sound intellectual framework for assessing the value of a company and making rational, fact-based decisions about how to invest in them with the help of the options market.

The book is split into three parts:

- Part I provides an explanation of what options are, how they are priced, and what they can tell you about what the market thinks the future price of a stock will be. This part corresponds to the second step of intelligent option investing listed earlier.
- Part II sets forth a model for determining the value of a company based on only a handful of drivers. It also discusses some of the behavioral and structural pitfalls that can and do affect investors' emotions and how to avoid them to become a better, more rational investor. This part corresponds to the first step of intelligent option investing listed earlier.
- Part III turns theory into practice—showing how to read the necessary information on an option pricing screen; teaching how to measure and manage leverage in a portfolio containing cash, stocks, and options; and going into detail about the handful of option strategies that an intelligent option investor needs to know to generate income, boost growth, and protect gains in an equity portfolio. This part corresponds to the final step of intelligent option investing listed earlier.

No part of this book assumes any prior knowledge about options or stock valuation. That said, it is not some sort of "Options for Beginners" or "My First Book of Valuation" treatment either.

Investing beginners will learn all the skills—soup to nuts—they need to successfully and confidently invest in the stock and options market. People who have some experience in options and who may have used covered calls, protective puts, and the like will find out how to greatly improve their results from these investments and how to use options in other ways as well. Professional money managers and analysts will develop a thorough understanding of how to effectively incorporate option investments into their portfolio strategies and may in fact be encouraged to consider questions about valuation and behavioral biases in a new light as well.

The approach used here to teach about valuation and options is unique, simple without being simpleminded, and extremely effective in communicating these complex topics in a memorable, vivid way. Readers used to seeing option books littered with hockey-stick diagrams and partial differential equations may have some unlearning to do, but no matter your starting point—whether you are a novice investor or a seasoned hedge fund manager—by the end of this book, I believe that you will look at equity investing in a new light.

Part I

OPTIONS FOR THE
INTELLIGENT INVESTOR

Don't believe anything you have heard or read about options.

If you listen to media stories, you will learn that options are modern financial innovations so complex that only someone with an advanced degree in mathematics can properly understand them.

Every contention in the preceding sentence is wrong.

If you listen to the pundits and traders blabbing on the cable business channels, you will think that you will never be successful using options unless you understand what "put backspreads," "iron condors," and countless other colorfully named option strategies are. You will also learn that options are short-term trading tools and that you'll have to be a razor-sharp "technical analyst" who can "read charts" and jump in and out of positions a few times a week (if not a few times a day) to do well.

Every contention in the preceding paragraph is so wrong that believing them is liable to send you to the poor house.

The truth is that options are simple, directional instruments that we understand perfectly well from countless encounters with them in our daily lives. They are the second-oldest financial instrument known to humanity—in a quite literal sense, modern economic life would not be possible without them. Options are instruments that not only can be used but *should* be used in long-term strategies; they most definitely should be traded in and out of as *infrequently* as possible.

The first part of this book will give you a good understanding of what options are, how their prices are determined, and how those prices fluctuate based on changes in market conditions.

There is a good reason to develop a solid understanding of this theoretical background: the framework the option market uses to determine the price of options is based on provably faulty premises that, while "approximately right" in certain circumstances, are laughably wrong in other circumstances. The faults can be exploited by intelligent, patient investors who understand which circumstances to avoid and which to seek out.

Without understanding the framework the market uses to value options and where that framework breaks down, there is no way to exploit the faults. Part I of this book, in a nutshell, is designed to give you an understanding of the framework the market uses to value options.

This book makes extensive use of diagrams to explain option theory, pricing, and investment strategies. Those readers of the printed copy of this book are encouraged to visit the Intelligent Option Investor website (www .IntelligentOptionInvestor.com) to see the full-color versions of the type of illustrations listed here. Doing so will allow you to visualize options even more effectively in the distinctive intelligent option investing way.

Chapter 1

OPTION FUNDAMENTALS

This chapter introduces what an option is and how to visualize options in an intelligent way while hinting at the great flexibility and power a sensible use of options gives an investor. It is split into three sections:

1. Option Overview: Characteristics, everyday options, and a brief option history.
2. Option Directionality: An investigation of similarities and differences between stocks and options. This section also contains an introduction to the unique way that this book visualizes options and to the inescapable jargon used in the options world and a bit of intelligent option investor–specific jargon as well.
3. Option Flexibility: An explanation of why options are much more investor-friendly than stocks, as well as examples of the handful of strategies an intelligent option investor uses most often.

Even those of you who know something about options should at the very least read the last section. You will find that the intelligent option investor makes very close to zero use of the typical hockey-stick diagrams shown in other books. Instead, this book uses the concept of a *range of exposure*. The rest of the book—discussing option pricing, corporate valuation, and option strategies—builds on this range-of-exposure concept, so skipping it is likely to lead to confusion later.

This chapter is an important first step in being an intelligent option investor. Someone who knows how options work does not qualify as being an intelligent option investor, but certainly, one cannot become an intelligent option investor without understanding these basic facts. The concepts discussed here will be covered in greater detail and depth later in this book. For now, it is enough to get a sense for what options are, how to think about them, and why they might be useful investment tools.

Characteristics and History

By the end of this section, you should know the four key characteristics of options, be able to name a few options that are common in our daily lives, and understand a bit about the long history of options as a financial product and how modern option markets operate.

Jargon introduced in this section is as follows:

Black-Scholes-Merton model (BSM)
Listed look-alike
Central counterparty

Characteristics of Options

Rather than giving a definition for options, I'll list the four most important characteristics that all options share and provide a few common examples. Once you understand the basic characteristics of options, have seen a few examples, and have spent some time thinking about them, you will start to see elements of *optionality* in nearly every situation in life.

An *option*

1. Is a contractual right
2. Is in force for a specified time
3. Allows an investor to profit from the change in value of another asset
4. Has value as long as it is still in force

This definition is broad enough that it applies to all sorts of options— those traded on a public exchange such as the Chicago Board Options Exchange and those familiar to us in our daily lives.

Options in Daily Life

The type of option with which people living in developed economies are most familiar is an insurance contract. Let's say that you want to fully insure your $30,000 car. You sign a contract (option characteristic number 1) with your insurance company that covers you for a specified amount of time (option characteristic number 2)—let's say one year. If during the coverage period your car is totaled, your insurance company buys your wreck of a car (worth $0 or close to it) for $30,000—allowing you to buy an identical car. When this happens, you as the car owner (or investor in a real asset) realize a profit of $30,000 over the market value of your destroyed car (option characteristic number 3). Obviously, the insurance company is bound to uphold its promise to indemnify you from loss for the entire term of the contract; the fact that you have a right to sell a worthless car to your insurance company for the price you paid for it implies that the insurance has value during its entire term (option characteristic number 4).

Another type of option, while perhaps not as widely used by everyday folks, is easily recognizable. Imagine that you are a struggling author who has just penned your first novel. The novel was not a great seller, but one day you get a call from a movie producer offering you $50,000 for the right to draft a screenplay based on your work. This payment will grant the producer exclusive right (option characteristic number 1) to turn the novel into a movie, as well as the right to all proceeds from a potential future movie for a specific period of time (option characteristic number 2)—let's say 10 years. After that period is up, you as the author are free to renegotiate another contract. As a struggling artist working in an unfulfilling day job, you happily agree to the deal. Three weeks later, a popular daytime talk show host features your novel on her show, and suddenly, you have a *New York Times* bestseller on your hands. The value of your literary work has gone from slight to great in a single week. Now the movie producer hires the Cohen brothers to adapt your film to the screen and hires George Clooney, Matt Damon, and Julia Roberts to star in the movie. When it is released, the film breaks records at the box office. How much does the producer pay to you? Nothing. The producer had a contractual right to profit from the screenplay based on your work. When the producer bought this right, your literary work was not worth much; suddenly, it is worth a great deal, and the producer owns the upside potential from the increase in value of your story (option characteristic number 3). Again, it is obvious that the right to the literary work has value for the entire term of the contract (option characteristic number 4).

Keep these characteristics in mind, and we will go on to look at how these defining elements are expressed in financial markets later in this chapter. Now that you have an idea of what an option looks like, let's turn briefly to a short history of these financial instruments.

A Brief History of Options

Many people believe that options are a new financial invention, but in fact, they have been in use for more than two millennia—one of the first historically attested uses of options was by a pre-Socratic philosopher named Miletus, who lived in ancient Greece. Miletus the philosopher was accused of being useless by his fellow citizens because he spent his time considering philosophical matters (which at the time included a study of natural phenomena as well) rather than putting his nose to the grindstone and weaving fishing nets or some such thing.

Miletus told them that his knowledge was in fact not useless and that he could apply it to something people cared about, but he simply chose not to. As proof of his contention, when his studies related to weather revealed to him that the area would enjoy a bumper crop of olives in the upcoming season, he went around to the owners of all the olive presses and paid them a fee to reserve the presses (i.e., he entered into a contractual agreement—option characteristic number 1) through harvest time (i.e., the contract had a prespecified life—option characteristic number 2).

Indeed, Miletus's prediction was correct, and the following season yielded a bumper crop of olives. The price of olives must have fallen because of the huge surge of supply, and demand for olive presses skyrocketed (because turning the olive fruit into oil allowed the produce to be stored longer). Because Miletus had cornered the olive press market, he was able to generate huge profits, turning the low-value olives into high-value oil (i.e., he profited from the change in value of an underlying asset—option characteristic number 3). His rights to the olive presses ended after the harvest but not before he had become very wealthy thanks to his philosophical studies (i.e., his contractual rights had value through expiration—option characteristic number 4).

This is only one example of an ancient option transaction (a few thousand years before the first primitive common stock came into existence), but as long as there has been insurance, option contracts have been a well-understood and widely used financial instrument. Can you imagine how little cross-border trade would occur if sellers and buyers could not shift the risk of transporting goods to a third party such as an insurance company? How many ships would have set out for the Spice Islands during the Age of Exploration, for instance? Indeed, it is hard to imagine what trade would look like today if buyers and sellers did not have some way to mitigate the risks associated with uncertain investments.

For hundreds of years, options existed as private contracts specifying rights to an economic exposure of a certain quantity of a certain good over a given time period. Frequently, these contracts were sealed between the producers and sellers of a commodity product and wholesale buyers of that commodity. Both sides had an existing exposure to the commodity (the producer wanted to sell the commodity, and the wholesaler wanted to buy it), and both sides wanted to insure themselves against interim price movements in the underlying commodity.

But there was a problem with this system. Let's say that you were a Renaissance merchant who wanted to insure your shipment of spice from India to Europe, and so you entered into an agreement with an insurer. The insurer asked you to pay a certain amount of premium up front in return for guaranteeing the value of your cargo. Your shipment leaves Goa but is lost off Madagascar, and all your investment capital goes down with the ship to the bottom of the Indian Ocean. However, when you try to find your option counterparty—your insurer—it seems that he has absconded with your premium money and is living a life of pleasure and song in another country. In the parlance of modern financial markets, your option investment failed because of *counterparty risk*.

Private contracts still exist today in commodity markets as well as the stock market (the *listed look-alike option market*—private contracts specifying the right to upside and downside exposure to single stocks, exchange-traded funds, and baskets is one example that institutional investors use heavily). However, private contracts still bring with them a risk of default by one's counterparty, so they are usually only entered into after both parties have fully assessed the creditworthiness of the other. Obviously, individual investors—who might simply want to speculate on the value of an underlying stock or exchange-traded fund (ETF)—cannot spend the time doing a credit check on every counterparty with whom they might do business.[1] Without a way to make sure that both parties are financially able to keep up their half of the option bargain, public option markets simply could not exist.

The modern solution to this quandary is that of the *central counterparty*. This is an organization that standardizes the terms of the option contracts transacted and ensures the financial fulfillment of the participating counterparties. Central counterparties are associated with securities exchanges and regulate the parties with which they deal. They set rules regarding collateral that must be placed in escrow before a transaction can be made and request additional funds if market price changes cause a counterparty's account to become undercollateralized. In the United States, the central counterparty for options transactions is the Options Clearing Corporation (OCC). The OCC is an offshoot of the oldest option exchange, the Chicago Board Option Exchange (CBOE).

In the early 1970s, the CBOE itself began as an offshoot of a large futures exchange—the Chicago Mercantile Exchange—and subsequently started the process of standardizing option contracts (i.e., specifying the exact per-contract quantity and quality of the underlying good and the expiration date of the contract) and building the other infrastructure and regulatory framework necessary to create and manage a public market. Although market infrastructure and mechanics are very important for the brokers and other professional participants in the options market, most aspects are not terribly important from an investor's point of view (the things that are—such as margin—will be discussed in detail later in this book). The one thing an investor must know is simply that the option market is transparent, well regulated, and secure. Those of you who have a bit of extra time and want to learn more about market mechanics should take a look through the information on the CBOE's and OCC's websites.

Listing of option contracts on the CBOE meant that investors needed to have a sense for what a fair price for an option was. Three academics, Fischer Black, Myron Scholes, and Robert Merton, were responsible for developing and refining an option pricing model known as the *Black-Scholes* or *Black-Scholes-Merton model*, which I will hereafter abbreviate as the BSM.

The BSM is a testament to human ingenuity and theoretical elegance, and even though new methods and refinements have been developed since its introduction, the underlying assumptions for new option pricing methods are the same as the BSM. In fact, throughout this book, when you see "BSM," think "any statistically based algorithm for determining option prices."

The point of all this background information is that options are not only not new-fangled financial instruments but in fact have a long and proud history that is deeply intertwined with the development of modern economies themselves. Those of you interested in a much more thorough coverage of the history of options would do well to read the book, *Against the Gods: The Remarkable History of Risk*, by Peter Bernstein (New York: Wiley, 1998).

Now that you have a good sense of what options are and how they are used in everyday life, let's now turn to the single most important thing for a fundamental investor to appreciate about these financial instruments: their inherent ability to exploit directionality.

Directionality

The key takeaway from this section is evident from the title. In addition to demonstrating the directional power inherent in options, this section also introduces the graphic tools that I will use throughout the rest of this book to show the risk and reward inherent in any investment—whether it is an investment in a stock or an option.

For those of you who are not well versed in options yet, this is the section in which I explain most of the jargon that you simply cannot escape when transacting in options. However, even readers who are familiar with options should at least skim through this explanation. Doing so will likely increase your appreciation for the characteristics of options that make them such powerful investment tools and also will introduce you to this novel way of visualizing them.

Jargon introduced in this section is as follows:

Call option	Moneyness
Put option	In the money (ITM)
Range of exposure	At the money (ATM)
Strike price	Out of the money (OTM)
Gain exposure	Premium
Accept exposure	American style
Canceling exposure	European style
Exercise (an option)	

Visual Representation of a Stock

Visually, a good stock investment looks like this:

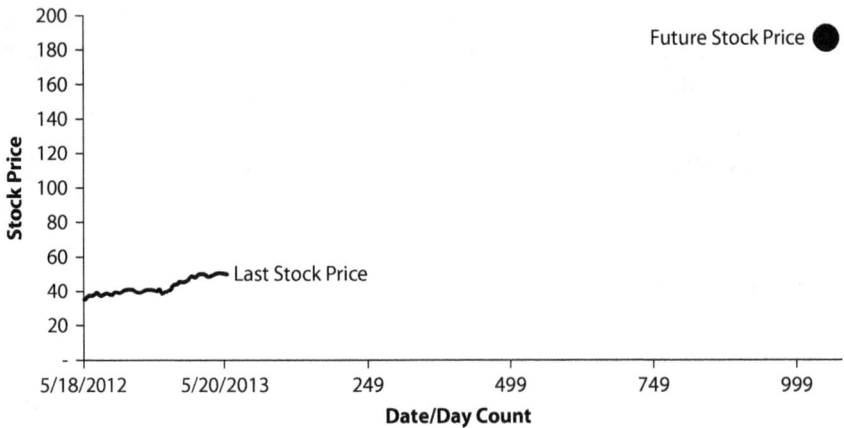

You can make a lot of mistakes when investing, but as long as you are right about the ultimate direction a stock will take and act accordingly, all those mistakes will be dwarfed by the success of your position.

Good investing, then, is essentially a process of recognizing and exploiting the directionality of mispriced stocks. Usually, investors get exposure to a stock's directionality by buying, or *going long*, that stock. This is what the investor's risk and reward profile looks like when he or she buys the stock:

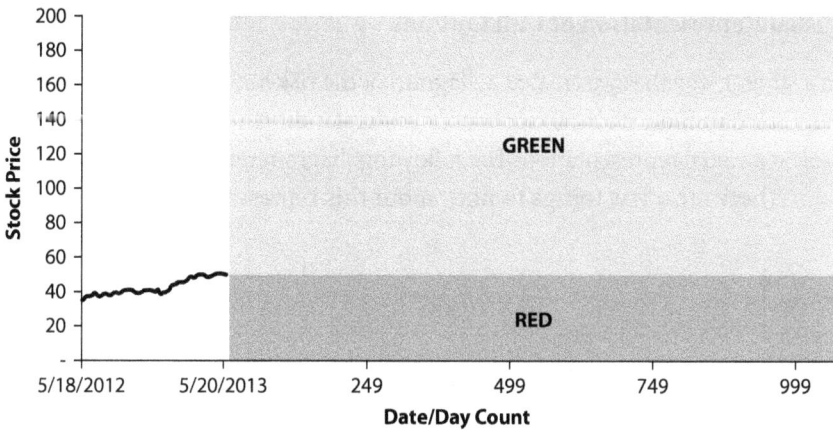

As soon as the "Buy" button is pushed, the investor gains exposure to the upside potential of the stock—this is the shaded region labeled "green" in the figure. However, at the same time, the investor also must accept exposure to downside risk—this is the shaded region labeled "red."

Anyone who has invested in stocks has a visceral understanding of stock directionality. We all know the joy of being right as our investment soars into the green and we've all felt the sting as an investment we own falls into the red. We also know that to the extent that we want to gain exposure to the upside potential of a stock, we must necessarily simultaneously accept its downside risk.

Options, like stocks, are directional instruments that come in two types. These two types can be defined in directional terms:

Call option   A security that allows an investor exposure to a stock's upside potential (remember, "Call up")

Put option   A security that allows an investor exposure to a stock's downside potential (remember, "Put down")

The fact that options split the directionality of stocks in half—up and down—is a great advantage to an investor that we will investigate more in a moment.

Right now, let's take a look at each of these directional instruments—call options and put options—one by one.

Visual Representation of Call Options

In a similar way that we created a diagram of the risk-reward profile of ownership in a common stock, a nice way of understanding how options work is to look at a visual representation. The following diagram represents a call option.

There are a few things to note about this representation:

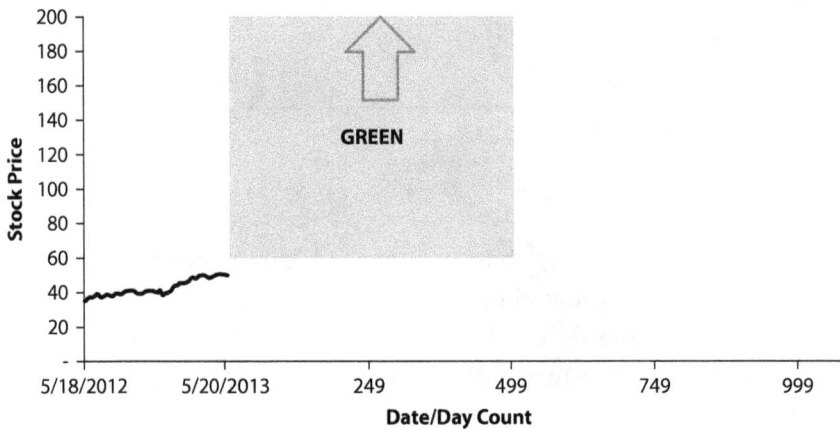

1. The shaded area (green) represents the price and time range over which the investor has economic exposure—I term this the *range of exposure*. Because we are talking about call options, and because call options deal with the upside potential of a stock, you see that the range of exposure lies higher than the present stock price (remember, "Call up").
2. True to one of the defining characteristics of an option mentioned earlier, our range of exposure is limited by time; the option pictured in the preceding figure expires 500 days in the future, after which we have no economic exposure to the stock's upside potential.
3. The present stock price is $50 per share, but our upside exposure only begins at $60 per share. The price at which economic exposure begins is called the *strike price* of an option. In this case, the strike price is $60 per share, but we could have picked a strike price at the market price of the stock, further above the market price of the stock (e.g., a strike price of $75), or even below the market price of the stock. We will investigate optimal strike prices for certain option strategies later in this book.

4. The arrow at the top of the shaded region in the figure indicates that our exposure extends infinitely upward. If, for some reason, this stock suddenly jumped not from $50 to $60 per share but from $50 to $1,234 per share, we would have profitable exposure to all that upside.
5. Clearly, the diagram showing a purchased call option looks a great deal like the top of the diagram for a purchased stock. Look back at the top of the stock purchase figure and compare it with the preceding figure: the inherent directionality of options should be completely obvious.

Any time you see a green region on diagrams like this, you should take it to mean that an investor has the potential to realize a gain on the investment and that the investor has *gained exposure.* Any time an option investor gains exposure, he or she must pay up front for that potential gain. The money one pays up front for an option is called *premium* (just like the fee you pay for insurance coverage).

In the preceding diagram, then, we have gained exposure to a range of the stock's upside potential by buying a call option (also known as a *long call*). If the stock moves into this range before or at option expiration, we have the right to buy the stock at our $60 strike price (this is termed *exercising an option*) or simply sell the option in the option market. It is almost always the wrong thing to exercise an option for reasons we discuss shortly.[2]

If, instead, the stock is trading below our strike price at expiration, the option is obviously worthless—we owned the right to an upside scenario that did not materialize, so our ownership right is worth nothing.

It turns out that there is special jargon that is used to describe the relationship between the stock price and the range of option exposure:

Jargon	Situation
In the money (ITM)	Stock price is within the option's range of exposure
Out of the money (OTM)	Stock price is outside the option's range of exposure
At the money (ATM)	Stock price is just at the border of the option's range of exposure

Each of these situations is said to describe the *moneyness* of the option. Graphically, moneyness can be represented by the following diagram:

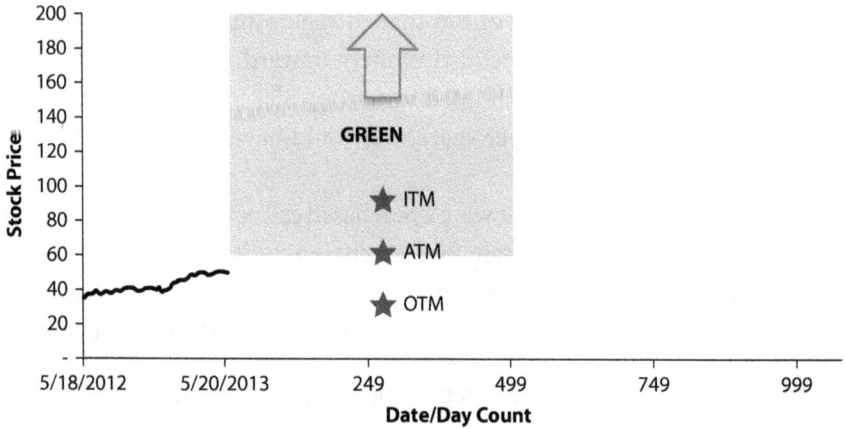

As we will discuss in greater detail later, not only can an investor use options to gain exposure to a stock, but the investor also can choose to accept exposure to it. Accepting exposure means running the risk of a financial loss if the stock moves into an option's range of exposure. If we were to accept exposure to the stock's upside potential, we would graphically represent it like this:

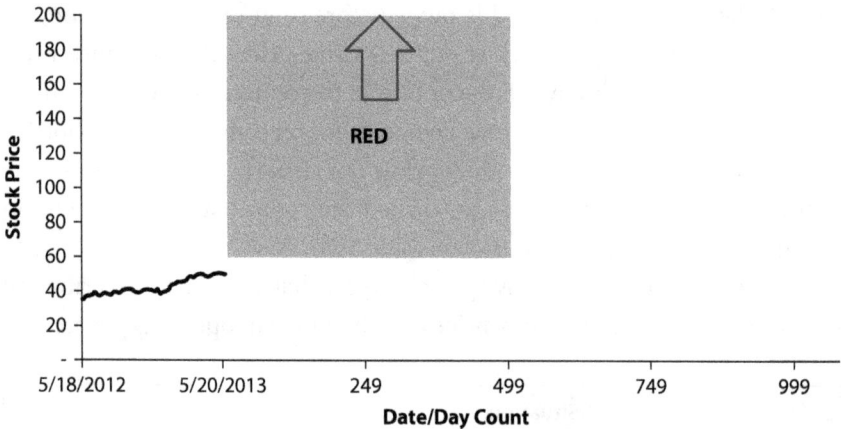

Any time you see a shaded region labeled "red" on diagrams like this, you should take it to mean that the investor has accepted the risk of realizing a loss on the investment and should say that the investor has *accepted exposure*. Any time an option investor accepts exposure, he or she gets to receive premium up front in return for accepting the risk. In the preceding example, the investor has accepted upside exposure by selling a call option (a.k.a. a *short call*).

In this sold call example, we again see the shaded area representing the exposure range. We also see that the exposure is limited to 500 days and that it starts at the $60 strike price. The big difference we see between this diagram and the one before it is that when we gained upside exposure by buying a call, we had potentially profitable exposure infinitely upward; in the case of a short call, we are accepting the possibility of an infinite *loss*. Needless to say, the decision to accept such risk should not be taken lightly. We will discuss in what circumstances an investor might want to accept this type of risk and what techniques might be used to manage that risk later in this book. For right now, think of this diagram as part of an explanation of how options work, not why someone might want to use this particular strategy.

Let's go back to the example of a long call because it's easier for most people to think of call options this way. Recall that you must pay a premium if you want to gain exposure to a stock's directional potential. In the diagrams, you will mark the amount of premium you have to pay as a straight line, as can be seen here:

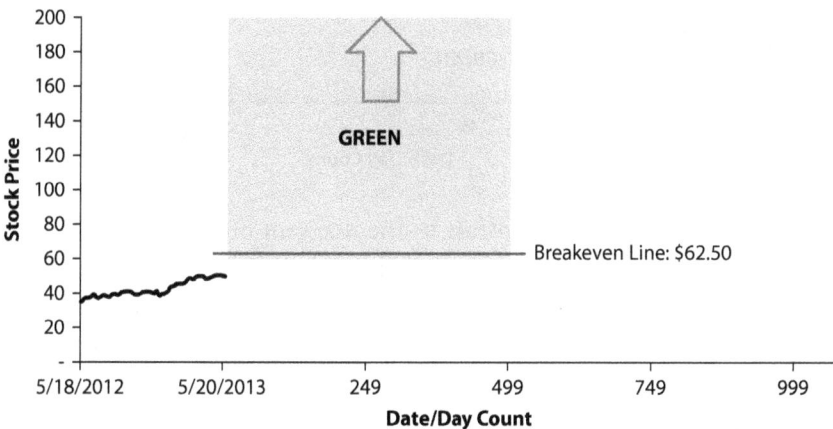

I have labeled the straight line the "Breakeven line" for now and have assumed that the option's premium totals $2.50.

You can think of the breakeven line as a hurdle the stock must cross by expiration time. If, at expiration, the stock is trading for $61, you have the right to purchase the shares for $60. You make a $1 profit on this transaction, which partially offsets the original $2.50 cost of the option.

It is important to note that a stock does not have to cross this line for your option investment to be profitable. We will discuss this dynamic in Chapter 2 when we learn more about the time value of options.

Visual Representation of Put Options

Now that you understand the conventions we use for our diagrams, let's think about how we might represent the other type of option, dealing with downside exposure—the put. First, let's assume that we want to gain exposure to the downside potential of a stock. Graphically, we would represent this in the following way:

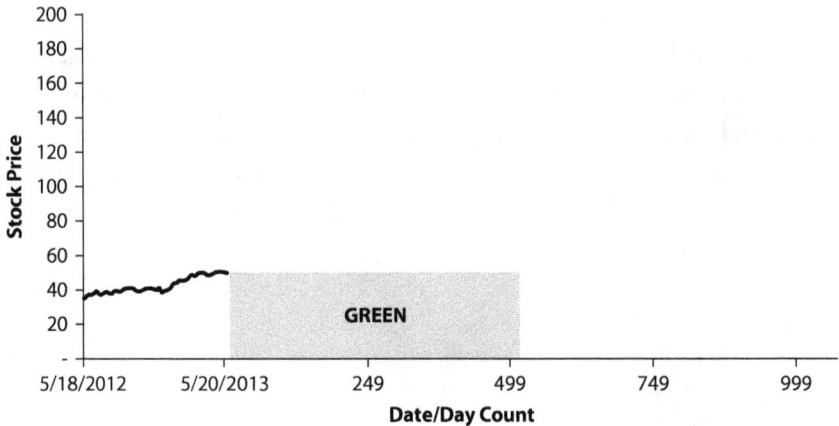

First, notice that, in contrast to the diagram of the call option, the directional exposure of a put option is bounded on the downside by $0, so we do not draw an arrow indicating infinite exposure. This is the same downside exposure of a stock because a stock cannot fall below zero dollars per share.

In this diagram, the time range for the put option is the same 500 days as for our call option, but the price range at which we have exposure starts at a strike price of $50—the current market price of the stock—making this an at-the-money (ATM) put. If you think about moneyness in terms of a range of exposure, the difference between out of the money (OTM) and in the money (ITM) becomes easy and sensible. Here are examples of different moneyness cases for put options:

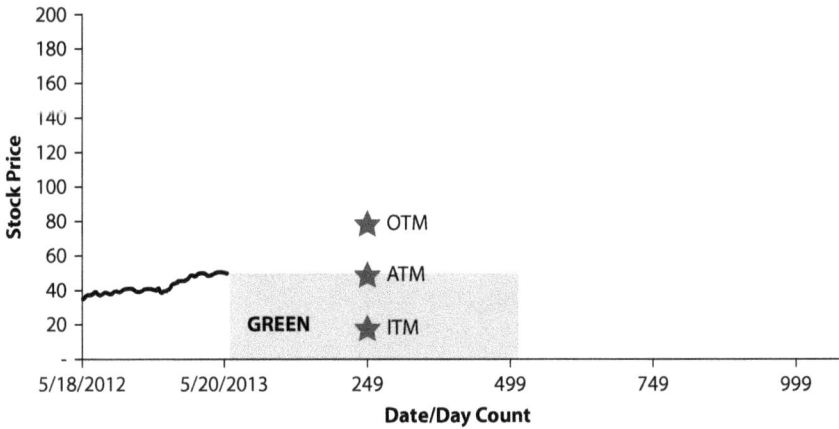

We are assuming that this put option costs $5, leading to a breakeven line of $45. This breakeven line is like an upside-down hurdle in that we would like the stock to finish below $45; if it expires below $50 but above $45, again, we will be able to profit from the exercise, but this profit will not be great enough to cover the cost of the option.

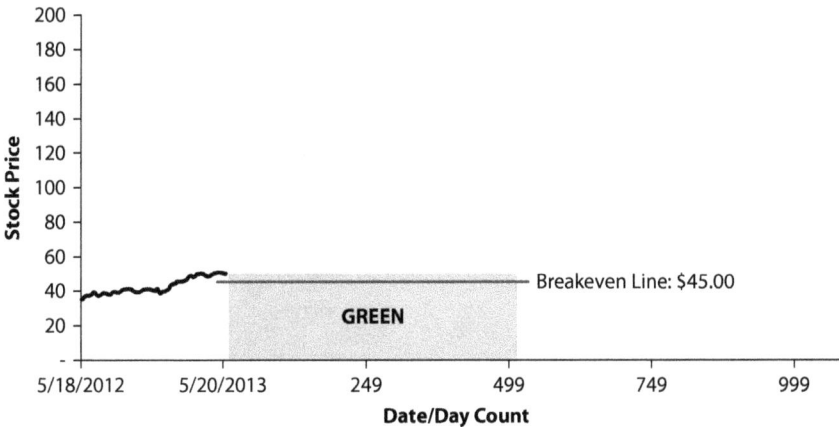

Obviously, if we can gain downside exposure to a stock, we must be able to accept it as well. We can accept downside exposure by selling a put; this book represents a sold put graphically like this:

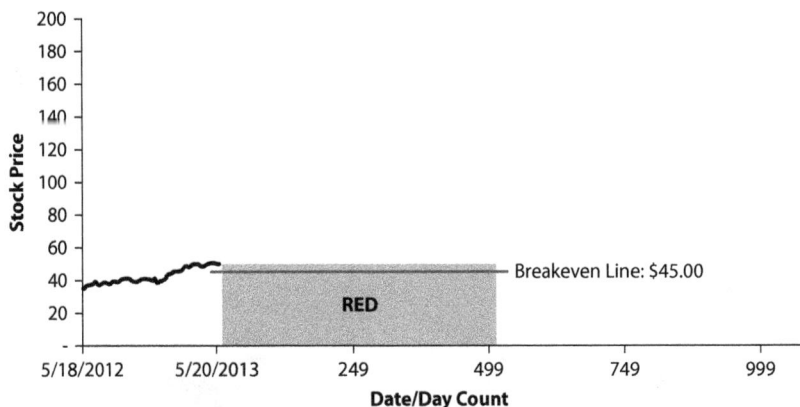

In this diagram, we are receiving a $5 premium payment in return for accepting exposure to the stock's downside. As such, as long as the stock expires above $45, we will realize a profit on this investment.

Visual Representation of Options Canceling Exposure

Let's take a look again at our visual representation of the risk and reward of a stock:

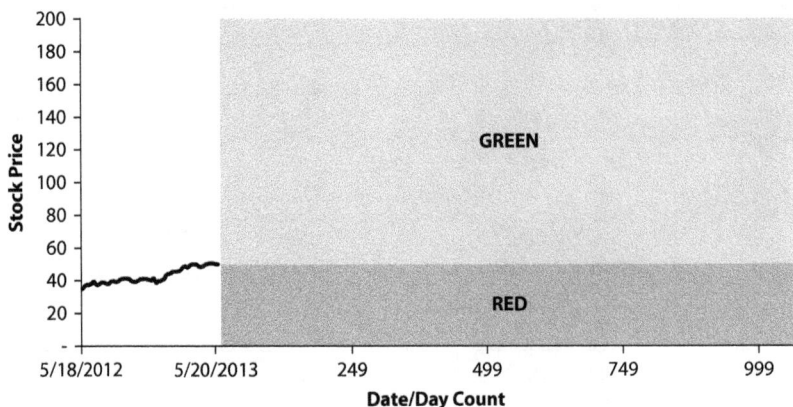

We bought this stock at $50 per share and will experience an unrealized gain if the stock goes up and an unrealized loss if it goes down. What might happen if we were to simultaneously buy a put, expiring in 365 days and struck at $50, on the same stock?

Because we are purchasing a put, we know that we are gaining exposure to the downside. Any time we gain exposure, we shade the exposure in green. Let's overlay this gain of downside exposure on the preceding risk-return diagram and see what we get.

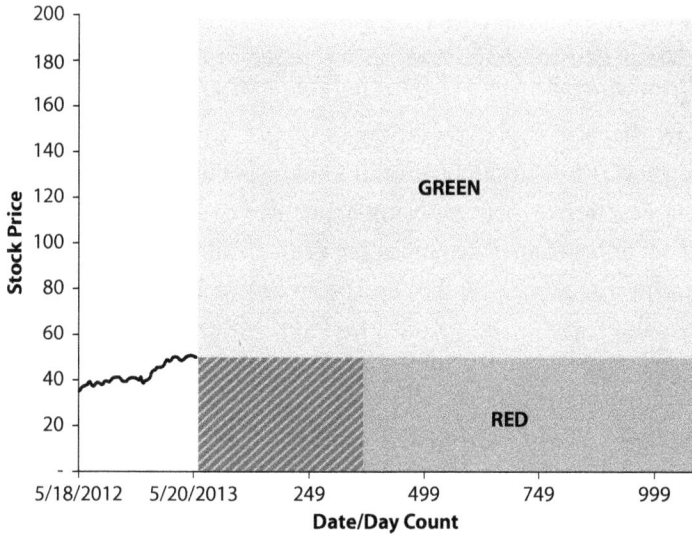

The region representing the downside exposure we gained by buying the put perfectly overlaps part of the region representing the downside exposure we accepted when we bought the stock. When there is a region such as this, where we are simultaneously gaining and accepting exposure, the two *exposures cancel out*, creating no economic exposure whatsoever.

From here on out, to show a canceling of economic exposure, we will shade the region in gray, like the following:

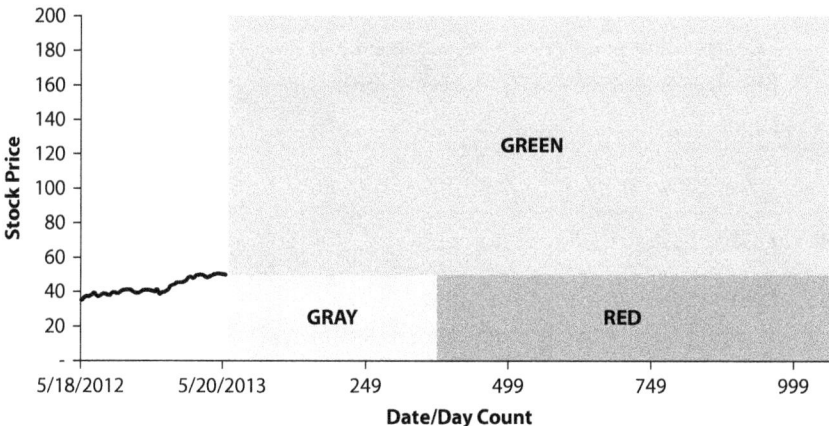

Any time a gain of exposure overlaps another gain of exposure, the potential gain from an investment if the stock price moves into that region rises. We will not represent this in the diagrams of this book, but you can think of overlapping gains as deeper and deeper shades of green (when gaining exposure) and deeper and deeper shades of red (when accepting it).

Now that you understand how to graphically represent gaining and accepting exposure to both upside and downside directionality and how to represent situations when opposing exposures overlap, we can move onto the next section, which introduces the great flexibility options grant to an investor and discusses how that flexibility can be used as a force of either good or evil.

Flexibility

Again, the main takeaway of this section should be obvious from the title. Here we will see the only two choices stock investors have with regard to risk and return, and we will contrast that with the great flexibility an option investor has. We will also discuss the concept of an effective buy price and an effective sell price—two bits of intelligent option investor jargon. Last, we will look at a typical option strategy that might be recommended by an option "guru" and note that these types of strategies actually are at cross-purposes with the directional nature of options that makes them so powerful in the first place.

Jargon introduced in this chapter is as follows:

Effective buy price (EBP)	Covered call
Effective sell price (ESP)	Long strangle
Leg	

Stocks Give Investors Few Choices

A stock investor only has two choices when it comes to investing: going long or going short. Using our visualization technique, those two choices look like this:

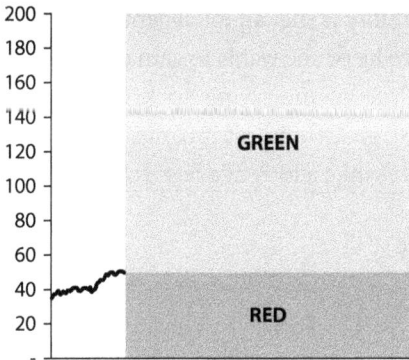

Going long a stock (i.e., buying a stock).

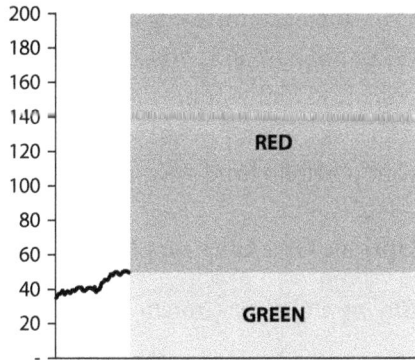

Going short a stock (i.e., short selling a stock).

If you want to gain exposure to a stock's upside potential by going long (left-hand diagram), you also must simultaneously accept exposure to the stock's downside risk. Similarly, if you want to gain exposure to a stock's downside potential by going short (right-hand diagram), you also must accept exposure to the stock's upside risk.

In contrast, option investors are completely unrestrained in their ability to choose what directionality to accept or gain. An option investor could, for example, very easily decide to establish exposure to the directionality of a stock in the following way:

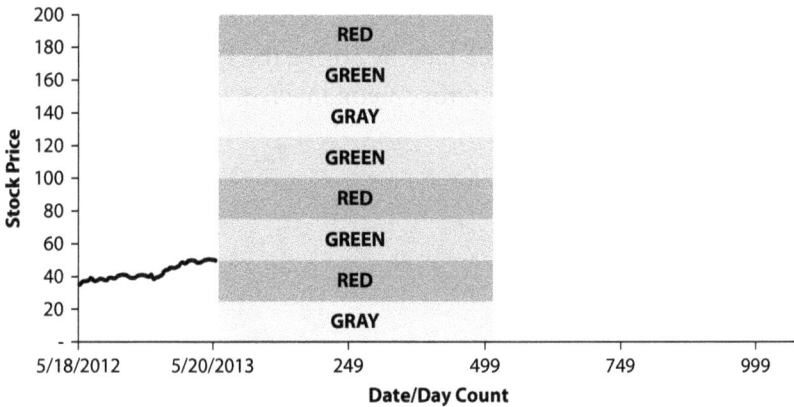

Why an investor would want to do something like this is completely beyond me, but the point is that options are flexible enough to allow this type of a crazy structure to be built.

The beautiful thing about this flexibility is that an intelligent option investor can pick and choose what exposure he or she wants to gain or accept in order to tailor his or her risk-return profile to an underlying stock. By tailoring your risk-return profile, you can increase growth, boost income, and insure your portfolio from downside shocks. Let's take a look at a few examples.

Options Give Investors Many Choices

Buying a Call for Growth

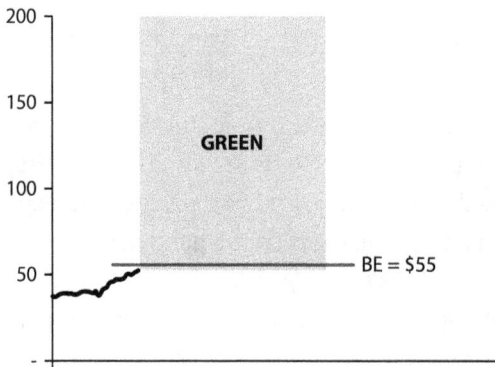

Above an investor is bullish on the prospects of the stock and is using a call option to gain exposure to a stock's upside potential above $50 per share. Rather than accepting exposure to the stock's entire downside potential (maximum of a $50 loss) as he or she would have by buying the stock outright, the call-option investor would pay an upfront premium of, in this case, $5.

Selling a Put for Income

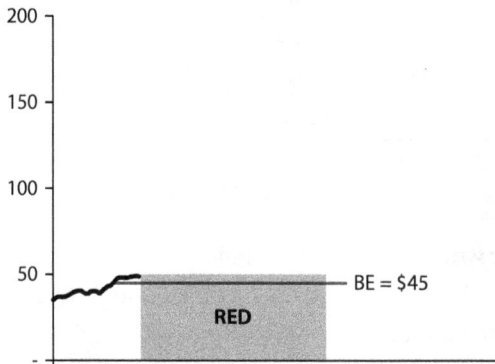

Here an investor is bullish on the prospects of the stock, so he or she doesn't mind accepting exposure to the stock's downside risk below $50. In return for accepting this risk, the option investor receives a premium—let's say $5. This $5 is income to the investor—kind of like a do-it-yourself dividend payment.

By the way, as you will discover later in this book, this is also the risk-return profile of a *covered call*.

Buying a Put for Protection

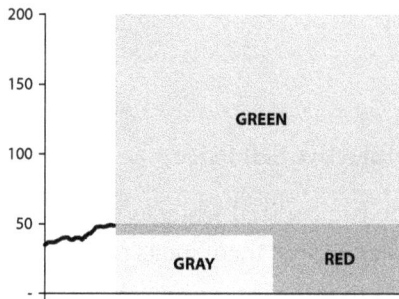

Above an investor wants to enjoy exposure to the stock's upside potential while limiting his or her losses in case of a market fall. By buying a put option struck a few dollars under the market price of the stock, the investor cancels out the downside exposure he or she accepted when buying the stock. With this protective put *overlay* in place, any loss on the stock will be compensated for through a gain on the put contract. The investor can use these gains to buy more of the stock at a lower price or to buy another put contract as protection when the first contract expires.

Tailoring Exposure with Puts and Calls

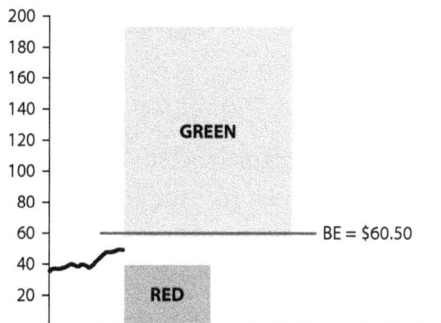

Here an investor is bullish on the prospects of the stock and is tailoring where to gain and accept exposure by selling a short-term put and simultaneously buying a longer-term call. By doing this, the investor basically subsidizes the purchase of the call option with the sale of the put option, thereby reducing the level the stock needs to exceed on the upside before one breaks even. In this case, we're assuming that the call option costs $1.50 and the put option trades for $1.00. The cash inflow from the put option partially offsets the cash outflow from the call option, so the total breakeven amount is just the call's $60 strike price plus the net of $0.50.

Effective Buy Price/Effective Sell Price

One thing that I hope you realized while looking at each of the preceding diagrams is how similar each of them looks to a particular part of our long and short stock diagrams:

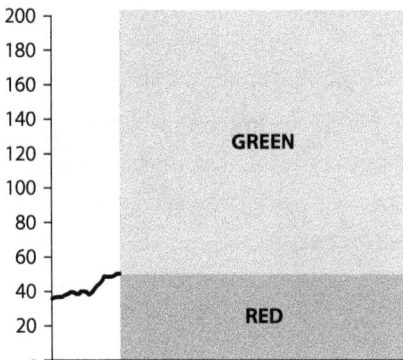

Buying a stock.　　　　Short selling a stock.

For example, doesn't the diagram labeled "Buying a call for growth" in the preceding section look just like the top part of the buying stock diagram?

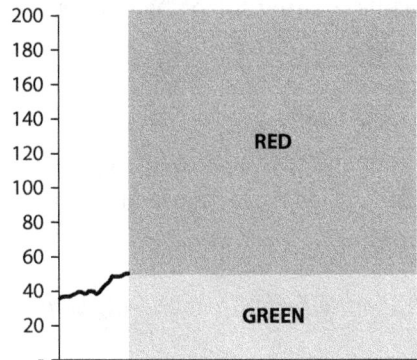

In fact, many of the option strategies I will introduce in this book simply represent a carving up of the risk-reward profile of a long or short stock position and isolating one piece of it. To make it more clear and easy to remember the rules for breaking even on different strategies, I will actually use a different nomenclature from *breakeven*.

If a diagram has one or both of the elements of the risk-return profile of buying a stock, I will call the breakeven line the *effective buy price* and abbreviate it *EBP*. For example, if we sell a put option, we accept downside risk in the same way that we do when we buy a stock:

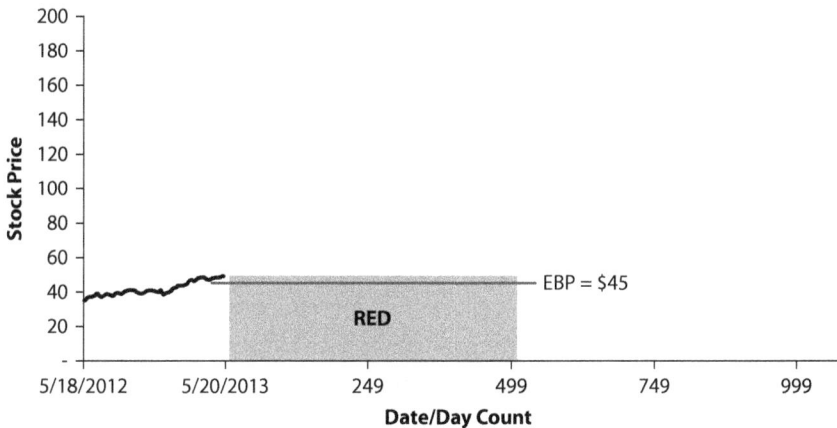

Basically, what we are saying when we accept downside risk is that we are willing to buy the stock if it goes below the strike price. In return for accepting this risk, we are paid $5 in premium, and this cash inflow effectively lowers the buying price at which we own the stock. If, when the option expires, the stock is trading at $47, we can think of the situation not as "being $3 less than the strike price" but rather as "being $2 over the buy price."

Conversely, if a diagram has one or both of the elements of the risk-return profile of short selling a stock, I will call the breakeven line the *effective sell price* and abbreviate it *ESP*. For example, if we buy a put option anticipating a fall in the stock, we would represent it graphically like this:

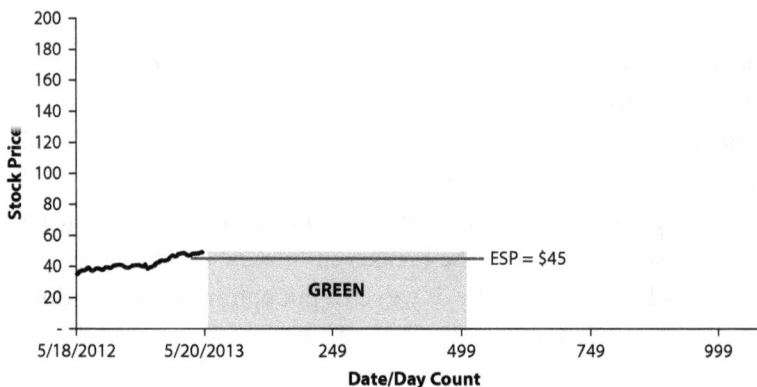

When a short seller sells a stock, he or she gets immediate profit exposure to the stock's downside potential. The seller is selling at $50 and hopes to make a profit by buying the shares back later at a lower price—let's say $35. When we get profit exposure to a stock's downside potential using options, we are getting the same exposure as if we sold the stock at $50, except that we do not have to worry about losing our shirts if the stock moves up instead of down. In order to get this peace of mind, though, we must spend $5 in premium. This means that if we hold the position to expiration, we will only realize a net profit if the stock is trading at the $50 mark less the money we have already paid to buy that exposure—$5 in this case. As such, we are effectively selling the stock short at $45.

There are some option strategies that end up not looking like one of the two stock positions—the flexibility of options allows an investor to do things a stock investor cannot. For example, here is the graphic representation of a strategy commonly called a *long strangle*:

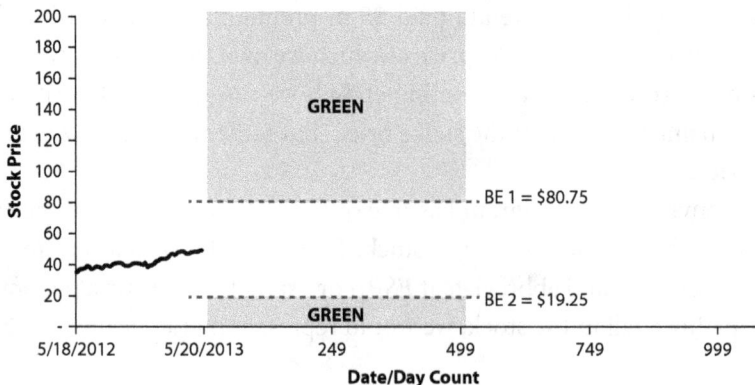

Here we have a stock trading at $50 per share, and we have bought one put option and one call option. The put option is struck at $20 and is trading for $0.35. The call option is struck at $80 and is trading for $0.40. Note that the top part of the diagram looks like the top part of the long-stock diagram and that the bottom part looks like the bottom part of the short-stock diagram. Because a stock investor cannot be simultaneously long and short the same stock, we cannot use such terminology as *effective buy* or *effective sell* price. In this case, we use *breakeven* and abbreviate it *BE*.

This option strategy illustrates one way in which options are much more flexible than stocks because it allows us to profit if the stock moves up (into the call's range of exposure) or down (into the put's range of exposure). If the stock moves up quickly, the call option will be *in the money*, but the put option will be far, far, far *out of the money*. Thus, if we are ITM on the call, the premium paid on the puts probably will end up a total loss, and vice versa. For this reason, we calculate both breakeven prices as the sum of both *legs* of our option structure (where a leg is defined as a single option in a multioption strategy). As long as the leg that winds up ITM is ITM enough to cover the cost of the other leg, we will make a profit on this investment. The only way we can fail to make a profit is if the stock does not move one way or another enough before the options expire.

Flexibility without Directionality Is a Sucker's Game

Despite this great flexibility in determining what directional investments one wishes to make, as I mentioned earlier, option market makers and floor traders generally attempt to mostly (in the case of floor traders) or wholly (in the case of market makers) insulate themselves against large moves in the underlying stock or figure out how to limit the cost of the exposure they are gaining and do so to such an extent that they severely curtail their ability to profit from large moves. I do not want to belabor the point, but I do want to leave you with one graphic illustration of a "typical" complex option strategy sometimes called a *condor*:

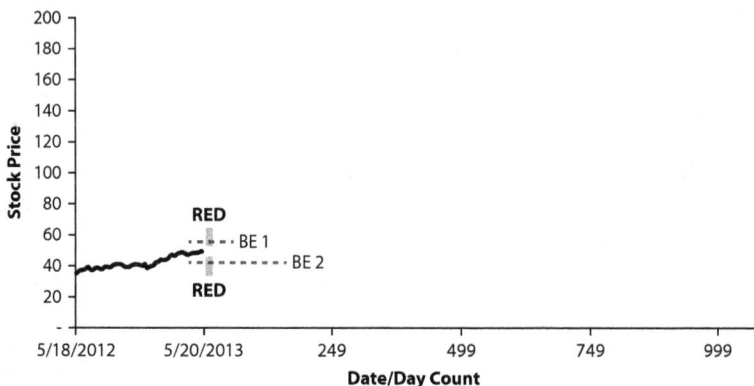

There are a few important things to notice. First, notice how much shorter the time frame is—we have moved from a 500-day time exposure to a two-week exposure. In general, a floor trader has no idea of what the long-term value of a stock should be, so he or she tries to protect himself or herself from large moves by limiting his or her time exposure as much as possible. Second, look at how little price exposure the trader is accepting! He or she is attempting to control his or her price risk by making several simultaneous option trades (which, by the way, puts the trader in a worse position in terms of breakeven points) that end up canceling out most of his or her risk exposure to underlying moves of the stock.

With this position, the trader is speculating that over the next short time period, this stock's market price will remain close to $50 per share; what basis the trader has for this belief is beyond me. In my mind, winning this sort of bet is no better than going to Atlantic City and betting that the marble on the roulette wheel will land on red—completely random and with only about a 50 percent chance of success.[3]

It is amazing to me that, after reading books, subscribing to newsletters, and listening to TV pundits advocating positions such as this, investors continue to have any interest in option investing whatsoever!

With the preceding explanation, you have a good foundation in the concept of options, their inherent directionality, and their peerless flexibility. We will revisit these themes again in Part III of this book when we investigate the specifics of how to set up specific option investments.

However, before we do that, any option investor must have a good sense of how options are priced in the open market. We cover the topic of option pricing in Chapter 2.

Chapter 2

THE BLACK-SCHOLES-MERTON MODEL

As you can tell from Chapter 1, options are in fact simple financial instruments that allow investors to split the financial exposure to a stock into upside and downside ranges and then allow investors to gain or accept that exposure with great flexibility. Although the concept of an option is simple, trying to figure out what a fair price is for an option's range of exposure is trickier. The first part of this chapter details how options are priced according to the Black-Scholes-Merton model (BSM)—the mathematical option pricing model mentioned in Chapter 1—and how these prices predict future stock prices.

Many facets of the BSM have been identified by the market at large as incorrect, and you will see in Part III of this book that when the rubber of theory meets the road of practice, it is the rubber of theory that gets deformed. The second half of this chapter gives a step-by-step refutation to the principles underlying the BSM. Intelligent investors should be very, very happy that the BSM is such a poor tool for pricing options and predicting future stock prices. It is the BSM's shortcomings and the general market's unwillingness or inability to spot its structural deficiencies that allow us the opportunity to increase our wealth.

Most books that discuss option pricing models require the reader to have a high level of mathematical sophistication. I have interviewed candidates with master's degrees in financial engineering who indeed had a very high level of mathematical competence and sophistication yet could not translate that sophistication into the simple images that you will see over the next few pages.

This chapter is vital to someone aspiring to be an intelligent options investor. Contrary to what you might imagine, option pricing is in itself something that intelligent option investors seldom worry about. Much more important to an intelligent option investor is what option prices imply about the future price of a stock and in what circumstances option prices are likely to imply the wrong stock prices. In terms of our intelligent option investing process, we need two pieces of information:

1. A range of future prices determined mechanically by the option market according to the BSM
2. A rationally determined valuation range generated through an insightful valuation analysis

This chapter gives the theoretical background necessary to derive the former.

The BSM's Main Job is to Predict Stock Prices

By the end of this section, you should have a big-picture sense of how the BSM prices options that is put in terms of an everyday example. You will also understand the assumptions underlying the BSM and how, when combined, these assumptions provide a prediction of the likely future value of a stock.

Jargon introduced in this section includes the following:

Stock price efficiency   Forward price (stock)
Lognormal distribution   Efficient market hypothesis (EMH)
Normal distribution   BSM cone
Drift

The Big Picture

Before we delve into the theory of option pricing, let me give you a general idea of the theory of option prices. Imagine that you and your spouse or significant other have reservations at a nice restaurant. The reservation time is coming up quickly, and you are still at home. The restaurant is extremely hard to get reservations for, and if you are not there at your reservation time, your seats are given to someone else. Now let's assume that in the midst of the relationship stress you are likely feeling at the moment, you decide to lighten the mood by betting with your spouse or significant other as to whether you will be able to make it to the restaurant in time for your seating.

If you were a statistician attempting to lighten the mood of the evening, before you placed your bet, you would have attempted to factor in answers to the following questions to figure out how likely or unlikely you would be to make it on time:

1. How long do you have until your reservation time?
2. How far away is the restaurant?
3. How many stop signs/stoplights are there, and how heavy is traffic?
4. What is the speed limit on the streets?
5. Does your car have enough gasoline to get to the restaurant?

Let's say that your reservation time is 6 p.m. and it is now 5:35 p.m. You realize that you will not be able to calculate an exact arrival time be-cause there are some unknown factors—especially how heavy traffic is and how often you'll have to stop at stoplights. Instead of trying to pick a point estimate of your arrival time, you decide to calculate the upper and lower bounds of a range of time over which you may arrive.

After assessing the input factors, let's say that your estimated arrival time range looks something like this:

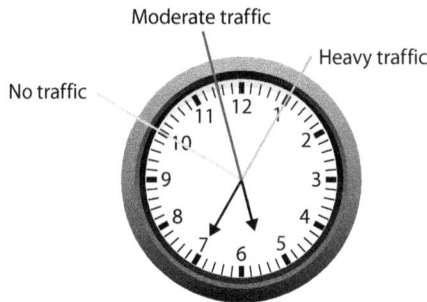

In other words, you think that your best chance of arrival is the 15-minute range between 5:50 and 6:05 p.m. If traffic is light, you'll make it toward the beginning of that interval; if traffic is heavy, you'll make it toward the end of that interval or may not make it at all. How willing would you be to bet on making it on time? How much would be a fair amount to bet?

This example illustrates precisely the process on which the BSM and all other statistically based option pricing formulas work. The BSM has a fixed number of inputs regarding the underlying asset and the contract itself. Inputting these variables into the BSM generates a range of likely future values for the price of the underlying security and for the statistical probability of the security reaching each price. The statistical probability of the security reaching a certain price (that certain price being a strike price at which we are interested in buying or selling an option) is directly tied to the value of the option.

Now that you have a feel for the BSM on a conceptual dining-reservation level, let's dig into a specific stock-related example.

Step-by-Step Method for Predicting Future Stock Price Ranges—BSM-Style

In order to understand the process by which the BSM generates stock price predictions, we should first look at the assumptions underlying the model. We will investigate the assumptions, their tested veracity, and their implications in Chapter 3, but first let us just accept at face value what Messrs. Black, Scholes, and Merton take as axiomatic.

According to the BSM,

- Securities markets are "efficient" in that market prices perfectly reflect all publicly available information about the securities. This implies that the current market price of a stock represents its fair value. New information regarding the securities is equally likely to be positive as negative; as such, asset prices are as likely to move up as they are to move down.
- Stock prices drift upward over time. This drift cannot exceed the risk-free rate of return or arbitrage opportunities will be available.
- Asset price movements are random and their percentage returns follow a normal (Gaussian) distribution.
- There are no restrictions on short selling, and all hedgers can borrow at the risk-free rate. There are no transaction costs or taxes. Trading never closes (24/7), and stock prices are mathematically continuous (i.e., they never gap up or down), arbitrage opportunities cannot persist, and you can trade infinitely small increments of shares at infinitely small increments of prices.

Okay, even if the last assumption is a little hard to swallow, the first three sound plausible, especially if you have read something about the *efficient market hypothesis* (EMH). Suffice it to say that these assumptions express the "orthodox" opinion held by financial economists. Most financial economists would say that these assumptions describe correctly, in broad-brush terms, how markets work. They acknowledge that there may be some exceptions and market frictions that skew things a bit in the real world but that on the whole the assumptions are true.

Let us now use these assumptions to build a picture of the future stock price range predicted by the BSM.

Start with an Underlying Asset

First, imagine that we have a stock that is trading at exactly $50 right now after having fluctuated a bit in the past.

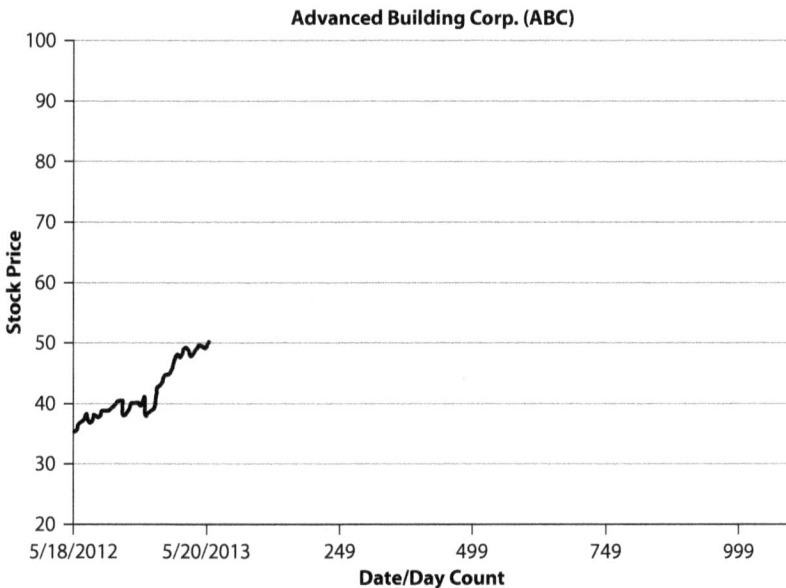

I am just showing one year of historical trading data and three years of calendar days into the future. Let's assume that we want to use the BSM to predict the likely price of this asset, Advanced Building Corp. (ABC), three years in the future.

The BSM's first assumption—that markets are efficient and stock prices are perfect reflections of the worth of the corporation—means that if there is no additional information about this company, the best prediction of its future price is simply its present price. In graphic terms, we would represent this first step in the following way:

Advanced Building Corp. (ABC)

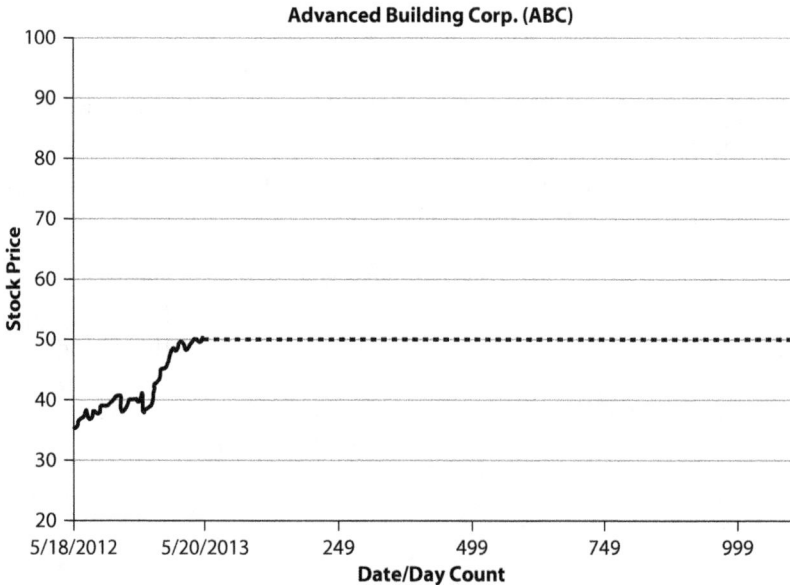

Here the dotted straight line represents a prediction of the future price of the stock at any point in time. However, to the extent that the world simply cannot stop spinning, news never stops flowing. Some of this news likely will have an impact on the economic value of the firm, but as stated earlier, according to the EMH, the incoming information is random and is just as likely to be positive for valuation as it is to be negative.

The first step of the BSM prediction is pretty raw. Stated simply, at this point in the process, the BSM predicts that the future price of the stock most likely will be the present price of the stock, with a possible range of values around that expected price randomly fluctuating from $0 to infinity.

To refine this decidedly unhelpful range, the BSM must incorporate its second axiom into its prediction methodology.

Calculate the Forward Price of the Stock

Looking at a long-range chart of stock markets, one fact sticks out: markets tend to rise over the long term. Although this is obvious to even a casual observer, the fact that markets tend to rise is contradictory to our first principal—that stocks are as likely to go up as they are to go down.

Indeed, if stocks in general did not go up, people would not think to invest in them as long as there were other investment choices such as risk-free bonds available. Thus the theorists modified their first assumption slightly, saying that stock prices are just as likely to go up as they are to go down over a very short period of time; over longer time periods, they would have to drift upward. The amount of this *drift* is set to the risk-free rate via a wonderfully elegant argument involving the no-arbitrage condition in the fourth assumption listed earlier.

Increasing the present price of the stock into the future at the risk-free rate generates what is known as the *forward price* of the stock. Here is what the forward price of our asset looks.

Advanced Building Corp. (ABC)

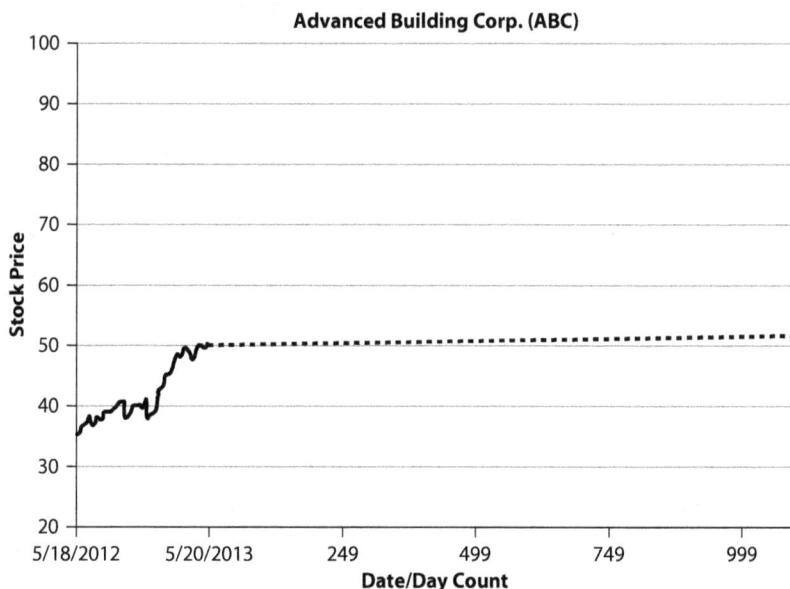

Here we see the stock being subject to risk-free drift—moving up steadily to $52 at the end of three years—this is the forward price. In terms of the BSM's prediction of the future stock price, this forward price line represents its most likely value.

The only slight modification to this calculation of forward price involves dividend-paying stocks. For dividend-paying stocks, the expected dividend serves as a downward drift that cancels out some of the upward drift of the risk-free rate. Simplistically, if the risk-free rate is 3 percent per year and the company has a dividend yield of 1 percent per year, the upward-drift term will be 2 percent (= 3 percent − 1 percent).

Add a Range around the Forward Price

Now even an academic would look at the preceding diagram and have his or her doubts that the model regarding whether the future price of this asset will ever be proven correct. This is when the academic will start to backpedal and remind us of the first axiom by saying, "Markets are efficient, but stock prices fluctuate based on new data coming into the market. Because good news is as likely to come into the market as bad news, stock prices should fluctuate up and down in equal probability." Because they are fluctuating randomly, our prediction should be a statistical one based on a range.

To make the predictive range more usable than our earlier condition (i.e., a predicted stock price between $0 and infinity), we must take a look at the next axiom—the percentage return of stocks follows a *normal* (also called *Gaussian*) distribution. A normal distribution is simply a bell curve, with which most people are very familiar in the context of IQ scores and other natural phenomena. A bell curve is perfectly symmetrical—the most commonly found value (e.g., an IQ of 100) is the value at the tallest point of the curve, and there are approximately as many instances of profound genius as there are of profound mental disability.

Note that the BSM assumes that percentage returns are normally distributed. In our graphs, we are showing price rather than percentage return on the vertical axis, so we will have to translate a percentage return into a price. Translating a percentage return into a price gives us a distribution that is skewed to the right called a *lognormal distribution*.

Thinking about stock prices for a moment, it becomes obvious that it is likely that stock prices will follow a skewed distribution simply because the price cannot fall any further than $0 per share but has no upward bound. For further evidence that this skewed distribution is correct, take a look at what happens to the prices of two stocks, both of which start initially at $50, but one of which decreases by 10 percent for three consecutive days and the other which increases by 10 percent for three consecutive days.

Losing Stock		Winning Stock	
Original price	$50.00	Original price	$50.00
Price after falling 10%	$45.00	Price after rising 10%	$55.00
Price after falling another 10%	$40.50	Price after rising another 10%	$60.50
Price after falling another 10%	$36.45	Price after rising another 10%	$66.55
Final difference from $50	**$13.55**	**Final difference from $50**	**$16.55**

Notice that even though both have changed by the same percentage each day, the stock that has increased has done so more than the losing stock has decreased. This experiment shows that if we assume a normal distribution of returns, we should wind up with a distribution that is skewed toward higher prices. Mathematically, this distribution is called the *lognormal curve*.

If we use the forward price as a base and then draw a cone representing the lognormal distribution around it, we end up with the following diagram:

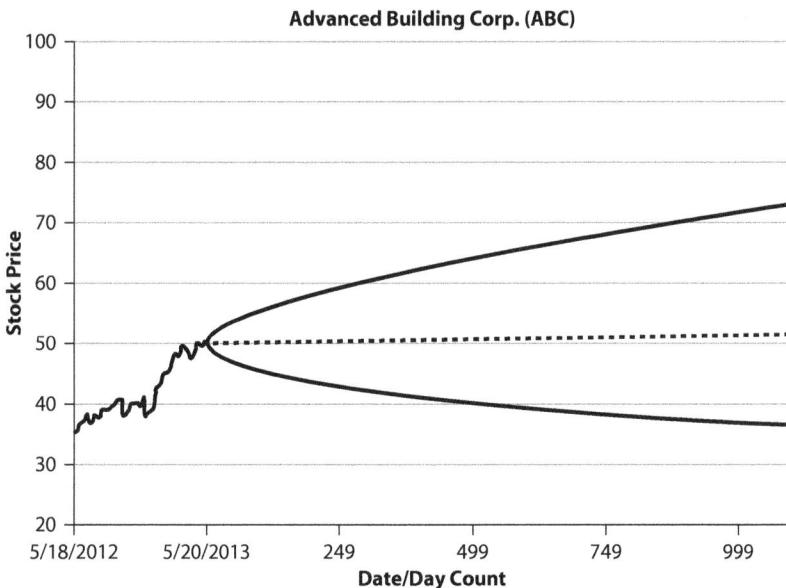

Advanced Building Corp. (ABC)

This diagram shows that the most likely future price projected by the BSM still lies along the straight dotted line, and the most likely range lies between the solid lines of the curve. In this diagram, note that even though the skew is subtle, the lower bound is closer to the forward price of the stock than is the upper bound. This confirms that the BSM's predictive model is consistent with its third assumption. It also gives us a much more sensible prediction of the future price of this stock than when we started out. We will term this graph the *BSM cone.*

According to the BSM, if you want to know the price at which a stock will trade at any point in the future, you can look within the bounds of the BSM cone. The prices within this cone are more likely to be near the forward price line and less likely to be near the lines of the cone itself. In a phrase, the BSM tells an investor, "If you want to know what the future price of a stock will be, look within the cone."

With the refinements we have made, we can say that our best guess for the value of this stock in three years will be $52, and the range of values between which the stock will most plausibly fall will be anywhere from around $37 to just over $70. One thing to note is that the cone as I have drawn it here does not, in fact, show the outline of the entire log-normal price distribution for the stock but rather just the *most plausible* range.

Also, as mentioned earlier, the likelihood of the stock price reaching each of the prices along the vertical axis is not equal. The most likely future value according to the BSM is the forward price. *Most likely* means, in the statistical sense, that there is a 50-50 chance that the stock will be above or below that line.

As one moves up the vertical (price) axis from the forward price line, the likelihood that the stock price will be above that point is progressively lower. By the time you reach the upper line of the cone, the chance that the stock price will be higher than that is only around 16 percent. Conversely, as you move down the vertical axis from the forward price line, the likelihood that the stock price will be below that point is progressively lower. By the time you reach the lower line of the cone, the chance that the stock price will fall lower than that is again around 16 percent.

Advanced Building Corp. (ABC)

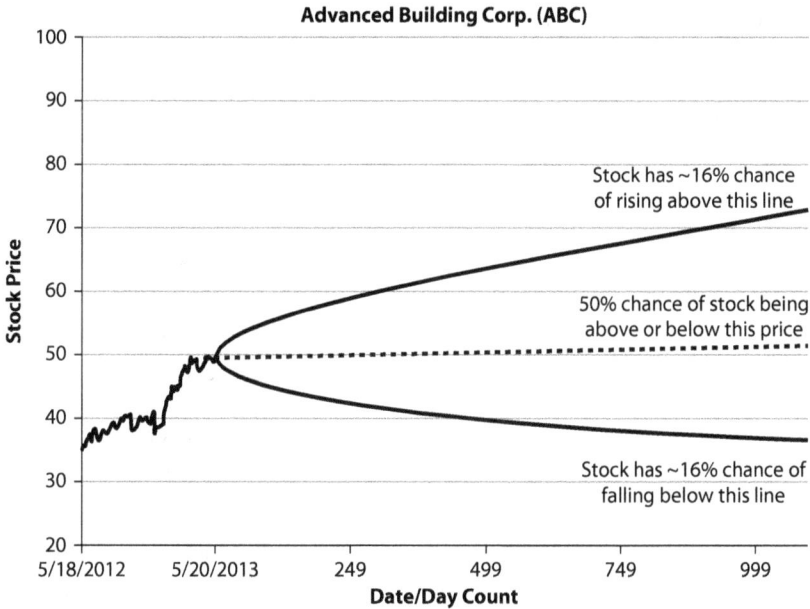

Because the BSM assumes that stock returns are lognormally distributed, and because the properties of the lognormal curve are very well understood by mathematicians, every single point on the vertical price axis is associated with a distinct probability. In other words, with just the few simple inputs we have discussed, the BSM mechanically churns out predictions of future stock prices by associating a future stock price with a theoretically derived probability.

Now that we know what the theory says and have created a prediction of the future price of a stock based on the theory, let's look at key areas where the BSM breaks down.

The BSM is Lousy at Its Main Job

By the end of this section, you will have a good understanding why the BSM—although a testament to human ingenuity and logical reasoning—is deeply flawed as a model to predict asset prices in general and stock prices specifically.

Jargon that will be introduced in this section is as follows:

Leptokurtic
Fat-tailed

Critiques of the Base Assumptions of the BSM

Before we head into the critique section, let us remind ourselves of the base assumptions of the BSM. When I introduced these assumptions earlier, I suggested that you should just accept them at face value, but this time around, let's look at the assumptions with a more critical eye.

- Securities markets are efficient in that market prices perfectly reflect all publicly available information about the securities. This implies that the current market price of a stock represents its fair value. New information regarding the securities is equally likely to be positive as negative; as such, asset prices are as likely to move up as they are to move down.
- Stock prices drift upward over time. This drift cannot exceed the risk-free rate of return, or arbitrage opportunities will be available.
- Asset price percentage returns follow a normal (Gaussian) distribution.
- There are no restrictions on short selling, and all hedgers can borrow at the risk-free rate. There are no transaction costs or taxes. Trading never closes (24/7), and stock prices are mathematically continuous (i.e., they never gap up or down), arbitrage opportunities cannot persist, and you can trade infinitely small increments of shares at infinitely small increments of prices.

Although the language is formal and filled with jargon, you need not be intimidated by the special terminology but should simply look at the assumptions from a commonsense perspective. Doing so, you will see how ridiculous each of these assumptions appears. Indeed, each one of them has either been proven wrong through experimental evidence (i.e., the first three assumptions) or is plainly false (the fourth assumption). Let's look at each assumption one by one.

Markets Are Efficient

The first two assumptions spring from a theory in financial economics called the *efficient market hypothesis* (EMH), which is strongly associated with the University of Chicago and which, more or less, still holds truck with many theorists to this day. Stock prices, under this theory, move in accordance with the *random-walk principal*—having a 50-50 chance of going up or down in a short time period because they are bought and sold on the basis of new information coming into the market, and this new information can be either good or bad.

The EMH proposes that there are different levels of efficiency in financial markets. The weakest form of efficiency holds that one cannot generate returns that are disproportionate to risk in a market simply by having access to information related to historical prices of the market (i.e., refuting so-called technical analysis). The strongest form of efficiency holds that even an investor with inside information about a company cannot generate returns that are disproportionate to the risk they assume by investing (this form is usually rejected even by supporters of the EMH).

In short, the EMH says that investors, in aggregate, dispassionately assess all available facts regarding the economic environment and rationally and methodically incorporate their well-informed expectations about likely future outcomes into their decisions to buy or sell a given stock. They always act in such a way as to maximize their utility in a rational, considered way.

Now, before running to your favorite search engine to look for academic papers refuting or defending the EMH, just step back and ask one simple question: Does this model of human behavior seem right to you? How many people on the road with you during rush hour or attending a sporting event or going holiday shopping seem to make calculated, rational, and well-considered decisions? When it comes to something dealing with money and investing, how many people do you know who act in the way just described? No matter what mathematical proof may or may not support the EMH, as a model of human behavior, the EMH simply does not ring true—to us at least.

Aside from the fundamental criticism that the EMH does not present a model of human behavior that seems, well, human, there have been empirical refutations of the EMH from almost its conception. Studies showing that stocks with low price-to-book ratios, price-to-sales ratios, and price-to-earnings ratios outperform those with high ratios have been well documented, and the effects mentioned seem to persist. One of my professors in business school, Graeme Rankine, helped to discover the so-called stock-split effect—the fact that stocks that split (i.e., the owners were simply told that for every share they previously owned, they now owned multiple shares, a change that should not have any effect whatsoever on the value of the firm) performed better after the split than those that did not split. More recently, Andrew Lo and Craig MacKinlay have demonstrated that financial markets are not efficient on even a weak basis but that they have some sort of a long-term price "memory" and seem to act more like an organic system than a mechanical one.

Later in this book we will discuss behavioral factors that affect investing, and in fact, several prominent behavioral economics theorists (Daniel Kahneman and Robert Shiller) have won Nobel prizes in economics as a result of their groundbreaking work in this field. In essence, what behavioral economics points out is that when given questions that test decision-making ability and process, most people—even highly trained people—do not make decisions in a way described by the tenants of the EMH. In fact, economists have found that experimentally, human decision makers are swayed by all sorts of issues that someone subscribing to the EMH would find irrational. Human decision makers do not, it turns out, act as perfectly rational economic animals as the EMH posits but rather are swayed by emotion, illusion, and ingrained prejudice that cause their decisions to be made in consistently flawed ways. Obviously, the experimental evidence that behavioral economics researchers have highlighted regarding how economic actors make decisions casts doubt on the basic premises of the EMH.

Indeed, proponents of EMH would argue (do argue in the case of Eugene Fama, a Nobel prize–winning economist at the University of Chicago and one of the intellectual godfathers of the EMH) that asset price bubbles cannot occur. If markets are efficient, they incorporate all available information regarding the likely future outcome of stocks and other financial assets in their present prices—meaning that even when prices are very high, as they were during the Internet boom and the mortgage finance boom, market participants' expectations are "rational." Fama has famously said, "I don't even know what a 'bubble' is."

This type of pedagogical rigidity in the face of clear evidence of the existence of bubbles and crashes, and in fact the enormous human costs that the bursting of bubbles bring about (e.g., in the wake of the bursting of the mortgage finance bubble), has soured many laypeople on the philosophical underpinnings of the EMH, even if they have never heard the term specifically mentioned. Academic responses to the tenants of the EMH from economists such as Nobel prize–winner Robert Shiller and Australian Steven Keen have been gaining strength and acceptance in recent years, whereas only a few years ago they would have been considered apostate and would have been ridiculed by "respectable" orthodox economists.

Whatever the arguments both for and against the EMH, if you are reading this book, you implicitly must hold the belief that stock markets are inefficient because by reading this book, you must be trying to "beat" the markets—an act that the EMH maintains is impossible. Although it is a pretty blunt tool for someone trying to accurately describe the complexity of markets, the one thing the EMH does have to recommend it is that if you hold to its assumptions, the mathematics describing asset prices is made much easier, and this ease leads to the ability to develop a pricing model such as the BSM.

In fact, although one of my favorite indoor sports is making fun of EMH assumptions, I do not disagree that, especially over short time frames and especially for certain types of assets, the EMH assumptions hold up pretty well and that the BSM is useful in describing likely price ranges. I discuss when the BSM is more useful and correct in Appendix A because in those instances an intelligent investor has a small chance of success. It goes without saying that intelligent investors choose not to invest in situations in which there is a small chance of success!

A good theory must be simple, but it also must be provably correct under all conditions. While the EMH is certainly simple, I maintain that it cannot be considered a good theory because it does not explain phenomena in financial markets correctly in all (most?) circumstances. This means that the first pillar on which the BSM is built is, for the purposes of intelligent investors, wrong.

Stock Returns Are Normally Distributed

A picture is worth a thousand words. Here is a picture of a normal distribution probability curve:

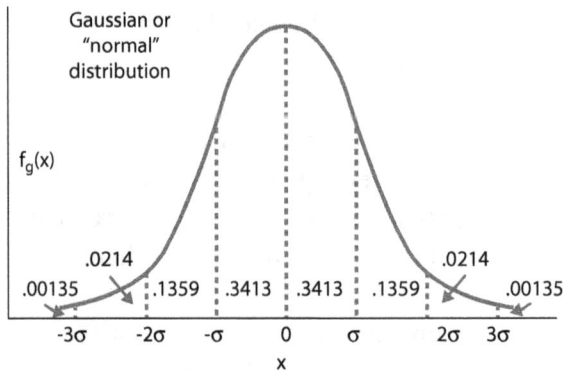

Gaussian or "normal" distribution

The numbers near the horizontal axis show the percent of cases in each region (e.g., between the 0 and σ, you see the number 0.3413—this means that for a normally distributed quantity such as IQ, you would expect 34.13 percent of cases to lie in that region), and the regions are marked off into numbers of standard deviations [denoted by the lowercase Greek letter sigma (σ)].

Now that you've seen a normal curve, let's take a look at daily returns for the Standard & Poor's 500 Index (S&P 500) over the past 50 years:

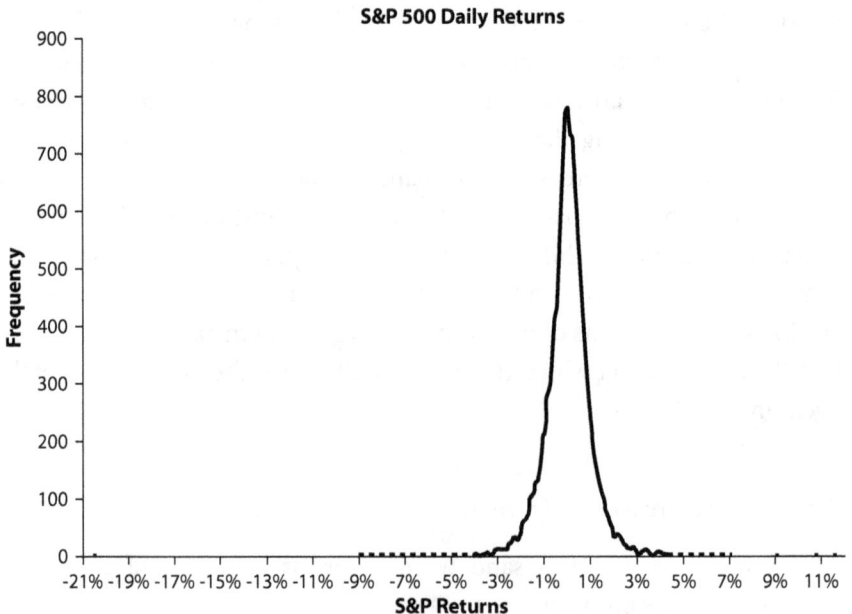

S&P 500 Daily Returns

There is a very easily recognizable difference between this curve and the preceding one—namely that this one looks much pointier than the other. However, a more profound difference can be seen by looking at the cases out near the –21 percent mark and the +11 percent mark. If the S&P 500's actual returns were normally distributed, these points simply would not exist—not for another billion years or so. The huge fall (a 20-standard-deviation event) might be expected to happen in financial markets every few billion years if in fact daily returns were normally distributed. Instead, they seem to happen about once every 70 years or so.

These observations should provide good anecdotal evidence that the assumption of normally distributed returns is unfounded. Indeed, empirical evidence has shown that stock market returns are what are termed strongly *leptokurtic* (a.k.a. *fat-tailed*) to the extent that it is not helpful to think of them as normal at all. The two characteristics of leptokurtic distributions are that (1) they are pointy and (2) they contain a relatively large proportion of extreme tail values. Some theorists think that the best way to understand stock returns is actually to conceive of them as multiple overlapping (and non-Gaussian) distributions. Whatever statistical distribution stock returns follow, it is certainly not Gaussian.

Option traders, in fact, took markets to be normally distributed until the great crash of 1987. After that time, the practitioner response to the obvious leptokurtic nature of stock price returns—charging a much higher than theoretically justified price for far out-of-the money (OTM) puts and far in-the-money (ITM) calls—came into being, and the *volatility smile*, a feature we will discuss in detail in Part III of the book, came into existence. This means that the second pillar on which the BSM is built is wrong.

Stock Prices Drift Upward at the Risk-Free Rate

On average, the compound annual growth of the stock market since 1926 has been on the order of 10 percent. The average annual compound growth of U.S. government Treasury bonds (our risk-free benchmark) has been on the order of 5 percent. Therefore, just comparing these averages, it would seem that stocks drift upward at roughly twice the risk-free rate.

Averages can be misleading, however, so in the following graph I have plotted the five-year rolling compound annual growth rate for both the S&P 500 and T-bonds:

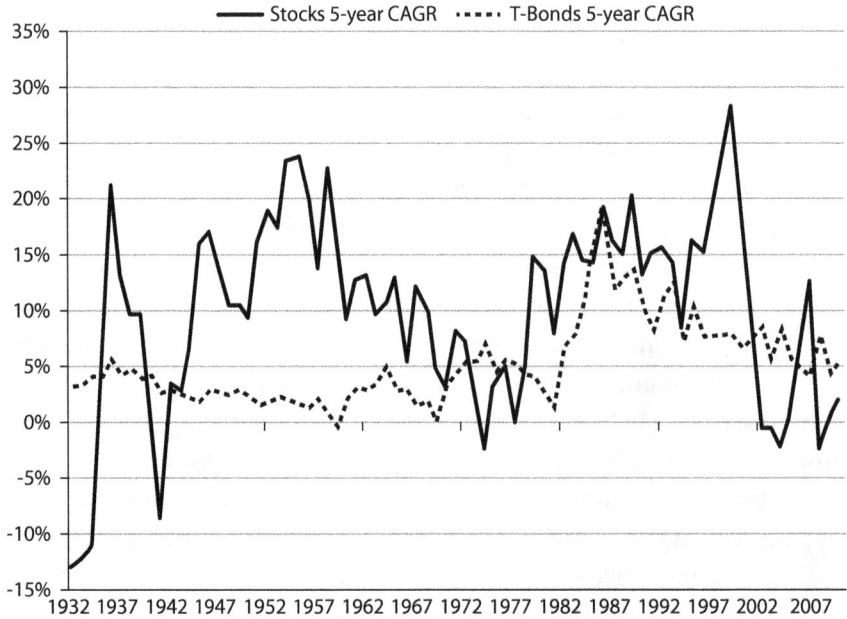

You can see that there are some significant outliers in the Great Depression area of the graph, but in general, stock returns are much higher than those of risk-free instruments on this rolling basis as well. In fact, if you asked me to guess what any randomly selected rolling five-year compound annual growth rate (CAGR) for stocks was going to be, I would probably pick a number like 13 percent and figure that I would at least be in the ballpark 80 percent of the time. Certainly, by looking at the preceding graph, you can tell that there is no reasonable basis to believe that stocks should increase anywhere around the rate of risk-free securities! As such, we can discard the third pillar of the BSM.

No Taxes, No Trading Restrictions, and All Market Participants Can Borrow at the Risk-Free Rate, Etc.

No comment, other than to say, "Ha!" With no pillars left, the edifice of the BSM crumbles in on itself after even just a cursory look.

The fact that the theoretical basis of option pricing is provably wrong is very good news for intelligent investors. The essence of intelligent option investing involves comparing the mechanically determined and unreasonable range of stock price predictions made by the BSM with an intelligent and rational valuation range made by a human investor. Because the BSM is using such ridiculous assumptions, it implies that intelligent, rational investors will have a big investing advantage. Indeed, I believe that they do.

Now that we have seen how the BSM forecasts future price ranges for stocks and why the predictions made by the BSM are usually wrong, let us now turn to an explanation of how the stock price predictions made by the BSM tie into the option prices we see on an option exchange such as the Chicago Board Option Exchange (CBOE).

Chapter 3

THE INTELLIGENT INVESTOR'S GUIDE TO OPTION PRICING

By the end of this chapter, you should understand how changes in the following Black-Scholes-Merton model (BSM) drivers affect the price of an option:

1. Moneyness
2. Forward volatility
3. Time to expiration
4. Interest rates and dividend yields

You will also learn about the three measures of volatility—forward, implied, and statistical. You will also understand what drivers affect option prices the most and how simultaneous changes to more than one variable may work for or against an option investment position.

In this chapter and throughout this book in general, we will not try to figure out a precise value for any options but just learn to realize when an option is clearly too expensive or too cheap vis-à-vis our rational expectations for a fair value of the underlying stock. As such, we will discuss pricing in general terms; for example, "This option will be much more expensive than that one." This generality frees us from the computational difficulties that come about when one tries to calculate too precise a price for a given option. The BSM is designed to give a precise answer, but for investing, simply knowing that the price of some security is significantly different from what it should be is enough to give one an investing edge.

In terms of how this chapter fits in with the goal of being an intelligent option investor, it is in this chapter that we start overlaying the range of exposure introduced in Chapter 1 with the implied stock price range given by the BSM cone that was introduced in Chapter 2. This perspective will allow us to get a sense of how expensive it will be to gain exposure to a given range or, conversely, to see how much we are likely to be able to generate in revenue by accepting exposure to that range. Understanding the value of a given range of exposure as perceived by the marketplace will allow us to determine what option strategy will be best to use after we determine our own intelligent valuation range for a stock.

Jargon introduced in this chapter is as follows:

Strike–stock price ratio	Volatility (Vol)
Time value	Forward volatility
Intrinsic value	Implied volatility
Tenor	Statistical volatility
Time decay	Historical volatility

How Option Prices are Determined

In Chapter 1, we saw what options looked like from the perspective of ranges of exposure. One of the takeaways of that chapter was how flexible options are in comparison with stocks. Thinking about it a moment, it is clear that the flexibility of options must be a valuable thing. What would it be worth to you to only gain upside to a stock without having to worry about losing capital as a result of a stock price decline?

The BSM, the principles of which we discussed in detail in Chapter 2, was intended to answer this question precisely—"What is the fair value of an option?" Let us think about option prices in the same sort of probabilistic sense that we now know the BSM is using.

First, let's assume that we want to gain exposure to the upside potential of a $50 stock by buying a call option with a strike price of $70 and a time to expiration of 365 days. Here is the risk-return profile of this option position merged with the image of the BSM cone:

Advanced Building Corp. (ABC)

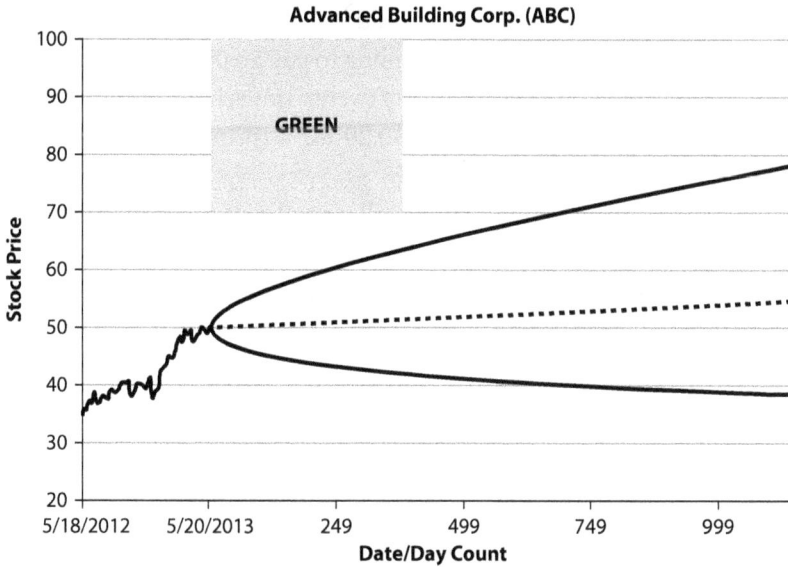

Notice that because this call option is struck at $70, the upside potential we have gained lies completely outside the cone of values the BSM sees as reasonably likely. This option, according to the BSM, is something like the bet that a seven-year-old might make with another seven-year-old: "If you can [insert practically impossible action here], I'll pay you a zillion dollars." The action is so risky or impossible that in order to entice his or her classmate to take the bet, the darer must offer a phenomenal return.

Off the playground and into the world of high finance, the way to offer someone a phenomenal return is to set the price of a risky asset very low. Following this logic, we can guess that the price for this option should be very low. In fact, we can quantify this "very low" a bit more by thinking about the probabilities surrounding this call option investment.

Remembering back to the contention in Chapter 2 that the lines of the BSM cone represent around a 16 percent probability of occurrence, we can see that the range of exposure lies outside this, so the chance of the stock making it into this range is lower than 16 percent. Let's say that the range of exposure sits at just the 5 percent probability level. What this means is that if you can find 20 identical investments like this and invest in all of them, only one will pay off (1/20 = 5 percent).

Thus, if you thought that you would win $1 for each successful investment you made, you might only be willing to pay $0.04 to play the game. In this case, you would be wagering $0.04 twenty times in the hope of making $1 once—paying $0.80 total to net $0.20 for a (probabilistic) 25 percent return.

Now how much would you be willing to bet if the perceived chance of success was not 1 in 20 but rather 1 in 5? With options, we can increase the chance of success simply by altering the range of exposure. Let's try this now by moving the strike price down to $60:

Advanced Building Corp. (ABC)

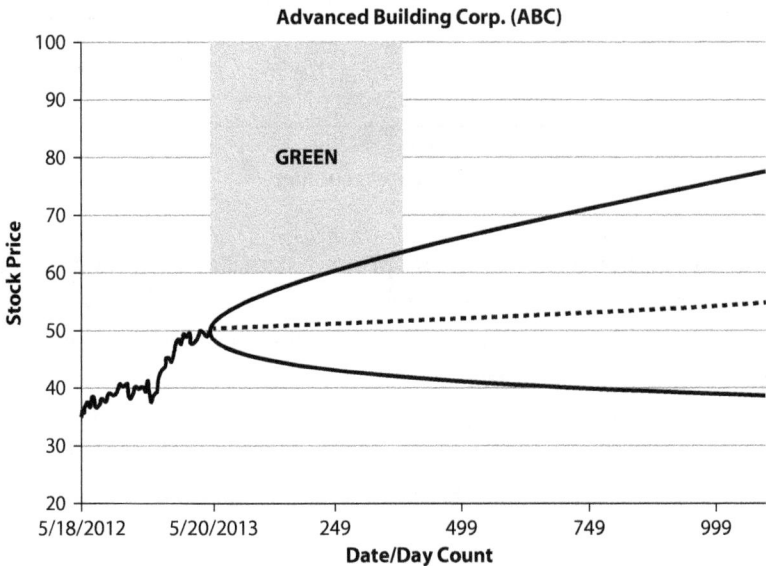

After moving the strike price down, one corner of the range of exposure we have gained falls within the BSM probability cone. This option will be significantly more expensive than the $70 strike option because the perceived probability of the stock moving into this range is material.

If we say that the chance of this call option paying its owner $1 is 1 in 5 rather than 1 in 20 (the range of exposure is within the 16 percent line, so we're estimating it as a 20 percent chance—1 in 5, in other words), we should be willing to pay more to make this investment. If we expected to win $1 for every five tries, we should be willing to spend $0.16 per bet. Here we would again expect to pay $0.80 in total to net $0.20, and again our expected percentage return would be 25 percent.

Notice that by moving the strike down from an expected 5 percent chance of success to an expected 20 percent chance of success, we have agreed that we would pay four times the amount to play. What would happen if we lowered the strike to $50 so that the exposure range started at the present price of the stock? Obviously, this at-the-money (ATM) option would be more expensive still:

Advanced Building Corp. (ABC)

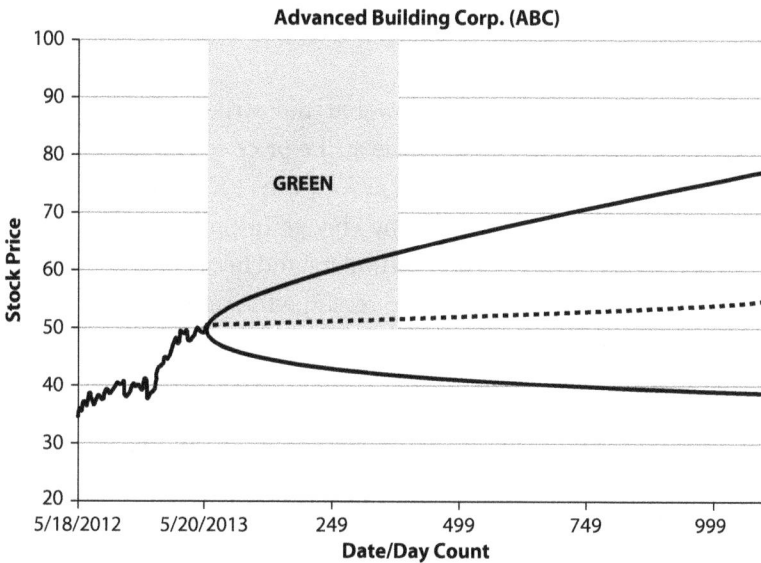

The range of upside exposure we have gained with this option is not only well within the BSM probability cone, but in fact it lies across the dotted line indicating the "most likely" future stock value as predicted by the BSM. In other words, this option has a bit better than a 50 percent chance of paying off, so it should be proportionally more expensive than either of our previous options.

The payouts and probabilities I provided earlier are completely made up in order to show the principles underlying the probabilistic pricing of option contracts. However, by looking at an option pricing screen, it is very easy to extrapolate annualized prices associated with each of the probability levels I mentioned—5, 20, and 50 percent.

The following table lists the relative market prices of call options corresponding to each of the preceding diagrams.[1] The table also shows the calculation of the call price as a percentage of the present price of the stock ($50) as well as the *strike–stock price ratio*, which shows how far above or below the present stock price a given strike price is.

Strike Price	Strike–Stock Price Ratio	Call Price	Call Price as a Percent of Stock Price
70	140%	$0.25	0.5
60	120%	$1.15	2.3
50	100%	$4.15	8.3

Notice that each time we lowered the strike price in successive examples, we lowered the ratio of the strike price to the stock price. This relationship (sometimes abbreviated as K/S, where K stands for strike price and S stands for stock price) and the change in option prices associated with it are easy for stock investors to understand because of the obvious tie to directionality. This is precisely the reason why we have used changes in the strike–stock price ratio as a vehicle to explain option pricing. There are other variables that can cause option prices to change, and we will discuss these in a later section.

I will not make such a long-winded explanation, but, of course, put options are priced in just the same way. In other words, this put option,

Advanced Building Corp. (ABC)

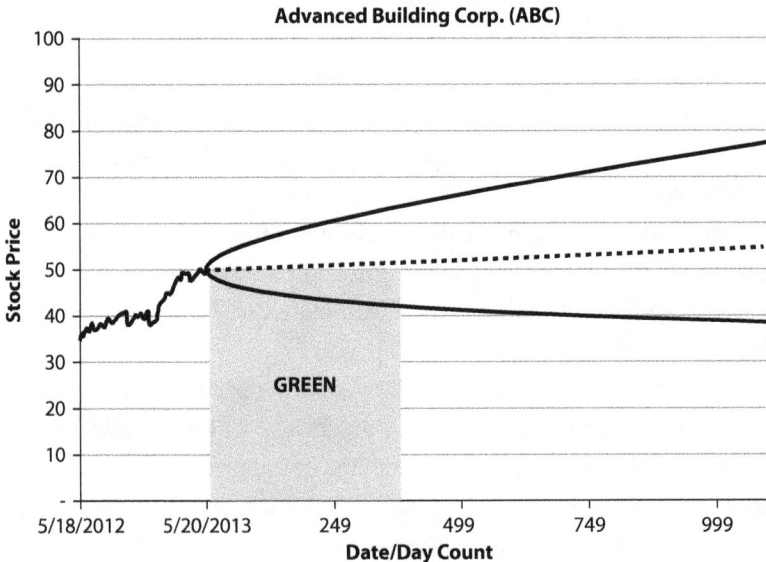

would be more expensive than the following put option, which looks like this:

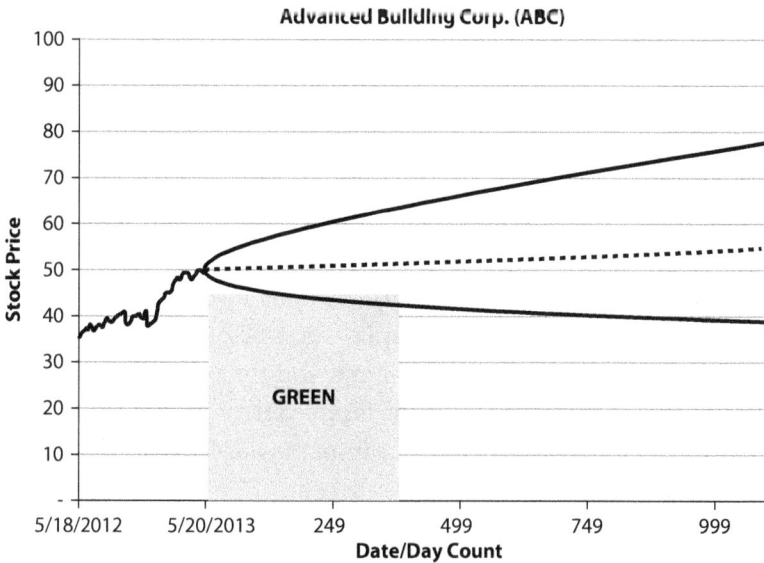

The former would be more expensive than the latter simply because the range of exposure for the first lies further within the BSM cone of probability than the latter.

We can extrapolate these lessons regarding calls and puts to come up with a generalized rule about comparing the prices of two or more options. Options will be more expensive in proportion to the total range of exposure that lies within the BSM cone. Graphically, we can represent this rule as follows:

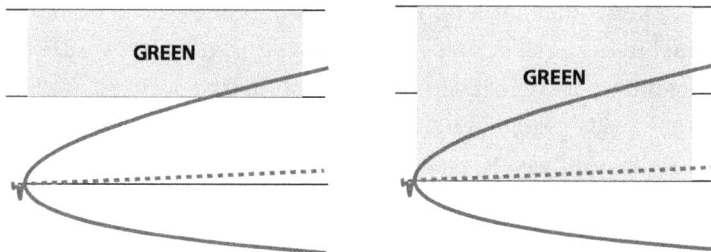

This call option will be much less   than this call option.
expensive...

This is so because the area of the range of exposure for the option on the left that is bounded by the BSM probability cone is much smaller than the range of exposure for the option on the right that is bounded by the same BSM probability cone.

Time Value versus Intrinsic Value

One thing that I hope you will have noticed is that so far we have talked about options that are either out of the money (OTM) or at the money (ATM). In-the-money (ITM) options—options whose range of exposure already contains the present stock price—may be bought and sold in just the same way as ATM and OTM options, and the pricing principle is exactly the same. That is, an ITM option is priced in proportion to how much of its range of exposure is contained within the BSM probability cone.

However, if we think about the case of an OTM call option, we realize that the price we are paying to gain access to the stock's upside potential is based completely on potentiality. Contrast this case with the case of an ITM call option, where an investor is paying not only for potential upside exposure but also for *actual* upside as well.

It makes sense that when we think about pricing for an ITM call option, we divide the total option price into one portion that represents the potential for future upside and another portion that represents the actual upside. These two portions are known by the terms *time value* and *intrinsic value*, respectively. It is easier to understand this concept if we look at a specific example, so let's consider the case of purchasing a call option struck at $40 and having it expire in one year for a stock presently trading at $50 per share.

We know that a call option deals with the upside potential of a stock and that buying a call option allows an investor to gain exposure to that upside potential. As such, if we buy a call option struck at $40, we have access to all the upside potential over that $40 mark. Because the stock is trading at $50 right now, we are buying two bits of upside: the actual bit and the potential bit. The actual upside we are buying is $10 worth (= $50 − $40) and is termed the *intrinsic value* of the option.

A simple way to think of intrinsic value that is valid for both call options and put options is *the amount by which an option is ITM*. However, the option's cost will be greater than only the intrinsic value as long as there is still time before the option expires. The reason for this is that although the intrinsic value represents the actual upside of the stock's price over the option strike price, there is still the possibility that the stock price will move further upward in the future. This *possibility for the stock to move further upward* is the potential bit mentioned earlier. Formally, this is called the *time value* of an option.

Let us say that our one-year call option struck at $40 on a $50 stock costs $11.20. Here is the breakdown of this example's option price into intrinsic and time value:

$10.00	Intrinsic value: the amount by which the option is ITM
+ $1.20	Time value: represents the future upside potential of the stock
= $11.20	Overall option price

Recall that earlier in this book I mentioned that it is almost always a mistake to exercise a call option when it is ITM. The reason that it is almost always a mistake is the existence of time value. If we exercised the preceding option, we would generate a gain of exactly the amount of intrinsic value—$10. However, if instead we sold the preceding option, we would generate a gain totaling both the intrinsic value and the time value—$11.20 in this example—and then we could use that gain to purchase the stock in the open market if we wanted.

Our way of representing the purchase of an ITM call option from a risk-reward perspective is as follows:

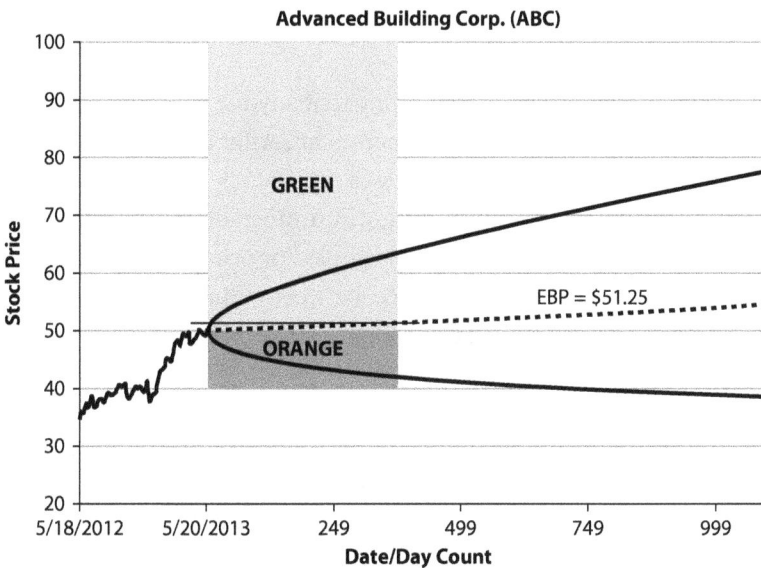

Advanced Building Corp. (ABC)

Usually, our convention is to shade a gain of exposure in green, but in the case of an ITM option, we will represent the range of exposure with intrinsic value in orange. This will remind us that if the stock falls from its present price of $50, we stand to lose the intrinsic value for which we have already paid.

Notice also that our (two-tone) range of exposure completely overlaps with the BSM probability cone. Recalling that each upper and lower line of the cone represents about a 16 percent chance of going higher or lower, respectively, we can tell that according to the option market, this stock has a little better than an 84 percent chance of trading for $40 or above in one year's time.[2]

Again, the pricing used in this example is made up, but if we take a look at option prices in the market today and redo our earlier table to include this ITM option, we will get the following:

Strike Price ($)	Strike–Stock Price Ratio (%)	Call Price ($)	Call Price as a Percent of Stock Price
70	140	$0.25	0.5
60	120	$1.15	2.3
50	100	$4.15	8.3
40	80	10.85	21.7

Again, it might seem confounding that anyone would want to use the ITM strategy as part of their investment plan. After all, you end up paying much more and being exposed to losses if the stock price drops. I ask you to suspend your disbelief until we go into more detail regarding option investment strategies in Part III of this book. For now, the important points are (1) to understand the difference between time and intrinsic value, (2) to see how ITM options are priced, and (3) to understand our convention for diagramming ITM options.

From these diagrams and examples it is clear that moving the range of exposure further and further into the BSM probability cone will increase the price of the option. However, this is not the only case in which options will change price. Every moment that time passes, changes can occur to the size of the BSM's probability cone itself. When the cone changes size, the range-of-exposure area within the cone also changes. Let's explore this concept more.

How Changing Market Conditions Affect Option Prices

At the beginning of Chapter 2, I started with an intuitive example related to a friendly bet on whether a couple would make it to a restaurant in time for a dinner reservation. Let's go back to that example now and see how the inputs translate into the case of stock options.

Dinner Reservation Example	Stock Option Equivalent
How long before seating time	*Tenor*[3] of the option
Distance between home and restaurant	Difference between strike price and present market price (i.e., strike–stock price ratio)
Amount of traffic/likelihood of getting caught at a stoplight	How much the stock returns are thought likely to vary up and down
Average traveling speed	Stock market *drift*
Gas expenditure	Dividend payout

Looking at these inputs, it is clear that the only input that is not known with certainty when we start for the restaurant is the amount of traffic/number of stoplights measure.

Similarly, when the BSM is figuring a range of future stock prices, the one input factor that is unknowable and that must be estimated is how much the stock will vary over the time of the option contract. It is no surprise, then, that expectations regarding this variable become the single most important factor for determining the price of an option and the factor that people talk most about when they talk about options—*volatility* (*vol*).

This factor is properly known as *forward volatility* and is formally defined as the expected one-standard-deviation fluctuation up and down around the forward stock price. If this definition sounds familiar, it is because it is also the definition of the BSM cone. To the extent that expectations are not directly observable, forward volatility can only be guessed at.

The option market's best guess for the forward volatility, as expressed through the option prices themselves, is known as *implied volatility*. We will discuss implied volatility in more detail in the next section and will see how to build a BSM cone using option market prices and the forward volatility they imply in Part III.

The one other measure of volatility that is sometimes mentioned is *statistical volatility* (a.k.a. *historical volatility*). This is a purely descriptive statistic that measures the amount the stock price actually fluctuated in the past. Because it is simply a backward-looking statistic, it does not directly affect option pricing. Although the effect of statistical volatility on option prices is not direct, it can have an indirect effect, thanks to a behavioral bias called *anchoring*. Volatility is a hard concept to understand, let alone a quantity to attempt to predict. Rather than attempt to predict what forward volatility should be, most market participants simply look at the recent past statistical volatility and tack on some cushion to come to what they think is a reasonable value for implied volatility. In other words, they mentally anchor on the statistical volatility and use that anchor as an aid to decide what forward volatility should be. The amount of cushion people use to pad statistical volatility differs for different types of stocks, but usually we can figure that the market's implied volatility will be about 10 percentage points higher than statistical volatility. It is important to realize that this is a completely boneheaded way of figuring what forward volatility will be (so don't emulate it yourself), but people do boneheaded things in the financial markets all the time.

However people come to an idea of what forward volatility is reasonable for a given option, it is certain that changing perceptions about volatility are one of the main drivers of option prices in the market. To understand how this works, let's take a look at what happens to the BSM cone as our view of forward volatility changes.

Changing Volatility Assumptions

Let's say that we are analyzing an option that expires in two years, with a strike price of $70. Further assume that the market is expecting a forward volatility of 20 percent per year for this stock. Visually, our assumptions yield the following:

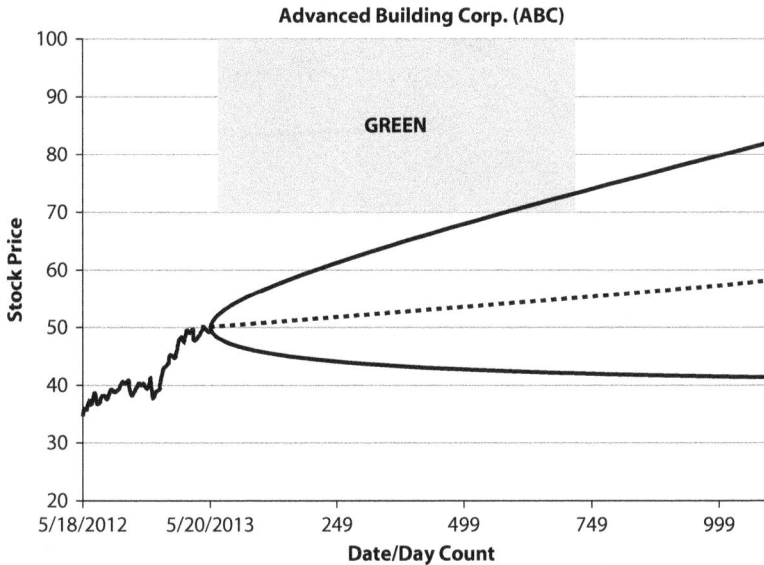

A forward volatility of 20 percent per year suggests that after three years, the most likely range for the stock's price according to the BSM will be around $41 on the low side to around $82 on the high side. Furthermore, we can tell from our investigations in Chapter 2 that this option will be worth something, but probably not much—about the same as or maybe a little more than the one-year, $60 strike call option we saw in Chapter 2.[4]

Now let's increase our assumption for volatility over the life of the contract to 40 percent per year. Increasing the volatility means that the BSM probability cone becomes wider at each point. In simple terms, what we are saying is that it is likely for there to be many more large swings in price over the term of the option, so the range of the possible outcomes is wider.

Here is what the graph looks like if we double our assumptions regarding implied volatility from 20 to 40 percent:

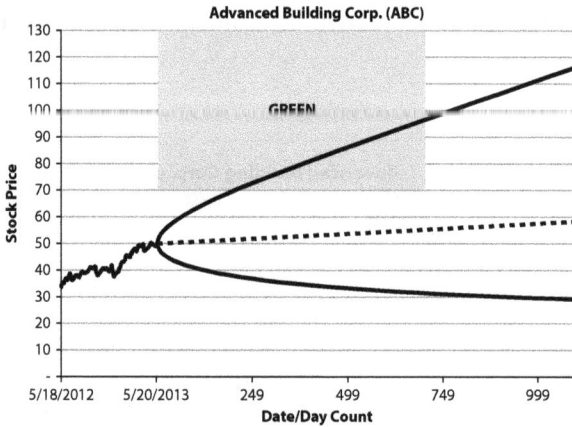

Compared with the preceding diagram, look how far into the exposure range the new BSM probability cone extends! Under an assumption of 40 percent per year forward volatility, the most likely price range for the stock as calculated by the BSM is around $30 to nearly $120.

Looking at the range of exposure contained within the new BSM probability cone, we can tell that the likelihood of the stock being at $70 or greater in two years is much higher than it was when we assumed a forward volatility of 20 percent. Because the area of the range of exposure contained within the new BSM cone is much greater, we can be sure that the option will be much more expensive now.

Let's now take a look at the opposite case—volatility is assumed to be half that of our original 20 percent per year assumption:

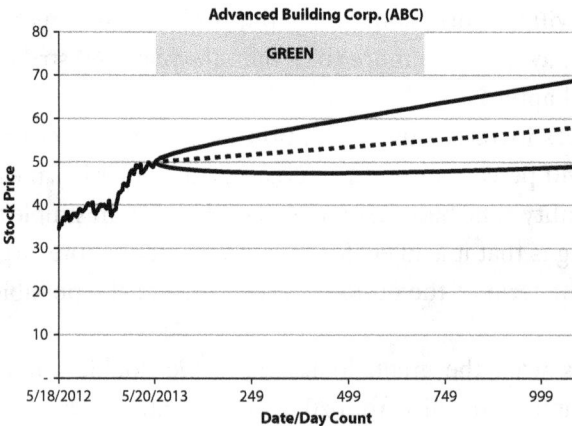

With this change in assumptions, we can see that the most likely range for the stock's price three years in the future is between about $50 and about $70. As such, the chance of the stock price hitting $70 in two years moves from somewhat likely (20 percent volatility in the first example) to very likely (40 percent volatility in the second example) to very unlikely (10 percent volatility in the third example) in the eyes of the BSM. This characterization of "very unlikely" is seen clearly by the fact that the BSM probability cone contains not one whit of the call option's exposure range.

In each of these cases, we have drawn the graphs by first picking an assumed volatility rate and then checking the worth of an option at a certain strike price. In actuality, option market participants operate in reverse order to this. In other words, they observe the price of an option being transacted in the marketplace and then use that price and the BSM model to mathematically back out the percentage volatility implied by the option price. This is what is meant by the term *implied volatility* and is the process by which option prices themselves display the best guesses of the option market's participants regarding forward volatility.

Indeed, many short-term option speculators are not interested in the range of stock prices implied by the BSM at all but rather the dramatic change in price of the option that comes about with a change in the width of the volatility cone. For example, a trader who saw the diagram representing 10 percent annualized forward volatility earlier might assume that the company should be trading at 20 percent volatility and would buy options hoping that the price of the options will increase as the implied volatility on the contracts return to normal.

This type of market participant talks about buying and selling volatility as if implied volatility were a commodity in its own right. In this style of option trading, investors assume that option contracts for a specific stock or index should always trade at roughly the same levels of implied volatility.[5] When implied volatilities change from the normal range—either by increasing or decreasing—an option investor in this vein sells or buys options, respectively. Notice that this style of option transaction completely ignores not only the ultimate value of the underlying company but also the very price of the underlying stock.

It is precisely this type of strategy that gives rise to the complex short-term option trading strategies we mentioned in Chapter 1—the ones that are set up in such a way as to shield the investor transacting options from any of the directionality inherent in options. Our take on this kind of trading is that although it is indeed possible to make money using these types of strategies, because multiple options must be transacted at one time (in order to control directional risk), and because in the course of one year many similar trades will need to be made, after you pay the transaction costs and assuming that you will not be able to consistently win these bets, the returns you stand to make using these strategies are low when one accounts for the risk undertaken.

Of course, because this style of option trading benefits brokers by allowing them to profit from the bid-ask spread and from a fee on each transaction, they tend to encourage clients to trade in this way. What is good for the goose is most definitely *not* good for the gander in the case of brokers and investors, so, in general, strategies that will benefit the investor relatively more than they benefit the investor's broker—like the intelligent option investing we will discuss in Part III—are greatly preferable.

The two drivers that have the most profound day-to-day impact on option prices are the ones we have already discussed: a change in the strike–stock price ratio and a change in forward volatility expectations. However, over the life of a contract, the most consistent driver of option value change is time to expiration. We discuss this factor next.

Changing Time-to-Expiration Assumptions

To see why time to expiration is important to option pricing, let us leave our volatility assumptions fixed at 20 percent per year and assume that we are buying a call option struck at $60 and expiring in two years. First, let's look at our base diagram—two years to expiration:

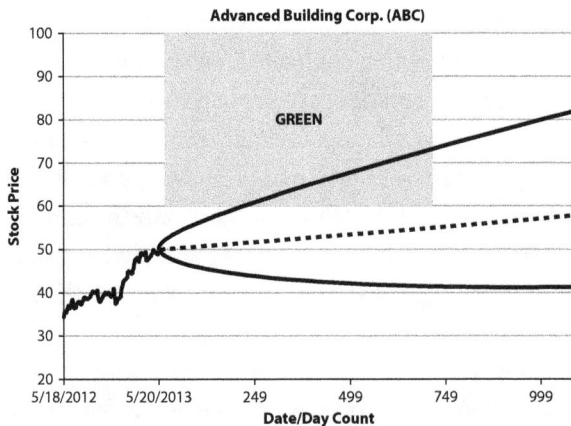

It is clear from the large area of the exposure range bordered by the BSM probability cone that this option will be fairly expensive.

Let's now look at an option struck at the same price on the same underlying equity but with only one year until expiration:

Advanced Building Corp. (ABC)

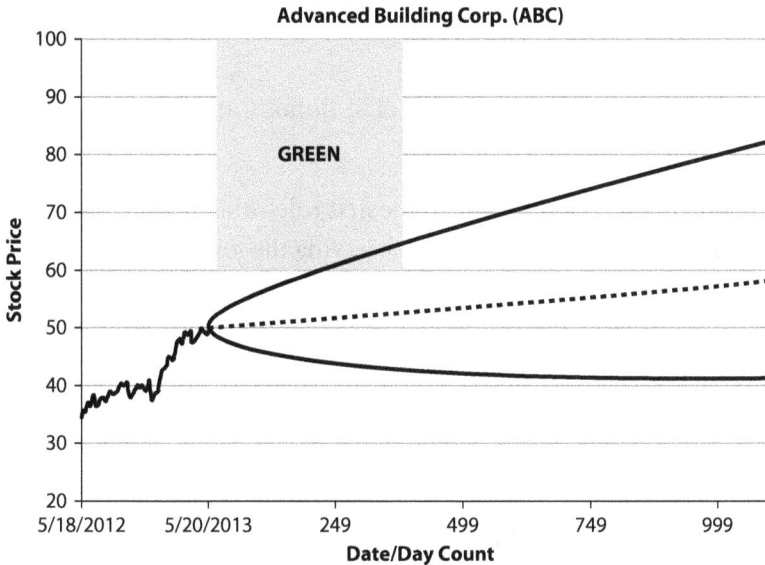

Consistent with our expectations, shortening the time to expiration to 365 days from 730 days does indeed change the likelihood as calculated by the BSM of a call option going above $60 from quite likely to just barely likely. Again, this can be confirmed visually by noting the much smaller area of the exposure range bounded by the BSM probability cone in the case of the one-year option versus the two-year one.

Indeed, even without drawing two diagrams, we can see that the chance of this stock rising above $60 decreases the fewer days until expiration simply because the outline of the BSM probability cone cuts diagonally through the exposure range. As the cone's outline gets closer to the edge of the exposure range and finally falls below it, the perceived chance falls to 16 percent and then lower. We would expect, just by virtue of the cone's shape, that options would lose value with the passage of time.

This effect has a special name in the options world—*time decay*. Time decay means that even if neither a stock's price nor its volatility change very much over the duration of an option contract, the value of that option will still fall slowly. Time decay is governed by the shape of the BSM cone and the degree to which an option's range of exposure is contained within the BSM cone. The two basic rules to remember are:

1. Time decay is slowest when more than three months are left before expiration and becomes faster the closer one moves toward expiration.
2. Time decay is slowest for ITM options and becomes faster the closer to OTM the option is.

Visually, we can understand the first rule—that time decay increases as the option nears expiration—by observing the following:

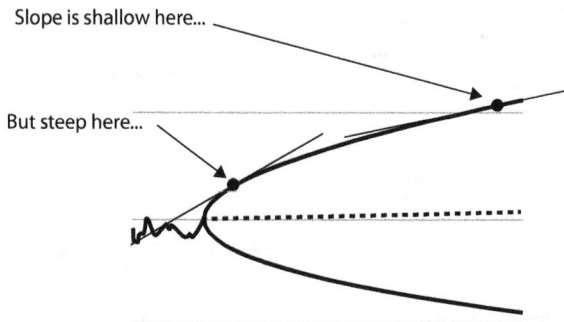

The steepness of the slope of the curve at the two different points shows the relative speed of time decay. Because the slope is steeper the less time there is on the contract, time decay is faster at this point as well.

Visually, we can understand the second rule—that OTM options lose value faster than ITM ones—by observing the following:

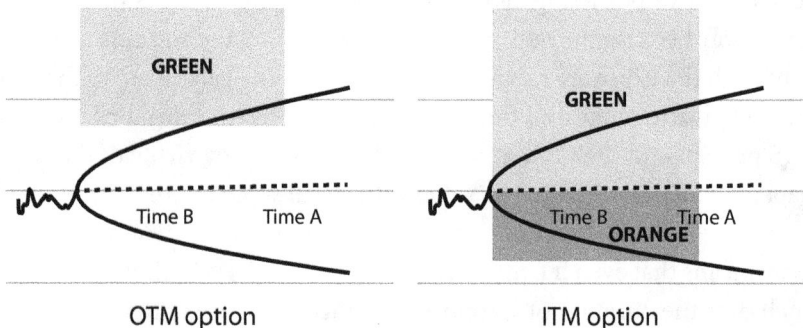

At time *A* for the OTM option, we see that there is a bit of the range of exposure contained within the cone; however, after some time has passed and we are at time *B*, none of the range of exposure is contained within the BSM cone. In contrast, at times *A* and *B* for the ITM option, the entire range of exposure is contained within the BSM cone. Granted, the area of the range of exposure is not as great at time *B* as it was at time *A*, but still, what there is of the area is completely contained within the cone.

Theoretically, time decay is a constant thing, but sometimes actual market pricing does not conform well to theory, especially for thinly traded options. For example, you might not see any change in the price of an option for a few days and then see the quoted price suddenly fall by a nickel even though the stock price has not changed much. This is a function of the way prices are quoted—often moving in 5-cent increments rather than in 1-cent increments—and lack of "interest" in the option as measured by liquidity.

Changing Other Assumptions

The other input assumptions for the BSM (stock market drift and dividend yield) have very small effects on the range of predicted future outcomes in what I would call "normal" economic circumstances. The reason for this is that these assumptions do not change the width of the BSM cone but rather change the tilt of the forward stock price line.

Remember that the effect of raising interest rates by a few points is simply to tilt the forward stock price line up by a few degrees; increasing your dividend assumptions has the opposite effect. As long as interest rates and dividend yields stay within typical limits, you hardly see a difference in predicted ranges (or option prices) on the basis of a change in these variables.

Simultaneous Changes in Variables

In all the preceding examples, we have held all variables but one constant and seen how the option price changes with a change in the one "free" variable. The thing that takes some time to get used to when one is first dealing with options is that, in fact, the variables don't all hold still when another variable changes. The two biggest determinants of option price are, as we've seen, the strike–stock price ratio and the forward volatility assumption. Because these are the two biggest determinants, let's take a look at some common examples in which a change in one offsets or exacerbates a change in the other.

Following are a few examples of how interactions between the variables sometimes appear. For each of these examples, I am assuming a shorter investment time horizon than I usually do because most people who get hurt by some adverse combination of variables exacerbate their pain by trading short-term contracts, where the effect of time value is particularly severe.

Falling Volatility Offsets Accurate Directional Prediction

Let's say that we are expecting Advanced Building Corp. to announce that it will release a new product and that we believe that this product announcement will generate a significant short-term boost in the stock price. We think that the $50 stock price could pop up to $55, so we buy some short-dated calls struck at $55, figuring that if the price does pop, we can sell the calls struck at $55 for a handsome profit. Here's a diagram of what we are doing:

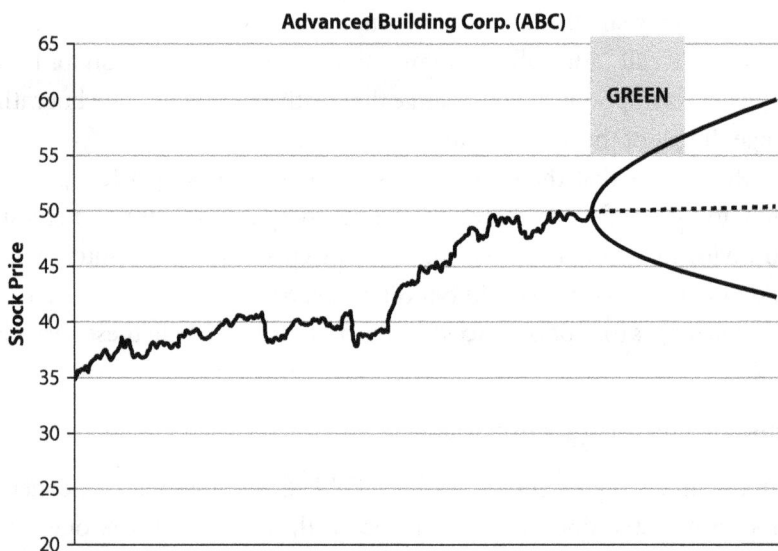

Advanced Building Corp. (ABC)

As you should be able to tell by this diagram, this call option should be pretty cheap—there is a little corner of the call option's range of exposure within the BSM cone, but not much.

Now let's say that our analysis is absolutely right. Just after we buy the call options, the company makes its announcement, and the shares pop up by 5 percent. This changes the strike–stock price ratio from 1.05 to 1.00. All things being held equal, this should increase the price of the option because there would be a larger portion of the range of exposure contained within the BSM cone.

However, as the stock price moves up, let's assume that not everything remains constant but that, instead, implied volatility falls. This does happen all the time in actuality; the option market is full of bright, insightful people, and as they recognize that the uncertainty surrounding a product announcement or whatever is growing, they bid up the price of the options to try to profit in case of a swift stock price move.

In the preceding diagram, we've assumed an implied volatility of 35 percent per year. Let's say that the volatility falls dramatically to 15 percent per year and see what happens to our diagram:

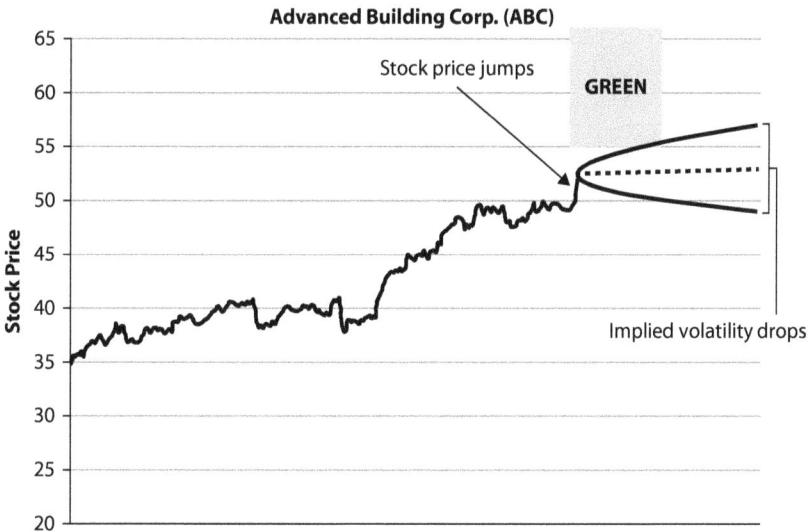

The stock price moves up rapidly, but as you can see, the BSM cone shrinks as the market reassesses the uncertainty of the stock's price range in the short term. The tightening of the BSM cone is so drastic that it more than offsets the rapid price change of the underlying stock, so now the option is actually worth less!

We, of course, know that it is worth less because after the announcement, there is only the smallest sliver of the call's range of exposure contained within the BSM cone.

Volatility Rise Fails to Offset Inaccurate Directional Prediction

Let's say that we are bullish on the Antelope Bicycle Co. (ABC) and, noting that the volatility looks "cheap," buy call options on the shares. In this case, an investor would be expecting to make money on both the stock price and the implied volatility increasing—a situation that would indeed create an amplification of investor profits.

We buy a 10 percent OTM call on ABC that expires in 60 days when the stock is trading for $50.

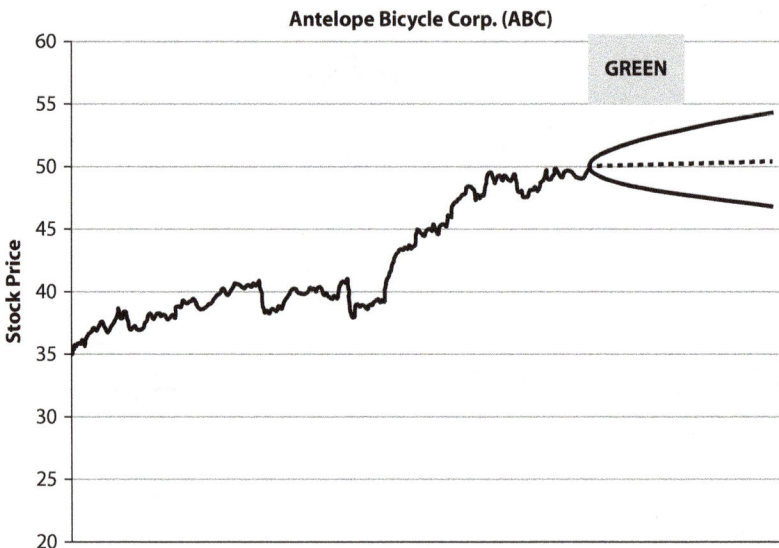

Antelope Bicycle Corp. (ABC)

GREEN

The next morning, while checking our e-mail and stock alerts, we find that ABC has been using a metal alloy in its crankshafts that spontaneously combusts after a certain number of cranks. This process has led to severe burn injuries to some of ABC's riders, and the possibility of a class-action lawsuit is high. The market opens, and ABC's shares crash by 10 percent. At the same time, the volatility on the options skyrocket from 15 to 35 percent because of the added uncertainty surrounding product liability claims. Here is what the situation looks like now:

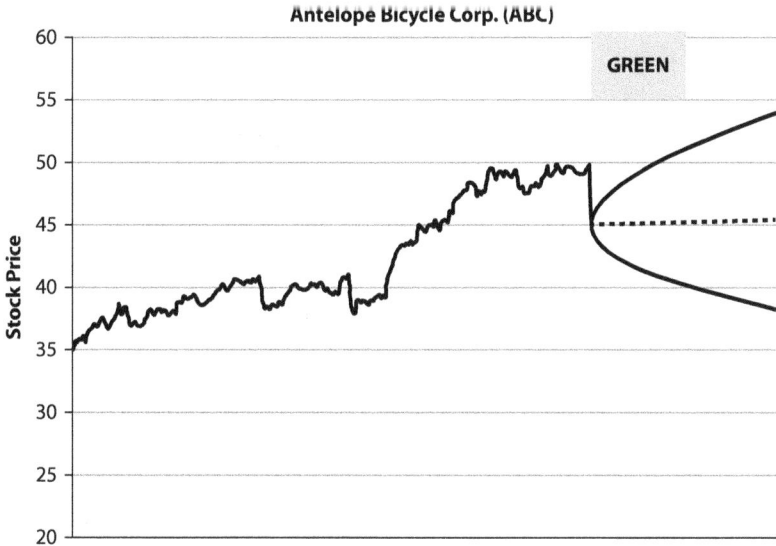

Antelope Bicycle Corp. (ABC)

This time we were right that ABC's implied volatility looked too cheap, but because we were directionally wrong, our correct volatility prediction does us no good financially. The stock has fallen heavily, and even with a large increase in the implied volatility, our option is likely worth less than it was when we bought it. Also, because the option is now further OTM than it originally was, time decay is more pronounced. Thus, to the extent that the stock price stays at the new $45 level, our option's value will slip away quickly with each passing day.

Rise in Volatility Amplifies Accurate Directional Prediction

These examples have shown cases in which changes in option pricing variables work to the investor's disadvantage, but it turns out that changes can indeed work to an investor's advantage as well. For instance, let's say that we find a company—Agricultural Boron Co. (ABC)—that we think, because of its patented method of producing agricultural boron compounds, is relatively undervalued. We decide to buy 10 percent OTM calls on it. Implied volatility is sitting at around 25 percent, but our option is far enough OTM that it is not very expensive.

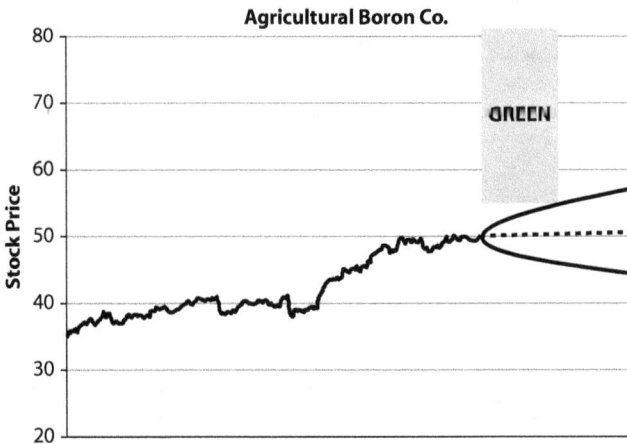

The morning after we buy these call options, chemical giant DuPont (DD) announces that it is initiating a hostile takeover and offering shareholders of ABC a 20 percent premium to the present market price—$60 per share. DuPont's statement mentions that it wants to gain exclusive access to ABC's boron processing technology. The market immediately thinks of German chemical giant BASF and believes BASF will make a higher counteroffer so as to keep ABC's revolutionary boron processing technology out of DuPont's hands. Because there is uncertainty surrounding the possibility of a counterbid and perhaps even the uncertainty that DuPont's offer will not be accepted, forward volatility on the contracts increases. The net result is this[6]:

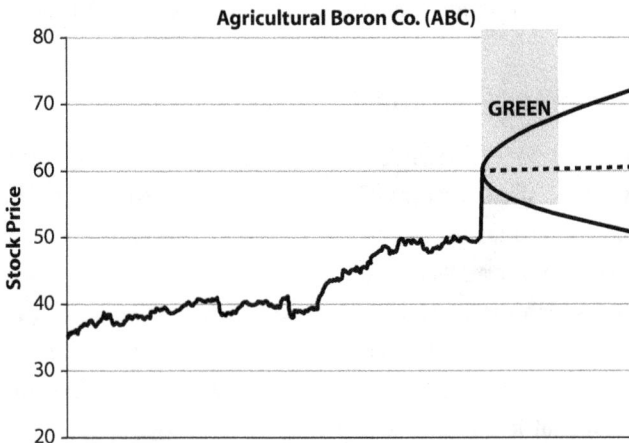

With this happy news story, our call options went from nearly worthless to worth quite a bit—the increase in volatility amplified the rising stock price and allowed us to profit from changes to two drivers of option pricing.

There is an important follow-up to this happy story that is well worth keeping in the back of your mind when you are thinking about investing in possible takeover targets using options. That is, our BSM cone widened a great deal when the announcement was made because the market believed that there might be a higher counteroffer or that the deal would fall through. If instead the announcement from DuPont was that it had made a friendly approach to the ABC board of directors and that its offer had already been accepted, uncertainty surrounding the future of ABC would fall to zero (i.e., the market would know that barring any antitrust concerns, DuPont would close on this deal when it said it would). In this case, implied volatility would simply fall away, and the call option's value would become the intrinsic value (in other words, there is no potential or time value left in the option). The situation would look like this:

Agricultural Boron Co. (ABC)

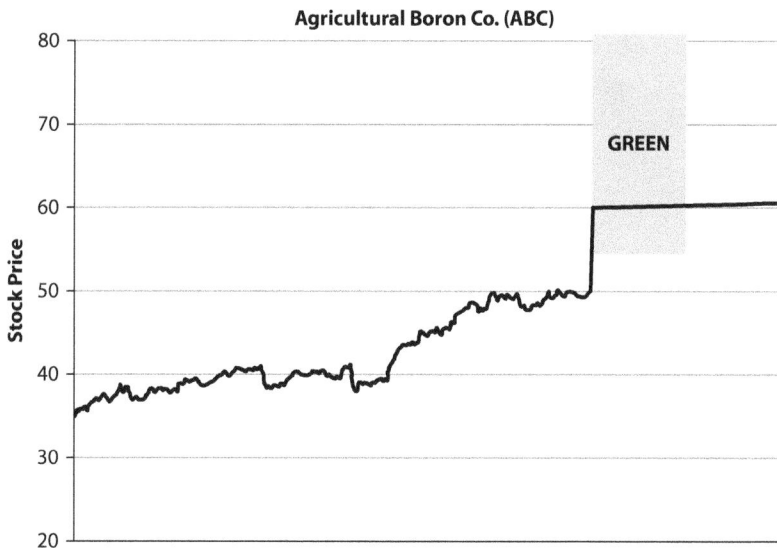

We would still make $5 worth of intrinsic value on an invested base that must have been very small (let's say $0.50 or so), but were the situation to remain uncertain, we would make much more.

You now have a good understanding of how options work and how they are priced from a theoretical perspective. Although it is clear from Chapter 2 that the BSM has its faults, it is undeniable that in certain times and under certain conditions, it works well. Please see Appendix A for a brief discussion of the situations in which the BSM is fairly good at pricing options—intelligent option investors will want to avoid these—and when it is poor—cases that present the most attractive chances for intelligent investors.

Now that you have a good idea of how options work and are priced, let's turn to how we can do a better job of predicting valuation ranges than the BSM does. This is the subject of Part II.

Part II

A SOUND INTELLECTUAL FRAMEWORK FOR ASSESSING VALUE

After reading Part I, you should have a very good theoretical grasp on how options work and how option prices predict the future prices of stocks. This takes us partway to the goal of becoming intelligent option investors.

The next step is to understand how to make intelligent, rational estimates of the value of a company. It makes no sense at all for a person to invest his or her own capital buying or selling an option if he or she does not have a good understanding of the value of the underlying stock.

The problem for most investors—both professional and individual—is that they are confused about how to estimate the value of a stock. As such, even those who understand how the Black-Scholes-Merton model (BSM) predicts future stock prices are not confident that they can do any better.

There is a good reason for the confusion among both professional and private investors: they are not taught to pay attention to the right things. Individual investors, by and large, do not receive training in the basic tools of valuation analysis—discounted cash flows and how economic transactions are represented in a set of financial statements. Professional investors are exquisitely trained in these tools but too often spend time spinning their wheels considering immaterial details simply because that is what they have been trained to do and because their compensation usually relies on short- rather than long-term performance. They have all the tools in the world but are taught to apply them to answering the wrong questions.

Part II of this book sets forth a commonsense approach to determining the value of a company. It aims to provide individual investors with the tools they need and to offer both individual and professional investors a framework that allows them to focus their attention on the most important things and ignore the rest.

Chapter 4 discusses what I call the *golden rule of valuation*. Chapter 5 looks at the only four things that can affect the long-term value of a stock and offers a way to estimate the value a company will create over its entire economic life. Chapter 6 investigates the behavioral biases and structural impediments working against us in our investment decisions and offers tools to avoid them.

In general, I have written these chapters to present the valuation framework from a conceptual perspective and have thus left out many details regarding financial statement line items and the like. These details are important, however, and it is unrealistic to think that you could translate theory into practice without knowing them. For this reason, I have provided a detailed valuation example on the Intelligent Option Investor website, complete with descriptions of all the financial statements I analyzed and explanations of the thought processes I used when doing the analysis.

Chapter 4

THE GOLDEN RULE OF VALUATION

Commit the following definition to memory:

> The value of an asset is the sum of the cash flows it creates on behalf of its owners over its economic life.

Contrary to popular opinion, valuation is easy. One does not need a master's degree in accounting or to be an expert in financial statement analysis to competently value a company and estimate a fair value range for a stock. The only thing a person needs is to internalize the preceding sentence and understand the handful of factors that affect the cash flows of a firm over time.

This chapter focuses on developing a theoretical framework using the *golden rule of valuation*—which you have already memorized—and looks at each part of that simple definition phrase by phrase, with each phrase a different section of the chapter. The sections are as follows:

1. The Value of an Asset: Here we offer a specific definition for an asset and discuss the distinction between value and price.
2. Cash Flows Generated on Behalf of the Owners: Specifies which cash flows we will measure when valuing an asset.
3. The Company's Economic Life: Breaks the life of the firm into three stages to help make the valuation process easier and more transparent.

For those new to the subject of valuation, I present an additional section that provides overviews of specific topics such as *time value of money* and *discount rates*, but even being unacquainted with these terms right now will not be a handicap.

Business is essentially a collection of very simple transactions—producing, selling, and investing excess profits. In my experience, one of the biggest investing mistakes occurs when people forget to think about business in terms of these simple transactions.

Having a firm grasp of valuation is an essential part of being an intelligent option investor. The biggest drawback of the BSM is its initial assumption that all stock prices represent the true values of the stocks in question. It follows that the best opportunity for investors comes when a stock's present price is far from its true intrinsic value. In order to assess how attractive an investment opportunity is, we must have a good understanding of the source of value for a firm and the factors that contribute to it. These are the topics of this chapter and the next.

In terms of our intelligent option investing process, we need two pieces of information:

1. A range of future prices determined mechanically by the option market according to the BSM
2. A rationally determined valuation range generated through an insightful valuation analysis

This chapter and the next give the theoretical background necessary to derive the latter.

Jargon to be introduced in this chapter is as follows:

Asset	Structural constraints
Demand-side constraints	Supply-side constraints
Owners' cash profit (OCP)	Expansionary cash flow
Free cash flow to owner(s) (FCFO)	Working capital

The Value of an Asset

The meaning of *asset*, in financial terms, is different from the vernacular meaning of "something I'd be upset about if it broke or was stolen." In financial terms, an *asset* is anything that can be owned that (1) was created through an expenditure and (2) has the capacity to generate revenues and/or to increase profits. Thinking about assets from the perspective of revenue creation and profit growth, it is clear that things such as family cars are usually not assets but are rather convenience items.

A collection of assets is also an asset—if you own a taxi cab, you own an asset; if you own a taxi-cab company, you also own an asset. Modern corporations are extremely complex, frequently with multiple business lines and operations in multiple states and countries and with assets comprised of machinery, land, and intellectual property. However, even though corporations are complex, they are still assets in the sense that they are a collection of discrete assets themselves.

An asset is created through an expenditure, so it follows that all assets have a price; this price may be greater or less than the asset's value. The distinction between the price of an asset and its value lies at the heart of what is known as *value investing*, so it is an important one to grasp. As an example, let's say that you would like to start a suburban taxi service, and frame the difference between price and value of the main asset you need to start this business: a car. In order for your business to be successful, the car you buy should be roomy, reliable, and attractive to customers. You do some research and decide to buy one of the two following cars—both of which fit your above-stated requirements:

1. 2013 Bentley Mulsanne: Manufacturer's suggested retail price (MSRP) of $300,000
2. 2013 Toyota Camry: MSRP of $28,000

The choice between the two cars for a typical taxi business is simple. The price of the Mulsanne is clearly too high. It is hard to imagine that the cash flows that would accrue to the owner of a Mulsanne taxi service would ever be enough to cover the cost of the car itself. In this case, the asset's value as a cab is much less than its price. In the parlance of modern financial theorists, a company paying the price of a Mulsanne for a car to start a suburban taxi service is "destroying shareholder value."

Obviously, it is not necessary to do complex calculations to see that value would be destroyed in this case with the purchase of the Bentley. We cannot be sure of what the value of a suburban taxi service is without some more information, but we can pretty easily guess that the cash generated from such a service would not be enough to pay off the price of the Mulsanne.

Whether the purchase of the Camry is a good idea or not is a bit more complicated. However, our conception of value for the service should not change, so our decision to invest will be driven completely by the relationship of the price of the Camry to our best idea for the value it can create. If the likely value of the car is higher than its price, it's an investment worth considering; if the likely value of the car is less than its price (as was the case in the Mulsanne), it is folly to do anything but walk away. If the likely value is much, much higher than the price, to the extent that it would provide you much more wealth than you might generate with another similarly sized, similarly risky investment, it would be irrational *not* to make the investment.

All of this—determination of the value and considerations surrounding investment—should seem very sensible to you. Indeed, it is only common sense. The problem is that when it comes to the investment process, many investors—professional and amateur alike—throw this common sense to the wind and start getting confused by what other people are saying about chart patterns and multiples and potential demand for a company's nascent product line.

I will talk about where this confusion might come from in Chapter 6.

Now that we have an understanding of what an asset is—something that can be owned, that is created through expenditures, and has the capacity to generate revenue or increase profits—let's investigate the next phrase in our golden rule: "cash flows generated on behalf of owners."

Cash Flows Generated on Behalf of Owners

Our taxi-cab entrepreneur buys the Camry—an act that, in the parlance of financiers, is called a *capital expense*—and opens the taxi service. In order to receive revenues, she will have to do a few things:

- Advertise
- Pay herself a salary
- Spend money to maintain the taxi in good working condition (gas, oil changes, etc.)
- Spend money on such things as insurance, licensing, mobile phone service, and banking and professional fees

Let's assume that the owner runs the business for an entire year, and she leaves what is left over after paying the preceding expenses in her bank account. At the end of the year, the owner is sitting on excess profits of $5,000. You might be tempted to say that this amount is the cash flow generated on behalf of the owner, but let's think about it more carefully for a moment.

The owner is a good businessperson, so she realizes that the Camry is not going to last forever. At some point, the owner will need to buy another one, so she wants to set some money aside for a down payment—let's say she sets aside $1,000.

Now the owner has $4,000 that is not spoken for—perhaps this is the amount of the total cash flow generated on behalf of the owner. It could be. The owner might simply be interested in running the business at the present level and may be content with the $4,000 in cash or so that she figures she can generate in excess of expenses every year. If so, the owner might pay herself a special "bonus" and use the $4,000 to go on a cruise.

However, let's say that the owner has an idea that she can schedule more efficiently if she uses an online ordering system that is tied into her accounting system. She thinks this online ordering system will allow her to schedule a few more fares a week just from improved order efficiency and will also save her a few hours a month 10-keying data into her accounting system. In other words, she believes that if she invests in the system, she will be able to increase the rate of growth of both revenues (through more fares per week) and profits (from the reduced time expended on bookkeeping). The online ordering system and related equipment cost $2,000.

If the owner does not spend the $2,000, she can be pretty confident that her business will keep buzzing along and will generate about $4,000 in cash flow for her the next year. If she spends the $2,000, she figures that she will be able to generate $4,500 next year—the extra $500 representing a nice return on her investment of 25 percent (= $500/$2,000). This extra return is at risk—it could be that the investment in the computerized system will not pay off, in which case the $2,000 she spent will simply be a waste—but if successful, the expenditure will pay for itself in just a few years.

If the taxi owner decides to spend the money on the new system, she ends up with $2,000 free and clear in her bank account. This money—the money that is left over after paying all her daily expenses, setting aside money for the maintenance of her business, and purchasing an asset designed to help her business expand—is the amount that we will term *cash flows generated on behalf of the owner.*

We have developed some terms to use in this book to describe each step of the process of generating cash flows on behalf of an owner. These are:

1. Owners' Cash Profit (OCP): Cash available to owners after all necessary direct costs of the business have been paid and after money is spent or set aside to maintain the business as a going concern (e.g., gas, insurance, maintenance, and setting aside funds for the next taxi).
2. Expansionary Cash Flows: Any money invested to try to generate more revenues or increase profit in the future. Expansionary cash flows are an investment, so are not guaranteed of being successful (e.g., online ordering system).
3. Free Cash Flow to Owners (FCFO): Any OCP left over after expansionary cash flows are made.

Free cash flow to owners is the quantity that we will measure and project to get an estimate of the value of a company.

From these descriptions, you can certainly identify the OCP, expansionary cash flows, and FCFO for our taxi entrepreneur. To analyze a public company, we need to associate these concepts with particular line items on a financial statement. On my website, I have a detailed valuation example (of enterprise software giant, Oracle) that shows what specific line items to estimate each of the quantities mentioned here.

Now that we have a good understanding of what cash flows we are looking at in order to value a company, let's investigate the phrase *over the company's economic life.*

The Company's Economic Life

The economic life of a company involves the firm struggling to generate cash flow subject to various constraints that change as the company grows older. When a company is young, like our taxi company, the main constraint it is likely to face is a *supply-side* one. Our taxi company has only one car and one driver. Assuming that the average ride for a customer lasts 15 minutes, the taxi company would be hard pressed to service more than about 40 customers a day or 240 customers a week (assuming a 10-hour work day and a 6-day work week). Because the taxi's capital resource base is small—one car—no matter how many potential customers may exist, the volume of service that may be provided is also small. This is a classic example of *supply-side constraints.*

Money and credit are like oxygen to a fire for supply-constrained companies. Given extra money—whether generated through operations, borrowed from a bank, or raised by selling shares to other part owners— our taxi company will be able to buy more cars and hire more drivers. If we think about these expenditures as investments, this is clearly an investor's dream because virtually any investment made is guaranteed to have good results.

"There is enough customer demand for 10 taxis in this town. We have three taxis and some money to invest. Let's buy another taxi." This is not a difficult or intellectually draining analytical process!

As long as the company has access to capital[1] and is producing something consumers want, the percentage growth rates of its revenues year over year during this stage of the business's economic life can be phenomenal; after all, if you own one cab and simply buy two others to serve a cab-starved region, your revenues are likely to show a year-over-year growth rate of somewhere around 200 percent.

FCFO during this time may, in fact, be negative—a company can fund itself through debt and actually pay more on expansionary projects than it receives in profits—but this does not mean that the business is bad, merely that it is facing supply-side constraints and trying to expand its capital base to meet the size of the market's demand.

We see this type of rapid growth in public companies all the time. Railroads in the 1800s, automobile companies in the 1900s, and Internet firms in the late 1990s all showed incredible revenue growth as customer demand swelled for products and services based on the latest technological advances.

If the taxi owner can navigate the process of raising money, eventually, she will have built up her capital base to match the size of the market opportunity. It is at this point that a company begins operating subject to *demand-side constraints*—constraints arising from the vagaries of competition and consumer choice.

When faced with demand-side constraints, the taxi cab owner is no longer concerned with finding new investment money to expand her capital base but rather with finding ways to keep her cash flows growing even though her capital base is sufficient to meet current customer demand. During this part of the company's economic life, investment decisions become more difficult. One possible investment choice is to spend money on systems or processes to make the operation more efficient. This will not affect *top-line* (i.e., revenue) growth but likely will increase the flow of cash to the owner by allowing for a higher proportion of revenues to be converted into profits.

Other investment possibilities for our demand-constrained taxi entrepreneur include opening an operation in another geographic area—maybe in the form of a joint venture (JV) with another entrepreneur in the new region who understands the local economy well—buying a rival taxi company, or indeed branching out to start some other business under the taxi company's umbrella.

In terms of our original example to illustrate FCFO, in this period, for a single car in her fleet, our taxi owner may be receiving the same $5,000 in profits, setting aside the same $1,000 for a replacement vehicle, paying the driver a $500 profit-sharing bonus, spending $700 for an improved lighting and security system for the lot in which she parks her fleet of cars, and squirreling away the rest in case the opportunity to buy the taxi company across town presents itself. The company may look as though it is generating $2,800 in FCFO (= $5,000 − $1,000 − $500 − $700), but in fact, in the owner's mind, that $2,800 may just be temporarily available. If a good, large investment opportunity presents itself, what had looked like free cash flow from years past might get used all at once in a major investment program.

To find examples of companies in this stage of development, one only needs to open the business section of the local newspaper. General Motors' JVs with Chinese carmakers to get a toehold in the burgeoning China market, Procter & Gamble buying Gillette Razors to boost its personal-care product lines, and Google stepping out of its turf of Internet search-based advertising to buy Motorola Mobility Systems and manufacturing mobile phones are all cases in point.

The growth of the taxi company's cash flows will depend on how good the potential investment opportunities are and how skillful the company's management is at exploiting those opportunities. If the opportunities are good and management is skillful, growth rates will continue to be high. They will certainly not be as high as during the "shooting fish in a barrel" investment environment when the company was supply constrained, but they will be higher than the growth rates of most of the companies in the larger economy.

At some point, however, good investment opportunities will become fewer and farther between. The taxi-cab company has bought up most of its regional competitors and is now constrained by the local regulator's rules against monopoly power and anticompetitive practices. The JV in a neighboring region did well, so our taxi owner bought out her partner and has expanded that business as far as it will go as well. She dallied with setting up a craft beer brewery (figuring that tipsy customers would be more likely to hire taxis) but abandoned that when it seemed like it was more trouble than it was worth.

In fact, the taxi owner noticed that in general, as her business grew larger, her investment opportunities seemed to generate less and less marginal improvement in cash flow to her. As with the case of the brewery, sometimes the extra money flowing in was simply not worth the time and hassle of running the new business.

So it goes in listed companies as well. Eventually, all the low-hanging investment fruit is picked and in placed in the company's basket, and getting that next apple requires more energy than it is worth. Looking at long data series of companies' profit growth, you can clearly see the downward trend over time as the investment opportunities become less and less compelling. Part of the problem for listed firms is not only the availability of good investment opportunities but also the fact that they have grown so large that it takes not only a compelling investment but also a compelling investment that is enormous in size to really move the needle. This is colloquially known as the *law of large numbers*.[2] Stated simply, this rule says that if you are really big, it is hard to grow really fast.

Now what?

The taxi cab company has been operating under an environment of demand constraints for some time, and the company—through acquisitions, expansion, and the like—has expanded as far as it can into its local economy. From here on, as long as no one invents a teleportation device (which would fairly quickly make taxis obsolete), its growth will depend on *structural constraints*—factors such as population growth, general economic conditions, and inflation.

If our taxi cab owner is smart, when faced with structural constraints, she will stop looking to invest the excess profits her company is generating every year and instead start paying herself a bonus (which she should invest wisely by buying a copy of this book, of course). In the world of listed companies, this bonus is termed a *dividend*.

There is, in fact, a structural speed limit for public companies as well—the rate of growth of the economy at large. And when a company is consistently growing at or near this structural rate, it is time for shareholders to demand to be paid dividends.

In the old days, before globalization, the rate of growth of the economy at large meant the growth rate of one's domestic economy. However, more and more, reduced trade barriers and cheap transportation cost have meant that the limiting growth rate is closer to that of the global economy. There are investing cases in which a company can potentially grow very quickly overseas, but for large, well-established firms (i.e, "Blue Chip" companies), usually their overseas exposure is much smaller or much less profitable than their domestic exposure, so the maximum growth rate ends up being pretty close to the domestic rate.

Thinking about this progression from start to finish, you can see that growth rates vary broadly in three stages—a startup stage (during which the firm faces supply constraints), an investment phase (during which the firm faces demand constraints), and a terminal phase (during which the firm faces structural constraints). It is important to realize that companies can sometimes jump between these growth stages, even though it is fairly rare.[3]

Throughout the life of a company, the firm is a machine generating profits and cash flows on behalf of its owners. I have said that the value of a company is the sum of the cash flows created by that company on behalf of its owners over its economic life. We only have one more tiny bit to investigate to have a complete understanding of this definition: how to sum up cash flows that are generated over time.

Time Value of Money: Summing Up Cash Flows Over Time

It turns out that summing up cash flows is not as easy as simply adding one year's cash flows to the next because the value of cash flows depends on when they are received. Have a hard time believing this? Look at this example: assume that you get stranded in the middle of the Mojave Desert and have to walk through the intense summer sun to find help at the next town. You stumble into a convenience store, suffering from acute dehydration—shaking, nauseous, and with an intense headache—but soon you realize that you have lost your wallet on the trek into town. The shopkeeper offers to loan you $5 now to buy drinks, but you will have to pay him $20 when you return with your wallet.

Of course, under the circumstances, your need is so great for the $5 worth of liquid now that you are glad to part with $20 a few hours later. In a sense, the difference between the two amounts is sort of an exchange rate between two different time periods. If you go to England, it takes one U.S. dollar to equal 0.66 of a British pound (let's assume). In the case of the Mojave convenience store, it takes 20 future dollars to equal 5 dollars right now.

This is the basic idea behind the *time value of money*. I will not go into detail behind this concept here (because it is discussed in detail in various online and print sources), but the main point is the one I made earlier: cash flows from different periods cannot be directly summed.

The main assumption behind modern finance is that cash flows that occur later are always worth proportionally less than cash flows that occur sooner. The formula to translate a future cash flow (CF) into its present value (PV) is

$$PV = CF \times e^{-rt}$$

where r is what is called the *discount rate*, e is the exponential function, and t is the time before the future cash flow is set to occur.

When one raises an exponent to a negative power, the result is a number smaller than one. This is just the mathematical translation of the phrase "a dollar today is worth more than a dollar tomorrow."[4]

Assuming we can forecast a future cash flow, the next most important question we should ask is what we should use for the discount rate.

According to the orthodox view of finance [embodied in something called the *capital asset pricing model* (CAPM), which is an idea closely related to the efficient market hypothesis (EMH)], there is a statistical formula that should generate the proper discount rate for any publicly traded asset by plugging in a few numbers. I will not go into detail as to why, but suffice it to say that I believe that the CAPM model's discount rate should be ignored by anyone who believes that stocks can be mispriced in the marketplace.

Abandoning orthodoxy, I advocate use of a 10 percent discount rate for most U.S. large- or medium-cap investments and about 12 percent for U.S. small- and microcap investments. The reason for this is that the market as a whole has generated compounded returns for the last century or so of around 10 percent per year. If you restrict yourself to the small-cap stock universe, that number increases to around 12 percent. By using 10 and 12 percent as fixed discount rates, the question I am answering is this: "If I expect this company to perform about as well as its peers, what is my best guess for what its peers will return?"[5] Using these set numbers allows you to measure different stocks according to a common yardstick, thereby taking out one source of error that one can make a mistake on in a valuation.

For now, let's just see what happens to a nominal payment of $100 per year when discounted at 10 and 12 percent. In the following graph, I have assumed that a payment of $100 is made at the end of the next 100 years. I discounted each of these payments at the discount rate listed and then kept the running sum of those discounted payments. Here is the graph:

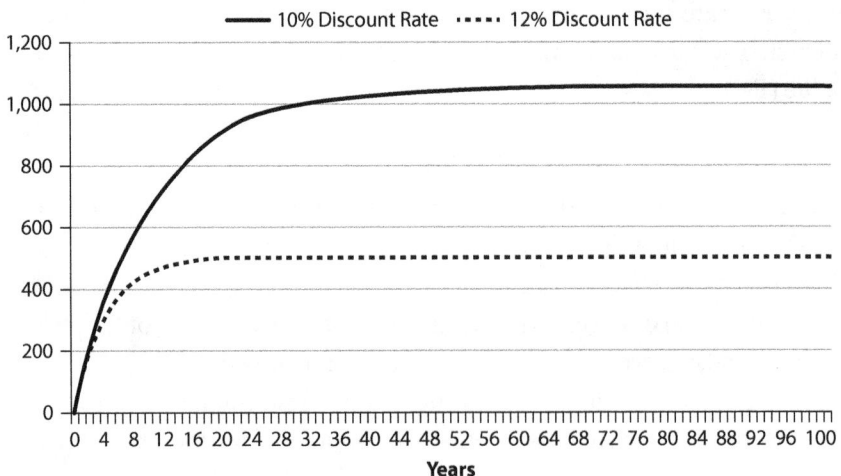

The interesting thing to note is how much the value is in the first 30 years or less of cash flows. At the 12 percent discount rate, the sum of the present value of all future cash flows trends toward around $506; at the 10 percent discount rate, the value levels off at $1,051. The points at which each of the curves level off represent the total value of the respective stream of cash flows. Using a 12 percent discount rate, the sum of the first 13 years of cash flows already exceeds 95 percent of the total $506 value—in other words, by year 14, it is almost the same as if you stop counting. At a 10 percent discount rate, it takes until year 29 to reach this point.

Thinking about this graph from a practical standpoint, it makes perfect sense. What if you loaned $100 to someone and he or she promised to repay you in 75 years. What value would you put on that promise of repayment? Nothing or next to nothing, I wager.

At a 10 percent discount rate, a promise to pay $100 in 75 years, using the preceding formula, is worth about $0.06; at a 12 percent discount rate, that promise is worth about $0.00001. These figures can surely be considered "next to nothing" and "nothing," respectively.

Look at the *golden rule of valuation* again:

> The value of an asset is the sum of the cash flows it creates on behalf of its owners over its economic life.

After the preceding discussion, its meaning now should be perfectly clear.

And now that you have a good grasp of the golden rule, let's take a look at the only four factors that can affect the value of a firm—I call them the *drivers of value*—and how we can analyze them to get a picture of what the company is worth.

Chapter 5

THE FOUR DRIVERS OF VALUE

In my experience, most people who analyze investments spend far too much time getting distracted by trivialities. These trivialities end up pulling them off course, confusing them, and creating valuation rationales that are so complex as to become gothic. Getting carried away with unimportant minutiae also contributes to the difficulties people have in making investing decisions—whether to invest in the first place and whether to decrease, increase, or close an investment.

This chapter introduces a process to estimate the value of a company—based on the *golden rule of valuation*—by singling out and analyzing only a handful of drivers. It seems counterintuitive, but you will see later in this book that less information actually counts for more in many circumstances, especially when valuing a company's stock. This chapter works hand in hand with Chapter 4 in teaching the skills of an intelligent option investor. Chapter 4 outlined how value accrues to the owner of a company. This chapter looks at the specific factors that allow that value to accrue.

Jargon introduced in this chapter is as follows:

Explicit forecast stage   Structural growth stage
Investment stage

Bird's Eye View of the Valuation Process

Before looking at each of the drivers in turn, let's first get an idea of the goal we are trying to reach from a high level. Our golden rule of valuation ties the value of a company to the cash flows it creates over time. Cash flows are created through the process we saw in the example of the taxi company in Chapter 4: revenues come in, present costs are paid, likely future costs are saved up for, and some investments may be undertaken to expand the business. Any cash that is left over after this process can be paid to the owners.

This is a pretty simple model, so it should not be hard to create a fairly accurate picture of how an individual company operates and how it is likely to operate in the future. All we need to understand is:

1. How revenues are likely to change
2. How efficiently a company is translating those revenues into profits
3. What proportion of the profits the company is investing in the growth of the business and how effective those investments are

Indeed, this picture also describes all the typical drivers of value for a company. There is one more driver, that I call "Balance Sheet Effects" and will describe in detail later in this chapter, but it is only applicable in a very few companies, so most of the time all you have to consider are the preceding three. In tabular format, the drivers are as follows:

Driver	Description
Revenue growth	How fast sales will likely increase
Profitability	How efficient the firm is in converting revenues to profits
Investment level and efficacy	Proportion of profits that must be invested to allow profits to grow in the future
Balance-sheet effects	The effect of hidden assets or liabilities on future cash flows

This seems like an easy enough task—just figure out three or maybe four things, and you are set—until you remember that you must make this analysis for the entire economic life of the firm. "How can I know what the revenues of this company are going to be 50 years in the future? What will its profitability be then? How should I know what kinds of investments it will be making?"

Indeed, having to forecast revenue growth and profitability 50, 75, or 100 years into the future for a company is an impossible task, and an investor would be foolish to even try (although in my consulting work I have seen financial models extending 50 years into the future).

Happily, the task of an intelligent investor can be made easier by doing three things:

1. Breaking up the economic life of a company into discrete stages and using shortcuts to make assumptions about what will happen in each stage
2. Recalling that based on the time value of money, future cash flows have increasingly shrinking present values
3. Focusing not on forecasting a single, exact number for each of the drivers but rather on developing a sensible best- and worst-case scenario for each one

Let's first look at shortcut number one: breaking up the economic life of a company into stages. It is not rocket science—the stages are short, medium, and long term. In the short term (0–3 or 5 years, let's say), we have a pretty easy time of thinking about how revenues, profitability, and investment levels are likely to change, so we can model the cash flows in this stage explicitly. For this reason, I call this the *explicit forecast stage.*

In the medium term (from the end of the short-term period to a point in time 5 or 10 years in the future for most companies), we would have a much more difficult time of forecasting explicit cash flows, so we dodge the difficulty by using a shortcut. We can see what investments are available to the company at present—whether the firm is supply- or demand-constrained—and what the company's track record has been regarding the outcomes of its past investments. Based on this analysis, we can say, "Considering the investment environment and management's skill in investing in the past, this firm's cash flows should be able to grow at an average rate of x percent during this period." Because this medium-term stage relies on the success of present investments, I call this the *investment stage.* Note, though, that mature companies—those that are already constrained by structural factors—will not, by definition, be able to grow any faster than the economy, no matter what investments they make. As such, for a mature firm in a mature industry, the investment stage usually does not have to be considered. The one case where it does is when a mature firm continues to invest in value-destructive projects. In this case, rather than factoring in above-normal growth, we should factor in below-normal growth because the owner's cash profit is eaten up by poor investments.[1]

In the long term (anything after the investment valuation stage), we know that a company will become constrained by structural factors and will, on average, only be able to grow as fast as the economy at large. Because of the structural constraints on growth, I call this the *structural growth stage.*

Pulling all these stages together in graphic format is instructive, and on careful inspection, we can also see something important about the second shortcut regarding the time value of money:

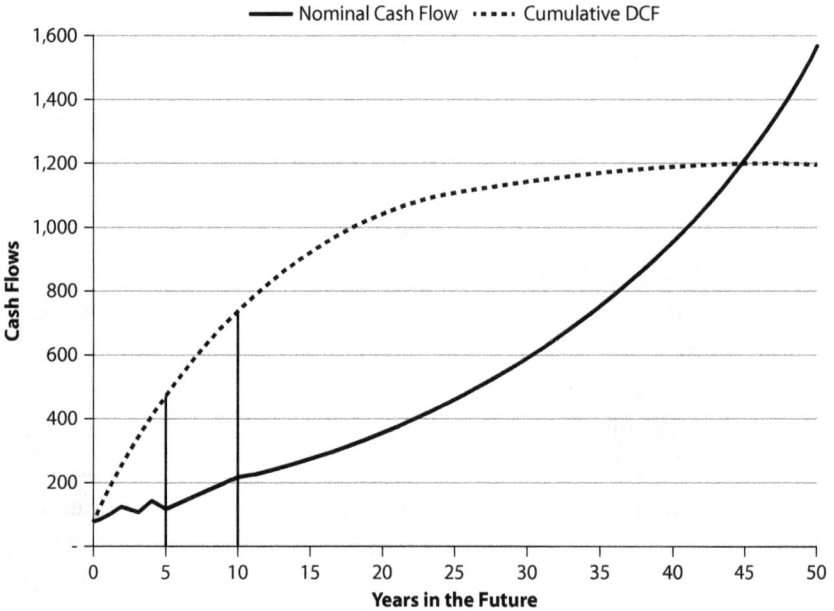

This diagram shows the nominal amount of cash flow generated by the company over a period of 50 years—represented by the solid line—overlain by its discounted value—represented by the dashed line. The explicit forecast stage is from zero to five years, the investment stage picks up after that and lasts five years, and the structural growth stage begins after that. You will notice that the dashed line starts to level off at a figure of around $1,200. The point at which that line levels off represents the total discounted value of those cash flows and, by extension, the value of this firm.

The explicit forecast stage assumes that cash-flow growth will vary up and down because of various competitive pressures that we have forecast based on our understanding of the business environment. In this diagram, the value of the discounted cash flows generated during the explicit forecast stage makes up 39 percent of the total value of the firm.

During the investment stage, we have assumed that the company's investments will be very successful and allow the firm to generate a growth in cash flows of 15 percent per year (suggesting that this is a company with a large number of high-quality investment possibilities). An assumption of a constant-percentage rate of growth implies that the resulting line will be an exponential curve, and indeed, we can see that exponential curve between the 5- and 10-year marks. In this example—assuming this quick 15 percent per year rate of growth—the sum of discounted cash flows generated during the investment stage makes up 23 percent of the total value of the firm.

The structural growth stage—covering years 11 onto forever—assumes that investment opportunities will dry up for the firm as it hits structurally based demand constraints and that cash flows from that point forward will grow at 5 percent per year. We are again assuming a constant-percentage growth per year that again will generate an exponential curve—this is the solid line starting after year 5 and continuing upward through year 50. Note, though, that the slope of the solid line during the structural growth stage is subtly shallower than the slope of the solid line during the investment stage. This subtle change of slope represents a pretty big slowdown from an average growth rate of 15 percent per year to only 5 percent per year. All in all, the discounted cash flows generated during the structural growth stage make up the remaining 38 percent of total value of this example firm.

Note how small a percentage of overall value cash flows generated during the explicit forecast stage represents—only 39 percent of the total. This obviously implies that more than three-fifths of the value of this stock is based on the cash flows generated in the investment and structural growth stages. The sadly amusing fact about almost all the target prices published by sell-side research companies (such as the big brokerage houses), the fair-value estimates published by third-party research companies, and the investment valuations used by buy-side companies (such as hedge and mutual funds) is that they are generated by analysts who spend the vast majority of their analytical energy on estimating only the explicit stage of the forecast—which proportionally makes up the least amount of value of a going concern—and only a tiny sliver of their time and energy on the most important, weightiest component of the forecast—future growth rates.

The best thing that we as intelligent investors can do is to understand the effect of medium- and long-term growth rates on the value of companies (this makes us less susceptible to being swayed by short-term, nonmaterial developments such as the delayed launch of a product line or the like) and to attempt to rationally analyze the amount of cash flows likely to be generated along all three of the stages.

The final shortcut we use to improve the quality of our valuations is to not make the mistake of false precision and try to forecast one "right" number for each of the valuation drivers but rather to develop an idea of what the best- and worst-case scenarios are for each of the drivers. There are some very compelling benefits to taking this tact that I will discuss in greater detail in Chapter 6 on behavioral biases and later when we talk about finding option investments in Chapter 7. In the end, what we should be looking to develop is a series of ranges for our drivers in the first two stages[2] that looks something like this:

Explicit Forecast Stage

	Best Case	Worst Case
Revenues	8%	5%
Profits	18%	12 %
Investment Level	30% of OCP	45% of OCP

Investment Stage

	Best Case	Worst Case	Duration
Growth of cash flows	15%	8%	10 years

One last thing to note is that although the number of drivers we need to consider and forecast is few, we really need to understand what makes each of these drivers vary. In Chapter 6, I will address the idea of *anchoring* more, but in short, it is the assumption that the next number in a series will be close to the last number in that series. This assumption is not necessarily true and can, in fact, be dangerously false. For instance, just because a firm has expanded revenues at an average annual percentage rate of 37 percent over the past few years does not mean that the next yearly increase needs to be 35, 30, or 25 percent or even positive.[3]

So making projections for each of the drivers should never be just a process of simply extrapolating past results. Making projections for each driver means really understanding what factors are influencing that driver and how those factors are likely to change in the future. Although this process of understanding the underlying factors and projecting driver values into the future is not as difficult or complex as neurosurgery or designing a manned spacecraft to Mars, it does require some creativity, insight, thought, and patience.

For an actual, specific example of a valuation done using this methodology, please see the detailed valuation example of Oracle posted on the Intelligent Option Investor (IOI) website www.IntelligentOptionInvestor .com. A general explanation of the valuation drivers, along with a few high-level examples, follows.

A Detailed Look at the Drivers of Value

Now that we have an idea of where we are going in our valuation process, let us take a look at each of the valuation drivers one by one.

Revenue Growth

Revenue growth is the first determinant of value for a company—if revenues are not coming in, it is obvious that cash will not flow to the company's owners. Organic revenue growth (i.e., that which does not come from acquiring another company) can come from

1. Increased volume of sales (selling more stuff)
2. Increased value of sales (selling stuff for more)

At the heart of understanding a company's revenues and forecasting the future growth rate of its revenues is understanding what the company is selling and to whom it is selling its product(s). The business model for a company such as Bentley that is selling $300,000 Mulsannes that we rejected for our taxi-cab company in Chapter 4 is going to be very different from that of the $30,000 Camry-selling Toyota.

Toyota has very little ability to raise prices—that is, to sell its stuff for more money—so it must sell more stuff. Bentley, on the other hand, has enormous pricing power—its customers are more sensitive to the image that the possession of a Bentley conveys to them than they are to the monetary cost of possession—and one of the ways Bentley maintains that pricing power is by restricting its production—selling less stuff, in other words. Understanding the interplay between selling more stuff and selling stuff for more is essential to understanding the first driver of value to a firm.

Some people—experienced analysts included—tend to look at revenues as year-over-year percent changes and simply extrapolate the recent percentage growth into the future. This is a big mistake and can be a very expensive one. Companies that are at the transition between the supply-constrained early growth period and the demand-constrained investment-based growth period can sometimes see some very rapid slowdowns in revenue growth from one year to the next. If you are trying to value a company as though its revenue stream will continue forever (or for a long time) or as though it were a supply-constrained startup—which is basically what people do when they extrapolate recent growth rate numbers too far into the future—you will estimate the value of the company as being too great. Likewise, when a company whose business tends to move with the business cycle—like a steel producer—is in a cyclic trough, and you assume that its business is going to keep growing at low rates or even shrinking far into the future, you will generate too low an estimate for the value of the firm.

Rather than extrapolating, really understanding the dynamics of the business is crucial. Most Wall Street analysts spend proportionally less of their time trying to figure out revenues than they do profit. In contrast, I usually suggest that people try to spend more time getting a very firm grasp of how a firm generates revenues. Who is buying the company's products or services and why are they buying those products or services rather than another's? Are customers using credit to buy the company's products or services? And if so, how tenuous is that line of credit? How many of the company's products might people need or want and how often would they be willing to buy them? These are all essential questions to answer, and once you have a good idea about them, you will have gone a long way to understanding the value of the company in which you are considering taking an ownership stake.

Profit generation, while undeniably an important factor, is for most companies, an almost mechanical process that is largely dependent upon the amount of revenues flowing into the firm. I will discuss why most of the market focuses so much on profitability in the next section, but readers who are interested in seeing what parts of a financial statement I believe are the most important to dig into when analyzing revenues, please consult the valuation example on the IOI website.

Profitability

Think back to our taxi-cab example in Chapter 4. After the first year of operation, our transportation entrepreneur had $5,000 in her bank account. She was planning to set $1,000 aside for a down payment on a new taxi in a few years' time, after her present car had used up its economic life; this would give her a total of $4,000 that she could decide how to spend—either on a Caribbean cruise or on a new computerized ordering system.

In this example, *profitability* means this $4,000 amount that we are calling owner's cash profit.

As I mentioned earlier, most sell-side analysts and market speculators spend their time trying to forecast profitability. Usually, the profitability they are trying to predict is an accounting line item such as earnings per share (EPS), earnings before interest and taxes (EBIT), or earnings before interest, taxes, depreciation, and amortization (EBITDA). The reason for this is simple: most sell-side analysts' target prices (and more than a few buy-side investment strategies) are generated by multiplying one of these quantities by some market multiple. For example, an analyst might say that the target price of $ABC = 7.8 \times EBITDA = \$27.50$ per share.

There are three main reasons why using multiples analysis to value a company should be used with circumspection.

First and foremost, there is no law of nature saying that a stock price has to be a certain multiple of some financial statement line item. Just because other companies in a given industry are trading between 7.5 and 8.5 times EBITDA doesn't mean that they can't trade for higher or lower, nor does it mean that another company has to trade within that range either.

Second, the financial statement quantities mentioned (EPS, EBIT, and EBITDA) can all vary fairly substantially because of various accounting technicalities and other measures that do not have a material impact on the firm's long-term value.

Last but not least, multiples imply future profitability growth rates, but simultaneously make these implied growth rates much less meaningful.

To illustrate this point, consider the following question: Which of the following predictions seems more transparent and testable?

1. I forecast this company's medium-term cash flows will grow at an average of 10 percent per year for five years followed by GDP-like growth afterward.
2. I forecast this company is worth 23.5 times next year's EPS estimates.

Clearly, the former is preferable, since by specifying the growth rates, you are forced to think of how that growth might be achieved. The latter gives no hint of growth rates, so in effect detaches the value of the company from the operational details of the firm.

There are a few reasons why Wall Street analysts love to publish multiples-based target prices that I will discuss in Chapter 6 when I introduce structural impediments. For the time being, just realize that what is good for an investment banker or equity sales trader is rarely good for an investor.

Discounting the efficacy and transparency of market multiples-based valuation is not the same as saying that profitability is not important—of course it is. However, profitability is, to a surprisingly large extent, governed by structural factors and profit margins tend to be quite similar between companies in the same industry. For many companies, this makes estimating best- and worst-case profit margins fairly easy.

For example, the grocery business is one in which a supermarket buys an item at a low price and sells it at a higher price. Because the items it sells are basically identical to the items sold at competitors' stores, and because there are numerous competitors serving essentially the same customer base in the same area, it is impossible for the supermarket to raise its prices very much or for very long before customers start switching to another store. Because of these industry dynamics, the range over which grocery chain profitability varies is quite narrow. We can see an illustration of this in the following table of three large-capitalization pure-play grocery stores:

Company (Ticker)	Market Cap	Avg. 3-year OCP Margin
Kroger (KR)	$23.9 B	1.5%
Whole Foods Mkt (WFM)	$14.1 B	4.9%
Safeway (SWY)	$7.9 B	1.4%

Data courtesy of YCharts.com

Here we see that even the fancy Whole Foods Market, which, in terms of grocery stores operates on a sell-stuff-for-more model, is still generating OCP margins (i.e., OCP divided by revenues) of less than 5 percent. Kroger and Safeway—two supermarkets operating on a sell-more-stuff model—have virtually identical profit margins.

Of course, not all businesses are as stable and predictable as grocery stores. There are four effects that can alter the profitability of a company: operational leverage, demand changes, environmental factors, and efficiency increases.

The single most important factor affecting the ability to predict profitability at a firm is something called operating leverage. I describe this factor in Appendix B and go into detail about how to estimate the effects of operating leverage in the example valuation posted on the Intelligent Option Investor website. The takeaway from this material is that for companies with a high degree of operating leverage, the amount of revenues coming in will hugely influence profitability. This dependence of profits on revenues provides a prospective investor in a company with high operational leverage more reason to understand the demand environment and how a firm generates revenues.

Of course, if there are changes in the demand environment that cause consumers' preferences to change away from the product a company is providing and toward another that it is not (e.g., consumers preferring electronic tablets made by Apple over PCs made by Dell), or changes in the supply environment that causes a company's capital base to be too large (e.g., American car companies' factories having too much capacity after the U.S. car market saturated in the early 1980s), profit margins are *not* likely to settle into an historical range but may materially increase (e.g., Apple, after the release of iPads, iPhones, and so on) or decrease (e.g., Dell, after Apple's release of iPads, iPhones, and so on). Being able to correctly forecast this type of secular shift is difficult, but can be extremely profitable.

In addition to these factors, there can be rapid drops and rises in profitability caused by changes in the economic environment. These might be company-specific events, such as a natural disaster destroying a supply of inventory, or economy-wide conditions, such as loose monetary policy encouraging consumers to use debt to make more purchases. While these kind of factors can have a large short-term effect on profitability, averaged over a longer time frame of a few years, most businesses' profit margins end up returning to a fairly dependable range.

Another case in which the normal profit range of a company may change is through improvements in productivity. And although improvements to productivity can take a long time to play out, they can be extremely important. The reason for this is that even if a company is in a stage in which revenues do not grow very quickly, if profit margins are increasing, profit that can flow to the owner(s) will grow at a faster rate than revenues. You can see this very clearly in the following table:

Year	0	1	2	3	4	5	6	7	8	9	10
Revenues ($)	1,234	1,271	1,309	1,348	1,389	1,431	1,473	1,518	1,563	1,610	1,658
Revenue growth (%)	—	3	3	3	3	3	3	3	3	3	3
OCP ($) [4]	432	445	497	485	514	544	560	637	625	708	746
OCP margin (%)	35	35	38	36	37	38	38	42	40	44	45
OCP growth rate (%)	—	3	12	-2	6	6	3	14	-2	13	5

Even though revenues grew by a constant 3 percent per year over this time, OCP margin (owner's cash profit/revenues) increased from 35 to 45 percent, and the compound annual growth in OCP was nearly twice that of revenue growth—at 6 percent.

Thinking back to the earlier discussion of the life cycle of a company, recall that the rate at which a company's cash flows grew was a very important determinant of the value of the firm. The dynamic of a company with a relatively slow-growing revenue line and an increasing profit margin is common. A typical scenario is that a company whose revenues have been increasing quickly may be more focused on meeting demand by any means possible rather than in the most efficient way. As revenue growth slows, attention starts to turn to increasing the efficiency of the production processes. As that efficiency increases, so does the profit margin. As the profit margin increases, as long as the revenue line has some positive growth, profit growth will be even faster.

This dynamic is worth keeping in mind when analyzing companies and in the next section, where I discuss the next driver of company value— investment level and efficacy.

Investing Level and Efficacy

After our taxi company owner generated profits, she had to figure out if she was going to invest those profits or spend them, and if she invested them, she had to figure out what investment project was best. Listed companies also face the same process and choices. Managers are responsible for investing owners' cash profits with the aim of generating greater profits in the future or for returning owners' cash profits to the owners via dividends.

Because modern companies are so large and have so many shareholders, most owners not only do not take an active role in shaping the investments of their company, but they also don't even realize that the investment process is taking place.[5] In this environment, there are unfortunately many instances in which the owners' cash profits are invested badly or otherwise squandered on wasteful projects. Ford paying top dollar to buy a decrepit Jaguar springs to mind, as does Time Warner's miserable purchase of AOL at the very peak of the tech bubble. But these egregious examples are certainly just the tip of the iceberg. Companies routinely make implicit capital spending decisions by refusing to close down an underperforming or obsolete business, thereby robbing owners of cash flows that should have been theirs and instead filling the wallets of consultants and employees.[6] Or the managers, realizing that their mature core business throws off an enormous amount of cash, decide to spend some of that cash on acquisitions of dubious economic benefit to the owners.[7] Luckily, managers can always find an investment banker or two who are ready to talk about the numerous "synergies" that will no doubt someday come to pass, and too often boards and shareholders blithely accept the decisions and, once made, do not demand an accounting of owner benefits as a result of the union.

Using an intelligent option investing framework, however, these heretofore hidden investment programs and their success or failure can be seen much more clearly. First, we must see how much of the owners' cash profits for the company were spent on investing projects and forecast the amount that will likely be invested in the future. The online valuation example provides an actual look at precisely what financial line items go into this calculation. Right now, it is enough to frame the term *investments* as any cash outflows on capital projects that the company is making over and above the cash outflows necessary to maintain the business as a going concern. Recall that in Chapter 4, I called this spending expansionary cash flows because they are designed to generate faster profit growth in the future.

The phrase *faster profit growth* should prompt the question, "Faster than what?" It is at this point that we think back to the discussion of the life cycle of a company. After a company has cleared its supply-side constraints, and after it has done all it can to increase profits in an environment of demand-side constraints, it bumps up against *structural constraints*. Structural constraints represent the long-run "speed limit" for the growth of a firm. Because there is a speed limit for a firm in the long run, it is logical that during the investment stage of a company's life we compare the investment-boosted growth with that structural speed limit.

The ultimate structural speed limit, as discussed earlier, is the nominal growth in U.S. gross domestic product (GDP). In this case, *nominal* means the GDP growth that includes the effect of inflation as well as the increase in economic activity. A graph of this nominal increase in GDP from the postwar period follows:

Nominal U.S. GDP (Billions of USD)
March 1997–September 2013

Note that I have displayed this on a logarithmic axis to show how consistent growth has been. The line representing U.S. nominal GDP swings above or below the straight trend line but seems to swing back toward the line eventually.

Over this very long period, the nominal GDP growth in the United States averaged just over 6 percent per year. If the investment projects of a company are generally successful, the company will be able to dependably grow its profits at a rate faster than this 6 percent (or so) benchmark. The length of time it will be able to grow faster than this benchmark will depend on various factors related to the competitiveness of the industry, the demand environment, and the investing skill of its managers.

Seeing whether or not investments have been successful over time is a simple matter of comparing OCP growth with nominal GDP. Let's look at a few actual examples. Here is a graph of my calculation of Walmart's OCP and OCP margin over the last 13 years:

Estimated Owners' Cash Profit and OCP Margin for Walmart

— Total Estimated OCP (LH)   •••• OCP Margin (RH)

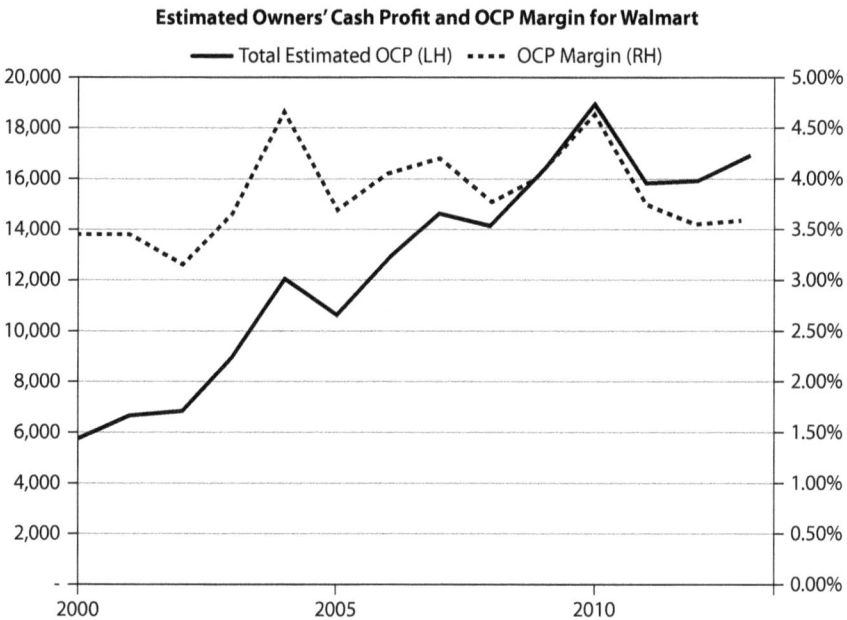

As one might expect with such a large, mature firm, OCP margin (shown on the right-hand axis) is very steady—barely breaking from the 3.5 to 4.5 percent range over the last 10 years. At the same time, its total OCP (shown on the left-hand axis) grew nicely as a result of increases in revenues. Over the last seven years, Walmart has spent an average of around 2 percent of its revenues on expansionary projects, implying that cash flow left for shareholders amounted to about \$0.02 (≈ \$0.045 – \$0.02) on every dollar, on average. How efficacious were these investments?

In the graph below, any point above the "0 ppt" horizontal axis indicates that Walmart's year-over-year OCP growth has exceeded the U.S. GDP by that amount, and vice versa. The year-over-year OCP growth statistics are fairly noisy, bouncing back and forth above and below growth in GDP; however, looking at a five-year compound annual growth rate (CAGR) tells the same story as the linear trend line on the chart: Walmart's growth has slowed significantly and now looks to be close to that of the economy at large on average. The rise in Walmart's fiscal 2010 result (which corresponds with calendar year 2009) is more a function of the company's revenues remaining resilient despite a U.S. recession than its growth outpacing a growing U.S. economy.

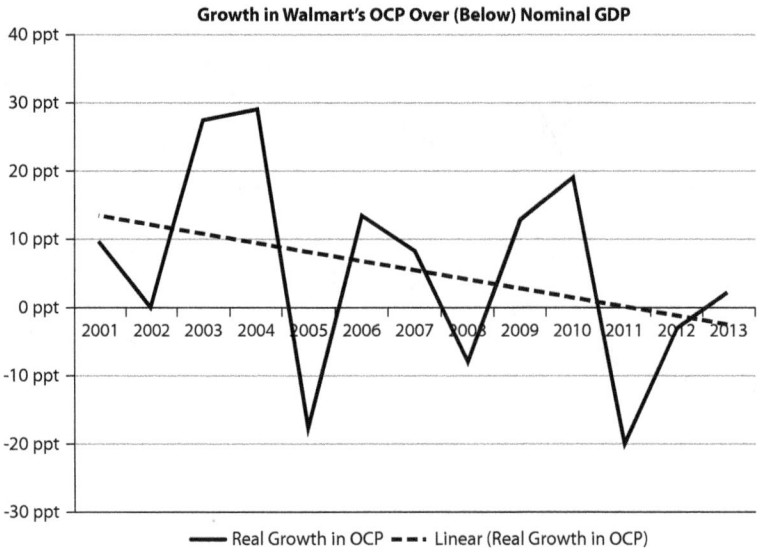

Growth in Walmart's OCP Over (Below) Nominal GDP

— Real Growth in OCP — ▪ · Linear (Real Growth in OCP)

To the credit of Walmart's management, the company has spent increasingly smaller proportions of revenues on expansionary projects over the last few years, perhaps in recognition that its expansionary projects were bringing in less bang for the buck over time.

In contrast, let's take a look at a firm whose investments seem to be adding considerable value—Oracle. First, let's take a look at its OCP margin:

Estimated OCP Margin for Oracle

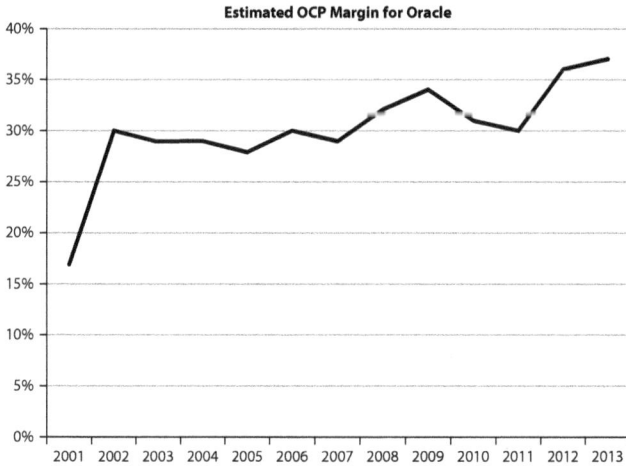

Other than the disastrous year of the tech bust in 2001, the company's OCP margin has held fairly steadily in the 30 percent range, but recently it has started to move toward the 35 percent level. Over the last five years, the company's expansionary spending has averaged around 15 percent of revenues per year, mainly through acquisitions. Because the expansionary spending is governed by its acquisitions, its investments are not uniform, and looking at the 2005–2008 period, the company was spending roughly half its revenues on expansion. Over this time period, how has Oracle's OCP growth been vis-à-vis GDP? Let's take a look:

Growth in Oracle's OCP Above (Below) Nominal GDP

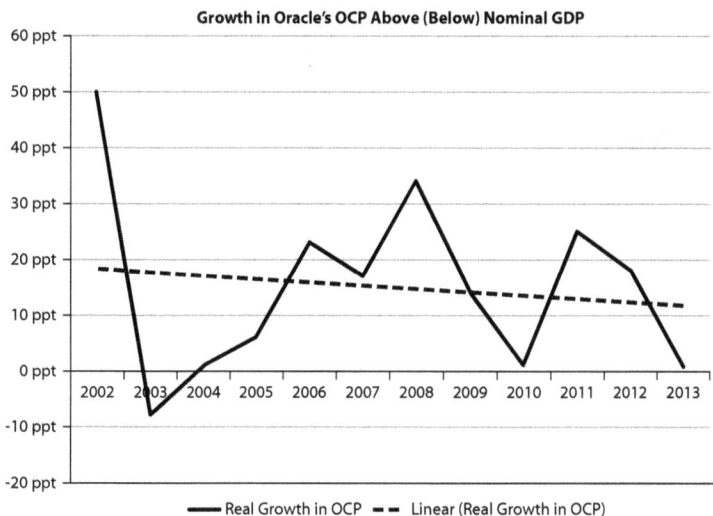

In contrast with Walmart, through this lens, we see that Oracle's investments have generally allowed its OCP to grow at a much faster rate than the economy at large (2010 was the year Oracle acquired Sun Microsystems, and the OCP that year is an artifact of that acquisition— I believe that its OCP that year was actually higher than stated here).

The beauty of this way of looking at companies is that the hidden or implicit investments a company is making will show up in this as well. I believe that, like many large companies, Walmart is finding that it must spend money on expansion because it is investing ineffectually through its internal business processes. One percent of revenues worth of expansionary cash flows per year—roughly 25 percent of owners' cash profits—is being spent so that the company can basically keep up with growth of the economy at large.

This discussion deals with investment efficacy. Investments— especially in the corporate environment, where one company completely takes control of another and must integrate the acquiree into its own business systems and culture—take time for results to be visible. As such, it is easy to see why the table at the start of this section showed investment efficacy affecting the medium-term results of the company—its growth rates in particular.

Understanding the interaction among these three drivers—revenue growth, profitability, and investing efficacy—allows an investor to take the biggest step toward valuing a stock. Occasionally, though, one must take what I call *balance-sheet effects* into consideration.

Balance-Sheet Effects

Let's think back to our taxi-cab service. Let's say that our owner decided that after the first year, the investment prospects for her firm were so good that she would buy two new cars. She thought that she could save money by buying two low-mileage, off-lease cars rather than new ones.

Before putting the cars into service, she cleans each of the cars thoroughly. While cleaning out the trunk of the first car, she finds a tightly wrapped brown paper package. Curious, she opens the package to find a pound of illegal drugs. She calls the police, who come to investigate. After looking over the situation, the police impound the car, telling our taxi entrepreneur that they had no estimate for when it would be returned.

The value of our taxi-cab company suddenly drops. Without the use of the car, there is no way for it to generate revenues. However, while revenues are not coming in, the company is still incurring costs (financing and insurance costs, in particular), so the new car is actually lowering the cash flow available to the owner. In the parlance of accounting experts, the company has experienced a nonoperational contingency that has resulted in a devaluation of one of its assets. This is a value-destroying balance-sheet effect.

The taxi company owner, upset with the turn of events and her bad luck in picking automobiles, grumbles as she gets back to work cleaning out the second car. Cleaning between the back seats, she finds a valid lottery ticket that was forgotten by the previous owner. Expecting a couple bucks worth of winnings, she checks the number and is more than overjoyed to find that she is holding the winning ticket for a $500,000 prize! The disappointment from the police impounding her other car melts away as she realizes this little slip of paper represents 125 years' worth (+$500,000/$4,000) of her company's first-year OCP. This is one heck of a positive balance-sheet effect.

The base assumption we make when we analyze a company is that all the assets on the balance sheet are operating assets—that they are being fully exploited to generate cash flows on behalf of owner(s). However, this is sometimes not a valid assumption to make. Sometimes the true value of assets can be hidden and remain hidden for some time.

On the hidden-asset side, one of the biggest jobs of the class of institutional investors known as *activist investors* is to dig into the operating details of a company to find assets that the company is not fully using or is using so badly that the company is not able to create maximum cash flows. Usually, the activist investor is looking to throw out the current management team and replace it with people he or she thinks can better use the assets. This is termed a *hostile takeover*, but it is important to remember that the term *hostile* is only valid from the perspective of the target's management team. An insightful activist investor with patience, foresight, and enough board seats to push through a change can be an enormous boon to investors in the company.

In the same way that there are hidden assets, there also can be hidden liabilities. Enron's complex transactions with its "special-purpose vehicles" are a vivid example of how dangerous hidden liabilities can be. Enron managers found ways to effectively channel financial transactions and obligations that they did not want on Enron's own books (namely, losses and liabilities) onto the books of off-shore entities. Even though the off-shore entities were established and controlled by Enron's management, they were not consolidated into Enron's own financial statements, so the transactions and obligations effectively disappeared from most investors' view. Several investor groups started putting two and two together and realized that the answer was less than four. Eventually, when the special-purpose vehicles became known by the investment community, it was obvious that there was much less equity for investors to own than they had thought previously, and the stock price plummeted.

Whereas hidden assets can be thought of as a winning lottery ticket stuck in between the seats of a used car, an old colleague of mine in the hedge fund world used to call hidden liabilities "snakes sleeping in a basket." Usually, it takes some time and familiarity with a company or industry to understand where these lottery tickets or snakes may reside, but most companies have them to a greater or lesser extent. Mostly, these hidden items are not material to valuation and thus can be ignored, but when they are not material, they can be truly powerful influences on valuation.

It is impossible to explain precisely where to look for these hidden items, but there are a few places one can typically start looking:

Lottery Tickets

1. Real estate carried at historical cost
2. Intellectual property (e.g., patents, copyrighted material, etc.)
3. Government connections (not as important in developed markets but could be vitally important in certain emerging markets)
4. Overfunded pensions

Snakes

1. Latent product/accident liability claims (e.g., asbestos, pollution remediation, etc.)
2. Manager malfeasance (e.g., price fixing, Foreign Corrupt Practices Act noncompliance, etc.)
3. Underfunded pensions
4. Off-balance-sheet corruption
5. Fraud

It's usually hard to find these, but if you do, you should try to make an assumption about the best- and worst-case financial impacts of these items and simply tack that onto whatever cash-flow projections you have made.

Tying It All Together

Throughout our analysis of a company's valuation drivers, our focus as investors should always be to estimate the free cash flow to owners that a firm will likely generate.

In the short-term, FCFO is driven by how fast revenues are growing, how efficiently the company is converting those revenues to profits, and how much of the profits the firm is spending on expansionary projects.

In the medium-term, FCFO is driven by how effective the investments the firm made in the preceding period are likely to be.

In the long-term FCFO is driven by structural constraints because a firm cannot grow faster than the economy at large.

Each driver has both best- and worst-case projections, so pooling all the best-case projections into a best-case FCFO scenario and all the worst-case projections into a worst-case FCFO scenario gives us an idea of the most and least cash flow that the firm will generate for us in the future (you can see an example of this on the Intelligent Option Investor website). Discounting those FCFO scenarios generates a present value range for the company. If we can find any balance-sheet effects, we add or deduct those effects from the value found from discounting the FCFO scenarios. This is the final valuation range of the company that we can compare to the market price of the stock. When the valuation range of a company and the price of a stock differ by a great amount, we have an opportunity to invest profitably.

Advanced Building Corp. (ABC)

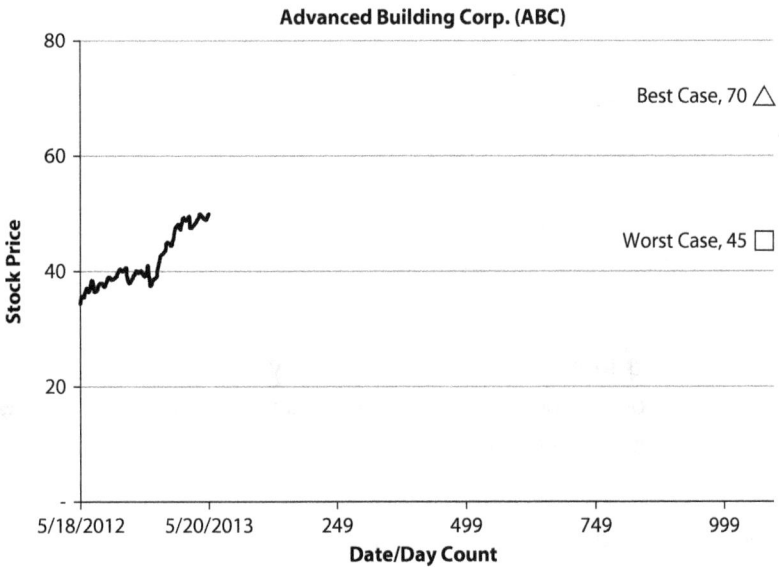

These are the general principles of intelligent investing, but again, the reader is invited to work through the detailed valuation example on the IOI website to help bring these general principles to life.

The preceding chapter on understanding the golden rule of valuation and this chapter on recognizing the valuation drivers are a great step toward building what Warren Buffett called a "sound framework for making [investment] decisions."

The one thing that I hope you have realized while reading this and the preceding chapter is what a simple and commonsense process valuation is. It is worth asking why—if rational valuation is such a simple process—do people generally have such a very difficult time investing and run into so many pitfalls.

To understand this, I now turn to an explanation of the behavioral biases and structural impediments that trip investors up and make suggestions on how to avoid them.

Chapter 6

UNDERSTANDING AND OVERCOMING INVESTING PITFALLS

You have seen that valuation is not a difficult thing. It requires understanding of a few key relationships, but it is basically a straightforward process most of the time.

Why then, do so many investors have such a hard time doing it well?

The main reason, I am sorry to say, is our nature as human beings and the weaknesses of our nature. This chapter discusses two facets of that—behavioral biases and structural impediments. The first facet—behavioral biases—involves how we as human beings try to figure out complex things and get caught in the process of doing so. The second facet—structural impediments—speaks about how we investors tend to buy—lock, stock, and barrel—into a game designed only for us to lose, whereas the winners' kids go to $50,000-a-year prep schools followed by a four-year tour of the Ivy Leagues.

There is hope. Don't despair. The first step to not falling for these pitfalls is simply to understand that they exist.

Obviously, being an intelligent option investor means investing intelligently, minimizing—as much as possible—the effects of irrational and emotional decision making. This chapter is designed to help you do just that.

Jargon introduced in this chapter is as follows:

X-system	Risk neutral
Risk seeking	Risk averse
C-seeking	Prospect theory

Behavioral Biases

Human intelligence evolved in an environment that is very different from the one in which we live today. Gone is the necessity to hunt and gather, protect ourselves from predators, and fashion our own shelter. In contrast, in our modern lives, we are safe from most environmental factors but are instead confronted with massive amounts of data. Groundbreaking photographer Rick Smolan, in his book, *The Human Face of Big Data* (Sausalito, CA: Against All Odds Productions, 2012), contends that a modern person processes more information in a single day than the typical sixteenth-century person processed in an entire lifetime. I am not sure if there is a scientific way of proving such a contention, but it does seem at least plausible.

In terms of investing, the mismatch between how our mental processes have evolved and the tasks that we expect them to carry out becomes an issue because, by and large, we are still using mental strategies that served our Stone Age ancestors well but that serve us investing denizens of the "Information Age" much less well.

The study of human bias in economic decision making is a big topic—called *behavioral economics* or *behavioral finance*—and it is not possible to cover it fully here. I will give a few examples here and suggest how you might work to counteract theses biases in your intelligent investing, but you are encouraged to study up on these issues themselves. It is a fascinating topic, and the more you learn, the more you will realize how much behavioral biases affect everyone's decision-making processes.

Here I will discuss three issues:

1. Love of symmetry
2. Confidence and overconfidence
3. Humans' kinky perception of risk

Love of Symmetry

Here is the chart of an asset that has had a smart 8.3 percent return in just 50 trading days. Is this thing likely to keep going up from here or fall back down after its relatively rapid rise?

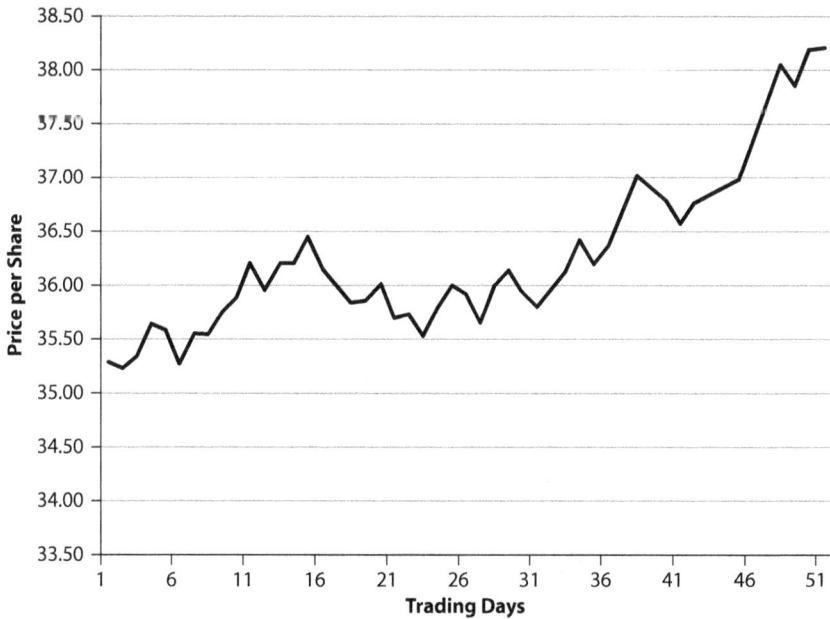

You would be correct if you answered, "Neither of the above." This is a chart I created using the random-number-generator function in Excel. Because Excel recalculates the values on the sheet any time a change is made, I could not get the next value in this series—the series changed as soon as I asked Excel to calculate the next day's return.

I have presented similar series to various groups, including groups of traders. It is fascinating to hear the predictions regarding this series and the reasoning behind the predictions. Usually, the crowd settles on an answer that is acceptable to most people (e.g., "It will probably go higher, but I'd set a stop loss at $37.25 and aggressively buy if it goes down to $35.50").[1]

Why do so many people see patterns where no patterns exist? Why do so many people put their faith in so-called technical analysis (which is neither technical nor analysis) even though they are just as likely to be successful consulting a Magic 8 Ball for investment advice?

To understand this, we need to realize that there are two separate human mental processes for analyzing and solving problems: *X-system* and *C-system.*

The X-system is in control of refleXive thought processes, and these processes take place in some very primitive areas of the brain. This system is extremely good at perceiving patterns and symmetry and can operate very quickly to solve common problems. It is also capable of multitasking. The C-system is in control of refleCtive thought processes, and these processes take place in parts of the brain associated with higher reasoning. This system works slowly to solve complex problems about which we have limited experience. Its ability to multitask is limited.

For an illustration of these two systems, consider this problem: you are walking in a house and are confronted with the following object:

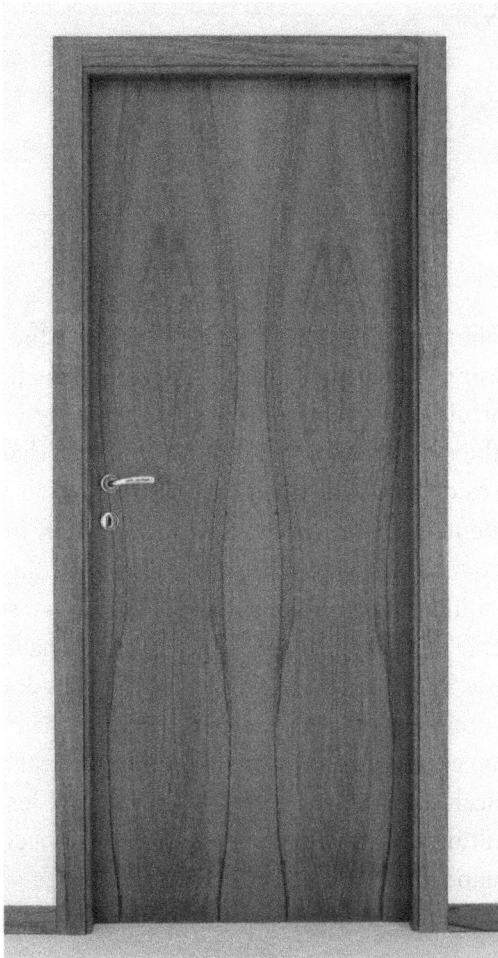

Your X-system recognizes this object as a door, quickly retrieves information about how to use objects of this type from your memory, and directs you to rotate the metal handle downward to open the door and move into the next room. You can solve this problem extremely quickly, with no conscious thought, even while you are doing something else, like speaking with a friend.

Now let's say that when you grab the handle and rotate it, rather than the door opening, the handle comes off in your hand. What do you do? Your mind automatically switches from X-system mode to C-system mode, and you begin to solve the problem of the closed door in a logical, systematic way. You would stop talking to your friend, push the door to see if it will open without the latch, bend down to take a look at the handle mechanism, and so on.

Throughout the process of attempting to solve this problem, you may switch back and forth between X-system and C-system processing, using your C-system as the controller and the X-system to check on prior solutions to similar problems you may have faced.

With this example, you likely have a good intuitive feel for the characteristics of the X- and C-systems, but for completeness's sake, here is a grid describing them:

X-System	C-System
Reflexive	Reflective
Good for recognizing symmetry and patterns and for solving commonly experienced problems	Good for analyzing complex, multistep problems outside previous experience
Operates quickly	Operates slowly
Separate processes do not interfere with one another, allowing for multitasking	Separate processes do interfere with one another, making multitasking difficult or impossible
Uses amygdala, basal ganglia, and temporal cortex—the areas of the brain associated with "fight or flight," reward training, identification of objects, and behavior	Uses anterior cingulate cortex, prefrontal cortex, medial temporal lobe, including the hippocampus—the areas of the brain associated with higher-order functions such as planning and control
Didactic style: analogy	Didactic style: mathematical proof
Psychologically comfortable and easy	Psychologically uncomfortable and difficult

The X-system is more psychologically comfortable to us (or to most of us) because it is the part of the brain we as a species have been using during most of our evolutionary history. The pattern-recognition portion of our brain is highly developed—so much so that even though computers such as Deep Blue can go toe to toe with chess grand masters, no computer has yet been designed that would be able to recognize a fork that is rotated 30 percent off center or a series of random items placed in front of it. Even the greatest computer "mind" cannot carry out a pattern-recognition task that is simple even for human infants.

In investing, humans tend to lean on this X-system pattern recognition and try to use shortcuts to analysis based on it. We have mental models for certain kinds of companies, certain kinds of information, and certain situations, and we attempt to escape uncomfortable, analytical C-system processing by allowing our X-system to match current conditions with those mental models.

When presented with a stimulus (e.g., bad quarterly earnings numbers), our tendency is to reflexively react rather than to analyze the information. This tendency is made more visceral because the X-system that is processing this stimulus is tied into the "fight or flight" response. We would rather act first, even if acting proves to be a detriment rather than a benefit.

This is a phenomenally difficult—I think impossible—bias to completely overcome. Although this bias can be extremely detrimental to us and our investing process, our highly developed X-system is also incredibly useful to us in our daily lives—allowing us to navigate the difficult problems presented by doors, car operation, and so on. I discuss how to recognize and work around X-system biases, how to use the X-system when it is useful to do so, and how to frame investment decisions using C-system processes in the valuation example of Oracle that can be found on the Intelligent Option Investor website. For now, let's look at another behavioral bias—overconfidence.

Confidence and Overconfidence

Scientific research has shown that humans do not feel comfortable with C-system-style analysis and tend to doubt the results of these processes. As mentioned earlier, C-system processes do not seem intuitive and certainly do not jibe with the satisfying off-the-hip decision making that seems to be prized culturally.

In what may seem like a counterintuitive reaction to this feeling of discomfort with C-system processes, you often find analysts and investors attempting to collect every scrap and shred of detail regarding a company's operations before making an investment decision. This phenomenon may have something to do not only with a certain discomfort with C-system processes but also with a natural human discomfort with the unknown. All investments are made in an environment of uncertainty, and uncertainty is an unsettling psychological state for humans to find themselves in. To ameliorate the discomfort from uncertainty, people have a tendency to attempt to gain control of the uncontrollable by not leaving any stone unturned in their analyses.

This may seem sensible, but in fact, studies have shown that more information does not help you to make better decisions—just the opposite, in fact. The first study showing this bias was done by a psychologist at the University of Oregon named Paul Slovic, who studied the accuracy and confidence of professional horserace handicappers.[2] Similar studies have been performed on other groups—medical doctors and stock brokers among them—and the results from subsequent studies have been very similar.

Professor Slovic gave professional handicappers varying amounts of information about horses running in a series of races and then asked them to make a prediction about the first-place finisher in each race. The handicappers were then asked to assess the confidence they had in their predictions. Slovic had the actual race results and compared the professionals' confidence with their actual accuracy. The results can be represented graphically as follows:

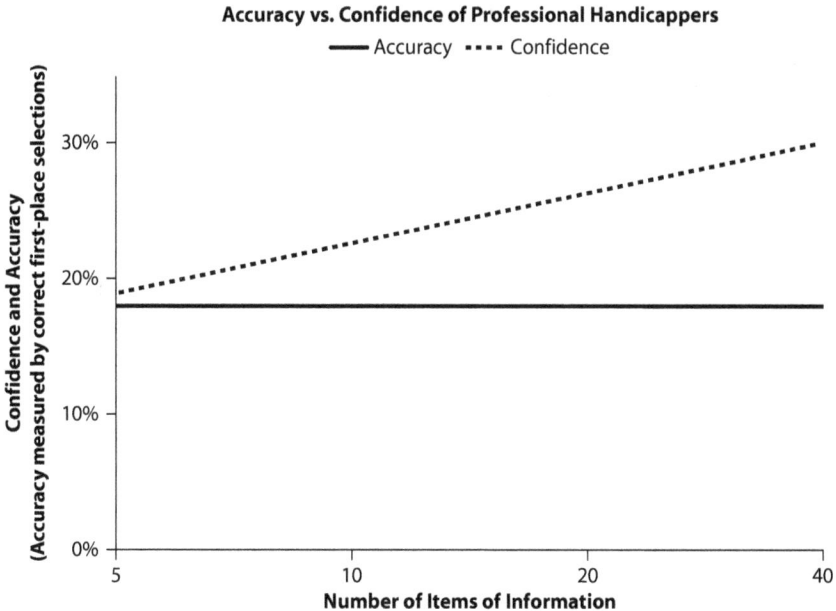

Accuracy vs. Confidence of Professional Handicappers

──── Accuracy ·· · · Confidence

Confidence and Accuracy
(Accuracy measured by correct first-place selections)

Number of Items of Information

This is an incredible graph. The horizontal line represents the accuracy of the expert predictions. The dotted line represents the confidence of the experts depending on the amount of information they had.

The fact that the predictive efficacy line remains horizontal and the confidence line increases so sharply indicates an interesting and, thinking about it, frightening facet of human behavior. Namely, even though the predictions made by the experts who had the most data were no more accurate in reality than those of their colleagues who had limited data, the ones with access to more and more data became more and more confident, to the extent that they were massively overconfident. Accuracy remains just under 20 percent, but confidence goes up to 30 percent—a 10 percentage point difference in perception (confidence) versus reality (accuracy)!

This behavioral bias has two large negative effects on investors. First is a tendency to spend too much time looking at too many nonmaterial minutiae until finally one cannot come to a decision regarding whether or not to invest—or, as it is colloquially known, *analysis paralysis.*

I think of the attempt to gather a huge amount of increasingly detailed information about an investment prospect as a sort of cosmic bargaining. The analyst or investor who spends hundreds of hours looking at very detailed information not material to the valuation is doing something akin to making a burnt offering of old. The analyst or investor is, in some sense, making a prayer to the market gods: "I will sacrifice a lot of time and mental effort learning about this company. Please reward me with positive returns this year."

In the attempt to bargain with the great unseen hand of the market, an analyst spends more and more time collecting increasingly less and less important information about the potential investment until the cost of collecting the extra information greatly outweighs the benefit of having gathered it. The big problem with very detailed analyses is that the closer one looks at a given problem, the more involved that problem becomes. Every fact has some supporting details, and each supporting detail has a few scenarios that may be associated with it. To do a really thorough job, you must look at each scenario in turn. Ah! But these scenarios turn out to be interrelated, so you must think about not only first-order changes in the scenarios but also secondary and tertiary ones as well. Soon the analyst or investor's spreadsheet model winds up being 45 tabs deep, and it still seems like there is more work that needs to be done before a decision can be made ("Where were those numbers regarding the depreciation of fixed assets at the Malaysian subbranch?! How can I invest if I don't know that?!"). At this point, the analysis has become thoroughly paralyzed, and frequently the investor will decide (after putting in all that hard work) just to drop the whole thing because he or she "can't get his or her head around" the valuation.

Another cost to gathering a great amount of detailed information is more subtle but no less dangerous. Let's say that the analyst has worked through all those secondary and tertiary scenarios and decides that the firm in question is undervalued. The company is trading for X and is worth "Y at a minimum." What is the analyst's confidence level in that Y valuation? If the scientific studies I mentioned earlier hold true, the analyst is 50 percent more confident than the position warrants. This is an unhealthy dose of overconfidence.

The investor hits the "Buy" button and hopes for the best. However, after a few quarters, some of the operational metrics at the firm begin to falter. The Capex project that was forecast to take 5 percent of sales in year one ends up taking closer to 9 percent. Sales are a bit lower than expected, and costs are a bit higher. But the investor has thought about all these possibilities and is still very confident in the valuation; these discrepancies are thus looked at like anomalies that will soon be corrected with another quarter or two of results. The situation can drag on for an extended time until suddenly the investor is confronted with the possibility that the firm is running out of cash, its new product line has failed, or whatever. The investor, once so confident, now has to face the unpleasant task of realizing a loss (why he or she may not want to realize a loss is discussed in the section "Humans' Kinky Perception of Risk" later).

"Love is blind." Unfortunately, overconfidence in an investment opinion can make one just as blind as love.

I believe that two facets of intelligent option investing can help to ameliorate these biases. First, recall that there are at most four—and most often only three—drivers determining company valuation. While you are reading about a company and analyzing its value, it is wise to constantly ask yourself two questions:

1. Is what I'm analyzing related to one of the drivers of company value?
2. Is what I'm analyzing material to the valuation?

Sure, there is some sort of satisfaction in knowing everything there is to know about coal-processing technology or oil reservoir structure and engineering, but recognize that this satisfaction is purely personal and is not going to make a bit of difference to the valuation. Understanding these kinds of technical details might help a tiny bit in understanding competitive dynamics in an industry, but the cost of learning them almost always exceeds the benefit from the knowledge. For any technical points you are trying to learn about as a layperson, there are likely two armies of engineers, specifically trained in that field, arguing with one another about whatever point you are learning about. No matter how large your bandwidth is, it is not likely that you will be able to make a more informed decision than those people. And if the final result is, "Company A will likely be able to produce coal at a slightly cheaper cost than Company B because of the geology where Company A has its mines," this is a fact that can be reasonably ensured by a few minutes on Wikipedia rather than by checking out books from the local university's engineering library.

Second, the online valuation example shows how you can create rational valuation ranges for a company, and I believe that those ranges can be very helpful. Estimating valuation ranges rather than tying themselves to point estimates of a specific stock value can help investors to remain more objective about information coming in and more observant of changing conditions. For example, if an investor sees one group of valuation ranges clustered near $30 and one group clustered near $50, the investor can objectively assess operational data coming in over time and decide which set of projected economic results the actual results will match. The investor may have thought the economic results underlying the $50 cluster were more likely, but as time goes on, he or she may see that the results leading to the $30 cluster are closer to the truth. In this case, the investor can be confident and happy about making accurate projections (because the investor projected both the $30 level and the $50 level), even if he or she is not particularly pleased with the investment outcome. This may be the psychological slack required to combat the last behavioral bias we will discuss—humans' kinky perception of risk.

Humans' Kinky Perception of Risk

Take a look at the following questions: First question: you have a choice between playing two games with the following monetary payoffs. Which game would you play?

- Game 1: 75 percent chance of winning $6,000 and a 25 percent chance of winning $0
- Game 2: 100 percent certainty of winning $4,000

Make a note of your choice. Second question: you have a choice between playing two games with the following monetary payoffs. Which game would you play?

- Game 3: 75 percent chance of losing $6,000 and a 25 percent chance of losing $0.
- Game 4: 100 percent certainty of losing $4,000

What was your answer to this question?

Mathematically, you should choose to play games 1 and 4—these are the rational choices. Most people irrationally would choose to play games 2 and 3. The expected payout of game 1 = 75 percent × $6,000 + 0 = $4,500. As such, game 1's outcome generates a higher expected payoff than game 2. If you chose game 2 in this instance, it would indicate that you are *risk averse.*

Reversing the conditions of the games to generate losses instead of profits, you can see that game 3 yields an expected loss ($4,500) that is greater than the expected loss of game 4 ($4,000). If you chose to play game 3 over game 4, this would indicate that you are *risk seeking* rather than risk averse.

Psychologists Amos Tversky and Daniel Kahnemann—two researchers who began the systematic study of behavioral biases—found that people tend to be risk averse with respect to gains and risk seeking with respect to losses and have coined the term *prospect theory* to describe this tendency.[3] To understand risk aversion and risk seeking, let's look at a simple betting example.

You offer a test subject a choice of either receiving a certain payment of a certain amount or receiving an amount based on the result of a fair bet such as a coin toss. If the coin comes up heads, the subject wins $100; if it comes up tails, the subject walks away with no payment. The expected payoff from the fair bet from a mathematical perspective is

$$\$100 \times 50\% + \$0 \times 50\% = \$50$$

Economists describe risk preferences for individuals on the basis of the fixed payment the individual would accept in order not to subject the payout to a risky outcome. The three risk preferences are

- Risk neutral
- Risk averse
- Risk seeking

The risk-neutral investor is completely rational. The mathematical expected payoff is $50, so the risk-neutral approach is not to accept any guaranteed payment other than $50 in lieu of making the bet. If you were to diagram the value the rational risk-neutral investor would assign to the expected value of a risky outcome (using what economists call a *utility curve*), you would get the following:

Risk-Neutral Utility Function

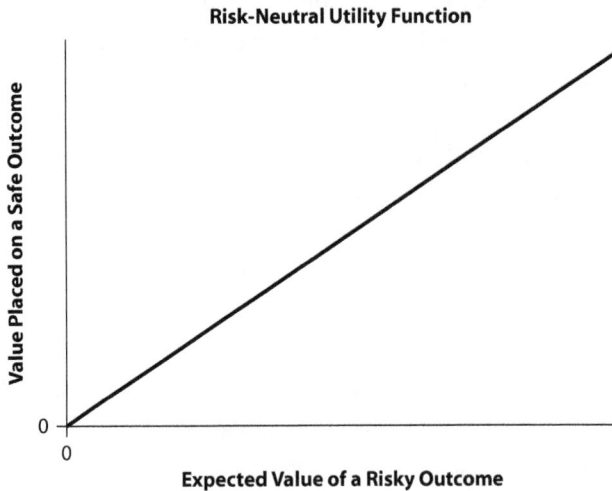

Because $50 is not a great deal of money to some people, they can and do remain risk neutral at this monetary level. Increase the potential payout to $1 million, and I guarantee that people will most happily demonstrate risk aversion.

Risk aversion is demonstrated by someone who would be willing to accept a guaranteed amount of less than the mathematically calculated expected payout in order to avoid putting the total payout at risk. For example, if you would prefer to accept a sure $45 instead of a 50 percent chance of winning $100, you are risk averse. The utility curve for a risk-averse investor would be represented like this:

Risk-Averse Utility Function

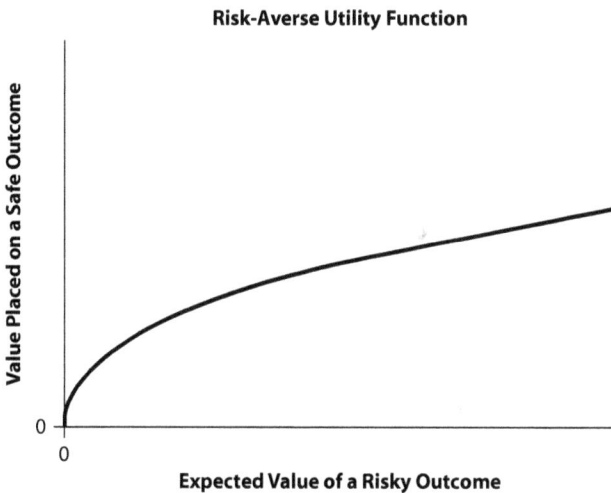

Most mentally healthy people with relatively low blood-alcohol levels are risk averse to a greater or lesser extent. As the amount in question becomes material (however the person in question defines *materiality*), the tendency toward risk aversion becomes much stronger.

Risk-seeking behavior is seen in gambling addicts and people with high enough blood-alcohol levels that they should not be operating heavy machinery. It is, of course, the converse of risk aversion: a risk seeker requires a higher guaranteed payment than the mathematically expected payout in order to forgo the bet. For instance, a risk seeker would not want to stop betting unless he or she was offered $60 or more for an expected-value bet of $50. The utility curve for a risk-seeking investor looks like this:

Risk-Seeking Utility Function

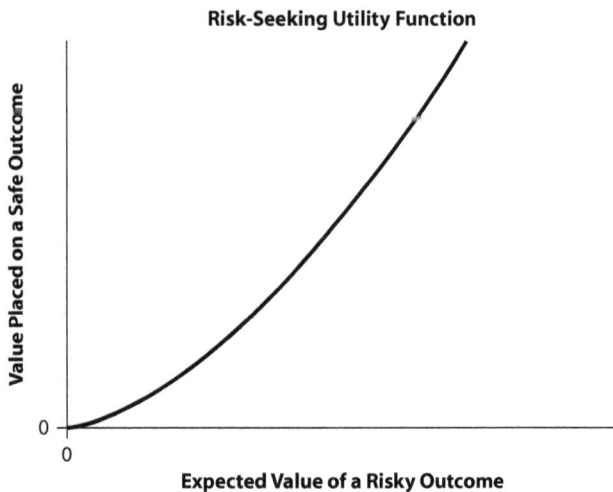

Risk seeking may seem implausible for anyone whose problems are not the feature of a daytime psychology talk show, but as you will see, each and every person reading this now likely displays risk seeking many times in an investing career.

If you read an Economics 101 textbook, you will learn that people are either risk neutral (professional economists always try hard to show that they are risk neutral because they generally pride themselves on being rational), risk averse, or risk seeking. In fact, we all display each of these profiles at different times depending on the situation. The unfortunate fact, discovered by Tversky and Kahnemann, is that humans tend to display the *least* helpful of each profile in different situations.

When we are winning, we tend to be risk averse. We have made 20 percent on an investment in a short time, and our tendency is to "take our money off the table" and realize our gains. The thing we fail to realize when we feel the pride and satisfaction of hitting the "Sell" button is that at the moment we close the position, our money is again sitting idle, and we are faced with the prospect of having to find another risky investment to replace the one we just closed.

Conversely, when we are losing, we tend to be risk seeking. For example, let's say that we have lost 60 percent on an investment. Is our natural tendency to sell that position? No. Because the value of our stake has fallen so much, we sense that any small movement up will be a big improvement to the present situation. We "let it ride" and hope for a lucky break. This is the action of someone who realizes that he or she has little to lose (because so much is lost already) and everything to gain—which, of course, is the very definition of desperation (and the day-to-day modus operandi of many hedge fund employees).

This variable risk profile is depicted by the following graph. The top-right quadrant shows a risk-averse profile—one would rather cap one's gains than let them ride. The bottom-left quadrant shows a risk-seeking profile—one would rather bet than realize one's losses.

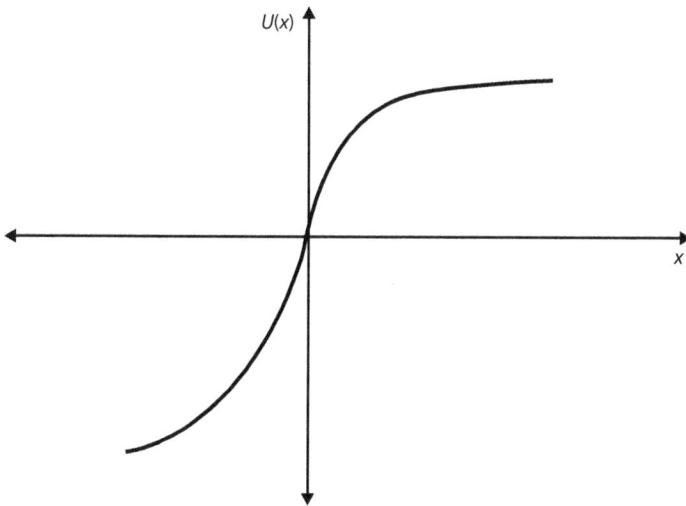

Prospect theory utility curve

Note how the curve in the upper right-hand quadrant looks like the risk-averse utility curve and that everything in the lower left-hand quadrant looks like the risk-seeking utility curve. This is an astounding graph, but perhaps an actual, visceral example would carry an even larger impact.

Think of the fellow who got in on the Google initial public offering, buying at $85 per share. A few months later, after more than doubling his money, he happily sells at just above $200 and again puts his capital at risk in another investment—starting over from square one in terms of making an investment decision.

Google (GOOG) Closing Price

This investor's thought at point *A*: "I am an investing genius! I just made a 100 percent return in a couple months—time to take my money off the table." However, after selling the shares and feeling the sense of relief that he had reduced his risk exposure to Google, he eventually grows dismayed about being hasty in realizing his gain:

Google (GOOG) Closing Price

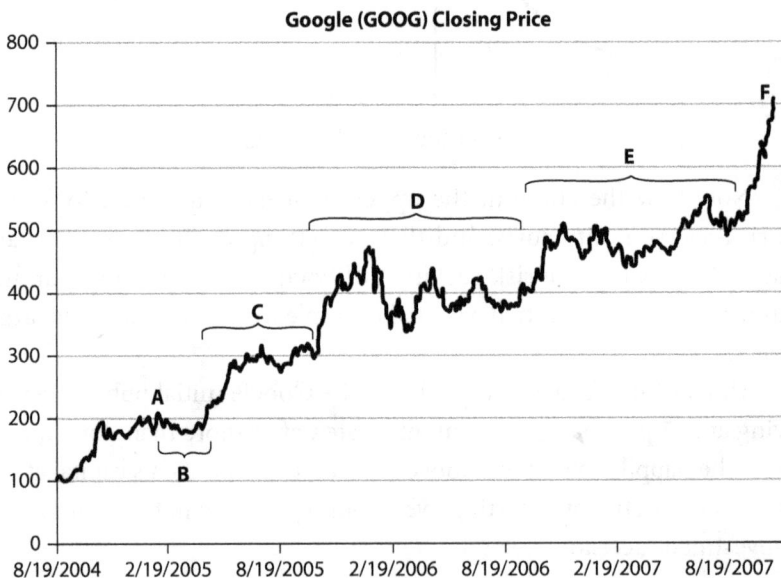

The investor's reasoning may have gone like this:

A	Original sale realizing profits
B	"I did the right thing."
C	"I left a little on the table, but it'll come back soon, and I'll buy some more then."
D	"Should I short Google?!"
E	"Aaaaaaaaaaaargh!"
F	Second purchase

Finally, after his mail carrier comments that she is retiring early after selling her Google position for $675 per share and a person at the country club buys a new Lexus using his Google sale proceeds, our kinked utility curve investor does the thing that social creatures tend to do when faced with uncertainty and remorse—follow the herd. He is happy that his limit order to buy at $695 is filled at midday and happier still that he made a gain of 3 percent after buying the shares.

Our hapless investor's bad sense of timing is good for us because his purchase of Google shares at the local 2007 market peak and ownership through the fall allow us to simultaneously follow the psychological pain he suffered on the stock chart and the utility function curve:

Google (GOOG) Closing Price

Thus an investor in Google at $695 feels pain extremely quickly when the value of the position drops slightly to the $620 per share level, let's say; this is indicated at position *A* in the diagram. However, as the price continues to decline (let's say to the $450 per share level indicated by position *B*), human decision makers have a tendency to say something like, "If only I could get $475 for my shares, I'd sell right now." If and when the shares do indeed reach $475, the curvature of the line in this quadrant implies that now the investor will require yet a higher guaranteed price (e.g., $525 per share) before he closes the bet. At some point, which may be one representing a significant loss of principal, the investor is largely inured to the prospect of further losses, and if the stock price goes far enough down, the investor is no longer tempted to bet on a small rise in price. This is the point that people usually sell—just as the $50 stock they bought is trading for $1.50 on the Pink Sheets!

This psychological effect is dreadfully difficult to overcome—perhaps impossible. However, again, I believe that the most important first step is having a rational, educated estimate of the fair value range of a company and understanding the drivers that go into the values making up that range.

Let's say that you bought a stock for $30 after having determined a low-end valuation of $39 and the high-end valuation around $50. Now a quarterly earnings announcement reports good numbers—data suggesting that the valuation cluster around $50 is closer to correct—and the stock advances by 10 percent—to $33.

Under these conditions, you are less likely to excitedly take your profits after the 10 percent up day because you know that the stock still has about 50 percent to go before it gets to your best-case valuation range. Again, understanding the drivers of valuation and having an appreciation for (and humility in the face of) the uncertainty involved in any projection of future conditions (as reflected by a valuation range) constitute the best way I have found to combat the deep-seated bias related to the kinks in our perception of risk.

Now we'll look briefly at structural impediments to rational investing before pulling together all the lessons learned so far to see how to invest intelligently using options.

Structural Impediments

We know that we have an enemy living inside of us in the form of the behavioral biases discussed earlier. If this weren't bad enough, we are attempting to invest intelligently in an environment not conducive to intelligence. In other words, not only must we battle an enemy within, but enemies without as well.

The enemies without are comprised of the forces arrayed against us—the owners of capital attempting to invest intelligently. These forces are part of the very structure that has developed to trade, manage, custody, analyze, and report on securities that is such an integral part of the investing process. They consist of the many explicit messages we as investors receive every week telling us that we should "trade like a pro" and the implicit messages that we don't know what we are doing so we should put our faith in this expert or the next if we hope to be successful.

At the heart of these structural issues is the distinction between principals and agents.

Principals versus Agents

You cannot talk about structural impediments without making the distinction between principals and agents. *Principals* are the owners of capital who invest in risky projects or assets with the expectation of generating a positive return. Principals can be like you and me—individuals with finite lives—or can be legal entities such as endowments or companies—which are theoretically perpetual actors. *Agents*, on the other hand, are the intermediaries who act on behalf of principals in return for salaries and who are paid for out of the capital of principals.

Any time a person is compensated for doing something, his or her own interests are on the line. When our own interests are on the line, we look for opportunities to protect and advance them. Unless a great deal of thought is put into how investment performance is measured and assessed and how compensation is awarded to agents as a result of that performance, in the process of advancing their own agendas, agents actually may end up working at cross-purposes to their principals. This tension between agents—who must work within the constraints of their industry to keep their jobs and advance their careers—and principals—who by and large are simply looking to save enough money to live comfortably in retirement and pass something on to their descendants—lies at the root of what I term *structural impediments.*

To investigate these structural impediments, we first need to figure out who is playing this investment game and what the rules are. To do this, I'll introduce the teams: the buy side and the sell side—both of which are agents—and the principals. With this knowledge, we can better avoid the structural pitfalls established by the agents largely for their own benefit.

The Buy Side

The buy side consists of agents hired by principals to invest and manage the principals' capital on their behalf. The most well-known buy-side players are mutual funds and hedge funds, but insurance companies, pension funds, and endowments also fit into this category. I tend to think of hedge funds and mutual funds as being different in approach from the others, so we'll look at these two groups separately.

Perhaps the attitude of mutual and large hedge fund players can best be summed up by the words of a professional money manager, who once told me, "Erik, no one ever got fired for not making money; they got fired for losing money." Most people unfamiliar with the money-management industry think that performance is paramount for the managers. In fact, investment performance is only a slightly inconvenient means to an end for money managers. For the owner of a hedge or mutual fund, the real name of the game is *assets under management* (AUM). AUM is the total amount of money a fund manages on behalf of its clients, and it is the main source of wealth for the owners of a fund. Mutual funds charge a *load* that represents a percentage of money clients leave with them to manage but are not usually directly rewarded for the performance of the fund. In the case of mutual funds, AUM is all important, and investment performance is merely a marketing tool. If fund A can generate good enough performance to stand prominently in the pack of other funds (i.e., "*x* percent of our funds beat their Lipper averages"), and rating companies such as Morningstar give the fund a positive rating, present customers of fund A are less likely to take their money to another fund, and customers of lower-performing funds will move their money to be managed by fund A. Of course, at the annual bonus time, fund employees are compensated in rough proportion to the performance of their investment recommendations, so there is an incentive for analysts and portfolio managers to perform well. However, if an analyst is interested in keeping his or her revenue stream coming in in the form of salary, the analyst quickly learns that the best route is usually the safest one.

This leads to a phenomenon known as *closet indexing*, where an investment fund's portfolio is so diversified that it effectively takes on a risk-return profile equivalent to the index (or whatever benchmark the fund is using to measure relative performance). A 2011 study by Martijn Cremers and colleagues concluded the following (italics added by author):

> In this paper we examine the prevalence of explicit and implicit (closet) indexing in equity mutual fund management across 30 countries. We find that although little explicit indexing exists as a proportion of assets under management [N.B.: There are few low-load index funds in proportion to "actively managed" funds] in almost all countries, a large amount of closet indexing exists. That is, *equity fund managers in many countries choose portfolios that track their stated benchmark closely.*

Or, to put it simply, whether an investor puts money into an active fund or an index fund, the investor mainly just gets the performance of the index. In addition, bonuses and salary increases are apportioned out on an annual basis, meaning that the natural investing time horizon for an analyst or money manager is only one year. Almost everyone in the industry feels a sense of excitement and relief at the beginning of a new year because they know they are starting out with a fresh slate. Clearly, the agents—the employees and owners of the funds—are not acting in the best interests of the principals (because they are charging fees but not providing much or any benefit), and the agents' investing time horizons are not, by and large, aligned with the investing time horizons of the principals (agents start again with a fresh slate every year whereas principals worry only about the value of their investment assets at some point in time, like college admission or retirement).

The same sort of dynamic occurs in the hedge fund industry, although with a bit of a twist. Large hedge funds usually are set up in a

"2-and-20" arrangement, where 2 percent of a client's money every year goes immediately to the manager (this is the *load* in a mutual fund), and 20 percent of profits (or profits over some benchmark) are apportioned out on a periodic basis. The owners of these prominent funds usually set up their businesses in such a way as to receive all the moneys based on AUM and leave the lion's share of the risky, performance-based payout to the portfolio managers and analysts hired to manage the money. The owners of large hedge funds, in other words, have compensation structures that are very similar to those of the owners of large mutual funds and so are concerned mainly with clients not moving their money to other hedge funds. For the owners of these funds, performance is, in a sense, just a necessary evil to their goal of generating wealth by safekeeping the wealth of others.

The owners of small hedge funds and the managers/analysts of all hedge funds lead a much more tenuous existence. This business is extremely competitive, and the continuation of these agents' salary- and bonus-generated revenue streams is extremely sensitive to recent performance. Small hedge fund owners are beholden to hedge funds of funds (HFoF)—another intermediary that funnels principals' capital to different hedge funds in return for a fee—and their money is extremely "fast." If a small fund manager does not outperform the appropriate benchmark in a given quarter or cannot convince the HFoF that performance lagged in the last quarter for some reason that will reverse itself in spades in the next quarter, it is very likely that the HFoF will pull its money from the fund. Similarly, a portfolio manager working for a large fund must, at least on an annual basis, prove to the hedge fund owner that his or her performance has been good enough or will soon be good enough to deserve a continued allotment of the clients' capital.

Strangely enough, as more and more hedge funds flood the market, soaking up opportunities to generate *alpha* (excess returns), hedge funds have come to display returns that are highly correlated with the underlying index. A recent research report published by Morgan Stanley told this tale in figures—the correlation between the Standard and Poor's 500 Index (S&P 500) and an index of hedge funds reached around 90 percent in mid-2013.[4] This does not mean that an individual hedge fund will engage in closet indexing as a mutual fund might, but it does mean that if you invest your money in multiple hedge funds to try to generate better performance, your returns will start looking a lot like the returns of the index at large.

Turning now to the next buy-side group—insurance companies, pension funds, and endowments—we see a different business model and different motivations for employees. In general, these buy-side businesses have much less pressure to generate superlative returns and exist as a sort of appendage of another primary business. Life insurance companies invest their clients' money but generally promise very limited returns—structuring agreements with clients in such a way as to ensure that if their investment decisions are at least minimally competent, they will be able to fulfill their promises to clients. As such, investments tend to be a default selection of blue chip equities and high-quality bonds. In this environment, the portfolio manager is not measured so much on his or her investment prowess but rather on his or her ability to allocate to bonds and stocks in a sensible enough proportion to be able to satisfy the insurance company's obligations to its clients when they come due. The real risk to the insurance company is not collecting enough fees or promising its clients too much. The investment horizon for these funds is something like 10 to 20 years.

Pension funds are much the same in terms of investment philosophy—if a portfolio manager allocates assets sensibly between high-grade corporate bonds and blue chip stocks, his or her career is basically safe. It is rare to find private sector entities now that even offer pensions to their employees and tougher still to think of examples of pensions that are adequately or overfunded (meaning that they have enough funds to meet their future obligations). Again, the investment horizon for these entities is a long 10 to 20 years.

Until rather recently, university endowments were very similar to insurance or pension funds, but they naturally have much longer investment time horizons because the money is usually not promised to any specific purpose in some limited time frame. Endowments usually allocate to a wider range of asset classes—including hedge funds, private equity funds, real estate, and so on—and several gifted portfolio managers at Harvard and Yale have done this to enormous effect on behalf of their schools in recent years. However, in general, asset selection or allocation risks are low for managers in this environment. Rather, the risks are much more related to the ability of managers to satisfy their schools' boards of governors that they are managing the school assets with propriety and foresight.

One undeniable fact to all buy-side firms is that as the entity grows larger, it becomes harder and harder to invest in anything but very large and liquid stocks. Even if you have a small cap position that increases by 100 percent in a single year, if your investment base is so large that the winning position's size is only 0.005 percent of the total AUM at the beginning of the year, it only represents 0.01 percent of the portfolio at the end of the year—hardly moving the needle in terms of excess performance.

To summarize the players in tabular format:

Player	Clients Are . . .	Time Horizon	Risk	Investment Paradigm
Hedge funds	Demanding, fast money	3 months to 1 year	Owner: Losing clients Managers: Not making risky enough bets	Anything that provides alpha
Mutual funds	Docile and uninformed	1 year	Breaking from the herd and seeing AUM drop	Closet indexing
Insurance companies and pension funds	Largely unaware of their investments	10 to 20 years	Not charging clients enough (insurance); not retiring before the pension is discontinued/ defaulted on (pensions)	AAA bonds and blue chip stocks—risk aversion
Endowments	Not born yet	10 years to 100 years	Losing confidence of board of governors	Wide asset-class level allocation with long-term perspective

Look back at this table. As a principal owner of capital, is there anything listed in the risk column that speaks to the risk of investing that you yourself have experienced or feel is most pressing to you?

The Sell Side

The sell side consists of companies whose job it is to connect principals (through their agents) who have capital with the financial markets.

Broker-dealers are the sell-side counterparties for institutional investors, whereas stock brokers and online brokers are the counterparties for individual ones.

The operative principle for this business is best summed up in the old adage, "Bears make money, and Bulls make money. Pigs get slaughtered." In other words, sell-siders do not care if the market goes up or down because their revenues depend only on investors accessing the market. The only way to lose this game is to get too greedy and take a risk position in a security that subsequently loses value.[5]

Sell-side players basically make money in proportion to how often their clients come to the market. As such, the sell side has a vested interest in getting its clients to trade as often as possible. Sell-side research groups hire very smart graduates from top universities and industry insiders who basically act as marketing arms for the firms' sales and trading desks. The more short-term "catalysts" the research group can find that might prompt a client to make a stock purchase or sale, the better for them. Research groups' bonuses are determined in large part by feedback from the sales and trading desk. Because the sales and trading team only makes money if a client trades, research that advocates long holding periods and infrequent trading is certainly not welcome, no matter how efficacious it might be.

The main duty of the people on the sales desks is to prompt clients to make a trading decision and to trade with them (rather than another bank), so salespeople spend a good bit of time making cold calls to hedge fund traders to give them some market "color" and point out opportunities to make short-term trades.

The End Result

The buy and sell sides interact with one another in such a way as to create an investing environment that values short-termism and dependence on large-capitalization stocks. The problem is that individual investors get wrapped up in these machinations and end up trying to act like agents when they are in fact principals. Agents, as we have seen, get paid a salary and bonus on the basis of various short-term factors that are, at best, neutral and, at worst, damaging to the interests of principals. Buy-side agents, as we have seen, are either relatively disinterested in investment performance (e.g., insurance companies and pension funds) or are interested only in relative outperformance over a very short time frame (e.g., hedge funds and mutual funds). Sell-side agents make money in proportion to trading volume and frequency, so they are happy to facilitate the enormous trade in a blue chip securities on behalf of a pension fund or the hundreds or thousands of individual trades in a day on behalf of an aggressive active hedge fund.

None of these agents are considering the economic value that may be created by the company in which they are investing, and in the attempt to maximize their own compensation, they are happy to ignore the long-term view in favor of a trade that will work within 90 days. Individual investors read sell-side research, and because the research analysts are so intelligent and well informed about various minutiae of a given company or industry, they think that the analysts' recommendations will help them in the long term. Business news channels offer a constant stream of pundits from both buy and sell sides pontificating about things that matter to them—short-term opportunities to generate a small advantage for the quarter—and that individual investors wrongly assume should be important to them as well.

An experienced technical analyst can find an investment opportunity in any chart pattern. A sell-side investment banker can always talk about why one company looks cheap in comparison with another in the same industry based on some ratio analysis that has a shelf life of about two weeks. Discount brokerages are happy to supply individual investors with sophisticated software and data packages that are "free" as long as the investors make a certain number of trades per month, and they encourage their clients to "trade like a pro."

The end result of these structural factors is that individual investors get caught in a mental trap that if they are doing anything different from what they see their highly paid agents doing, they must be doing something wrong. This is reinforced by one behavioral bias I mentioned in passing earlier—*herding*—the human tendency to try to find safety in following the lead of others rather than risk independent action.

In general, any information or strategy that does not hone in on the long-term economic value of a company should be considered by intelligent investors to be a red herring and ignored. No individual investor is being compensated with respect to short-term or relative performance, so information that is purported to give them advantages in this realm should be taken with a grain of salt.

Now that you have a good idea of the theory behind options from Part I and the theory of how to assess rational valuation ranges for a stock without falling into behavioral or structural traps from Part II, let's apply this knowledge to the practical task of investing. Part III discusses how to apply the principles of intelligent stock valuation to option investing and shows how to tilt the balance of risk and reward in our favor.

Part III

INTELLIGENT OPTION INVESTING

Now that you understand how options work and how to value companies, it is time to move from the theoretical to the practical to see how to apply this knowledge to investing in the market. With Part III of this book, we make the transition from theoretical to practical, and by the time you finish this part, you will be an intelligent option investor.

To invest in options, you must know how to transact them; this is the subject of Chapter 7. In it, you will see how to interpret an option pricing screen and to break down the information there so that you can understand what the option market is predicting for the future price of a stock. I also talk about the only one of the Greeks that an intelligent option investor needs to understand well—delta.

Chapter 8 deals with a subject that is essential for option investors—leverage. Not all option strategies are levered ones, but many are. As such, without understanding what leverage is, how it can be measured and used, and how it can be safely and sanely incorporated into a portfolio, you cannot be said to truly understand options.

Chapters 9–11 deal with specific strategies to gain, accept, and mix exposure. In these chapters I offer specific advice about what strike prices are most effective to select and what tenors, what to do when the expected outcomes of an investment materially change, and how to incorporate each strategy into your portfolio. Chapter 11 also gives guidance on so-called option overlay strategies, where a position in a stock is overlain by an option to modify the stock's risk-reward profile (e.g., protective puts for hedging and covered calls for generating income).

Unlike some books, this book includes only a handful of strategies, and most of those are very simple ones. I shun complex positions for two reasons. First, as you will see, transacting in options can be very expensive. The more complex an option strategy is, the less attractive the potential returns become. Second, the more complex a strategy is, the less the inherent directionality of options can be used to an investor's advantage.

Simple strategies are best. If you understand these simple strategies well, you can start modifying them yourself to meet specific investing scenarios when and if the need arises. Perhaps by using these simple strategies you will not be able to chat with the local investment club option guru about the "gamma on an iron condor," but that will be his or her loss and not yours.

Chapter 12 looks at what it means to invest intelligently while understanding the two forms of risk you assume by selecting stocks in which to invest: market risk and valuation risk.

Chapter 7

FINDING MISPRICED OPTIONS

All our option-related discussions so far have been theoretical. Now it is time to delve into the practical to see how options work in the market. After finishing this chapter, you should understand

1. How to read an option chain pricing screen
2. Option-specific pricing features such as a wide bid-ask spread, volatility smile, bid and ask volatility, and limited liquidity/ availability
3. What delta is and why it is important to intelligent option investors
4. How to compare what the option market implies about future stock prices to an intelligently determined range

In terms of where this chapter fits into our goal of becoming intelligent option investors, obviously, even if you have a perfect understanding of option and valuation theory, if you do not understand the practical steps you must take to find actual investment opportunities in the real world, all the theory will do you no good.

New jargon introduced in this chapter includes the following:

Closing price	Bid implied volatility
Settlement price	Ask implied volatility
Contract size	Volatility smile
Round-tripping	Greeks
Bid-ask spread	Delta

Making Sense of Option Quotes

Let's start our practical discussion by taking a look at an actual option pricing screen. These screens can seem intimidating at first, but by the end of this chapter, they will be quite sensible.

	Call						Description		Put					
Last	Chng	Bid	Ask	Impl. Bid Vol.	Impl. Ask Vol.	Delta		Last	Chng	Bid	Ask	Impl. Bid Vol.	Impl. Ask Vol.	Delta
							▼ JUL 26 '13							
0.86	-0.23	0.91	0.94	21.672%	24.733%	0.8387	31	0.09	+0.01	0.07	0.09	22.812%	24.853%	-0.1613
0.23	-0.14	0.24	0.26	20.380%	21.722%	0.4313	32	0.45	+0.10	0.39	0.42	20.456%	22.469%	-0.5689
0.02	-0.04	0.02	0.04	19.627%	22.988%	0.0631	33	1.15	+0.11	1.17	1.20	19.851%	24.612%	-0.9373
C0.00			0.02	N/A	62.849%	0.0000	37	C4.99		4.90	5.25	N/A	85.803%	-1.0000
C0.00			0.02	N/A	72.188%	0.0000	38	C5.99		4.85	7.25	N/A	203.970%	-1.0000
C0.00			0.02	N/A	81.286%	0.0000	39	C6.99		5.40	8.90	N/A	267.488%	-1.0000
							▼ AUG 16 '13							
C12.01		10.35	13.30	N/A	201.771%	0.9580	20	C0.00			0.02	N/A	77.739%	-0.0420
C11.01		9.30	12.40	N/A	192.670%	0.9598	21	C0.00			0.02	N/A	70.681%	-0.0402
C10.01		8.40	11.35	N/A	175.779%	0.9620	22	C0.00			0.02	N/A	63.514%	-0.0380
1.16	-0.17	1.17	1.19	19.408%	20.098%	0.7053	31	0.33	+0.02	0.33	0.34	19.958%	20.303%	-0.2948
0.54	-0.14	0.56	0.58	18.405%	18.997%	0.4743	32	0.76	+0.09	0.71	0.73	18.577%	19.170%	-0.5261
0.22	-0.06	0.20	0.22	17.721%	18.491%	0.2461	33	1.40	+0.14	1.35	1.38	17.954%	19.011%	-0.7545
C0.00			0.01	N/A	25.587%	0.0357	37	C4.99		4.95	5.30	N/A	41.423%	-0.9652
C0.00			0.01	N/A	29.201%	0.0392	38	C5.99		4.65	6.55	N/A	61.602%	-0.9616
C0.00			0.02	N/A	35.855%	0.0482	39	C6.99		6.70	7.30	N/A	52.378%	-0.9524
							▼ SEP 20 '13							
C12.02		11.75	11.90	N/A	55.427%	0.9897	20	C0.00			0.02	N/A	50.831%	-0.0103
C11.03		10.70	12.35	N/A	123.903%	0.9869	21	C0.01			0.03	N/A	48.233%	-0.0131
C10.04		9.50	10.10	N/A	64.054%	0.9834	22	C0.00		0.01	0.05	37.572%	46.993%	-0.0166
1.65	-0.13	1.65	1.68	22.720%	23.311%	0.6325	31	0.84	+0.07	0.80	0.82	22.989%	23.384%	-0.3679
1.06	-0.12	1.08	1.10	22.019%	22.407%	0.4997	32	1.23	+0.05	1.23	1.25	22.284%	22.672%	-0.5008
0.66	-0.07	0.65	0.67	21.378%	21.813%	0.3606	33	1.88	+0.16	1.79	1.82	21.453%	22.106%	-0.6402
C0.06		0.04	0.05	20.455%	21.147%	0.0463	37	C5.03		4.95	5.55	N/A	36.111%	-0.9558
0.03	0.00	0.01	0.03	19.050%	22.144%	0.0266	38	C6.00		6.15	6.30	17.134%	30.947%	-0.9757
0.02		0.01	0.02	21.354%	23.409%	0.0155	39	C6.99		6.85	7.55	N/A	44.342%	-0.9871
							▼ JAN 17 '14							
C12.05		11.55	12.30	N/A	54.689%	0.9712	20	C0.11		0.11	0.13	37.790%	38.919%	-0.0318
C11.07		10.05	12.00	N/A	66.920%	0.9628	21	C0.15		0.13	0.17	35.385%	37.587%	-0.0406
C10.10		9.85	10.00	0.000%	35.642%	0.9535	22	C0.19		0.17	0.19	34.172%	35.246%	-0.0503
C2.58		2.44	2.48	23.193%	23.656%	0.5890	31	1.80	+0.09	1.75	1.78	23.567%	23.914%	-0.4120
1.93	-0.09	1.91	1.93	22.845%	23.072%	0.5118	32	2.27	+0.12	2.22	2.25	23.145%	23.485%	-0.4879
1.42	-0.14	1.45	1.48	22.218%	22.553%	0.4324	33	2.73	+0.04	2.76	2.80	22.479%	22.925%	-0.5665
0.38	-0.06	0.39	0.41	21.148%	21.460%	0.1664	37	C5.57		5.70	5.80	21.404%	22.967%	-0.8294
C0.30		0.27	0.29	20.913%	21.374%	0.1258	38	C6.43		6.50	6.85	19.420%	26.265%	-0.8690
C0.22		0.18	0.21	20.899%	21.581%	0.0923	39	C7.35		7.40	7.85	18.411%	28.715%	-0.9025
							▼ JAN 16 '15							
12.10	-0.30	12.10	12.20	30.523%	32.597%	0.9064	20	0.68	0.00	0.66	0.68	33.203%	33.497%	-0.0906
3.40	-0.26	3.50	3.60	24.198%	24.854%	0.5354	32	4.25	+0.09	4.15	4.25	25.378%	26.033%	-0.4520
1.69	-0.10	1.70	1.75	23.081%	23.426%	0.3336	37	C7.27		7.30	7.40	24.054%	24.745%	-0.6521

I pulled this screen—showing the prices for options on Oracle (ORCL)—on the weekend of July 20–21, 2013, when the market was closed. The last trade of Oracle's stock on Friday, July 19, was at $31.86, down $0.15 from the Thursday's close. Your brokerage screen may look different from this one, but you should be able to pull back all the data columns shown here. I have limited the data I'm pulling back on this screen in order to increase its readability. More strikes were available, as well as more expiration dates. The expirations shown here are 1 week and 26, 60, 180, and 544 days in the future—the 544-day expiry being the longest tenor available on the listed market.

Let's first take a look at how the screen itself is set up without paying attention to the numbers listed.

Calls are on the left, puts on the right.

All the strikes for each selected expiry are listed grouped together.

This query was set up to pull back three strikes at the three moneyness regions (20–22, 29–31, 37–39). The 1-week options and the LEAPS did not have strikes at each of the prices I requested.

Strike prices and expirations are listed here.

You can tell the stock was down on this day because most of the call options are showing losses and all the put options are showing gains.

Now that you can see what the general setup is, let's drill down and look at only the calls for one expiration to see what each column means.

				Call				Description
Last	Chnq	Bid	Ask	Impl. Bid Vol.	Impl. Ask Vol.		Delta	
								▼ SEP 20 '13
C12.02		11.75	11.90	N/A	55.427%	◆	0.9897	20
C11.03		10.70	12.35	N/A	123.903%	◆	0.9869	21
C10.04		9.50	10.10	N/A	64.054%	◆	0.9834	22
1.65	-0.13	1.65	1.68	◆ 22.720%	23.311%	◆	0.6325	31
1.06	-0.12	1.08	1.10	◆ 22.019%	22.407%	◆	0.4997	32
0.66	-0.07	0.65	0.67	◆ 21.378%	21.813%	◆	0.3606	33
C0.06		0.04	0.05	◆ 20.455%	21.147%	◆	0.0463	37
0.03	0.00	0.01	0.03	◆ 19.050%	22.144%	◆	0.0266	38
0.02	+0.01	0.01	0.02	◆ 21.354%	23.409%	◆	0.0155	39

Red
(loss)

Green
(gain)

Last

This is the last price at which the associated contract traded. Notice that the last price associated with the far in the money (ITM) strikes ($20, $21, $22) and one of the far out-of-the-money (OTM) strikes ($37) have the letter "C" in front of them. This is just my broker's way of showing that the contract did not trade during that day's trading session and that the last price listed was the closing price of the previous day. *Closing prices* are not necessarily market prices. At the end of the day, if a contract has not traded, the exchange will give an indicative closing price (or *settlement price*) for that day. The Oracle options expiring on August 16, 2013, and struck at $20 may not have traded for six months or more, with the exchange simply "marking" a closing price every day.

One important fact to understand about option prices is that they are quoted in per-share terms but must be transacted in contracts that represent control of multiple shares. The number of shares controlled by one contract is called the *contract size*. In the U.S. market, one standard contract represents control over 100 shares. Sometimes the number of shares controlled by a single contract differs (in the case of a company that was acquired through the exchange of shares), but these are not usually available to be traded. In general, one is safe remembering that the contract size is 100 shares.

You cannot break a contract into smaller pieces or buy just part of a contract—transacting in options means you must do so with indivisible contracts, with each contract controlling 100 shares. Period. As such, every price you see on the preceding screenshot, if you were to transact in one of those options, would cost you 100 times the amount shown. For example, the last price for the $31-strike option was $1.65. The investor who bought that contract paid $165 for it (plus fees, taxes, and commissions, which are not included in the posted price). In the rest of this book, when I make calculations regarding money spent on a certain transaction, you will always see me multiply by 100.

Change

This is the change from the previous day's closing price. My broker shows change only for contracts that were actively traded that day. It looks like the near at-the-money (ATM) strikes were the most active because of the two far OTM options that traded; one's price didn't change at all, and the other went up by 1 cent. On a day in which the underlying stock fell, these calls theoretically should have fallen in price as well (because the K/S ratio, the ratio of strike price to stock price, was getting slightly larger). This just shows that sometimes there is a disconnect between theory and practice when it comes to options.

To understand what is probably happening, we should understand something about market makers. *Market makers* are employees at broker-dealers who are responsible for ensuring a liquid, orderly securities market. In return for agreeing to provide a minimum liquidity of 10 contracts per strike price, market makers get the opportunity to earn the *bid-ask spread* every time a trade is made (I will talk about bid-ask spreads later). However, once a market maker posts a given price, he or she is guaranteeing a trade at that price. If, in this case (because we're dealing with OTM call options), some unexpected positive news comes out that will create a huge rise in the stock price once it filters into the market and an observant, quick investor sees it before the market maker realizes it, the investor can get a really good price on those far OTM call options (i.e., the investor could buy a far OTM call option for 1 cent and sell it for 50 cents when the market maker realizes what has happened. To provide a little slack that prevents the market maker from losing too much money if this happens, market makers usually post prices for far OTM options or options on relatively illiquid stocks that are a bit unreasonable—at a level where a smart investor would not trade with him or her at that price. If someone trades at that price, fine—the market maker has committed to provide liquidity, but the agreement does not stipulate that the liquidity must be provided at a reasonable price. For this reason, frequently you will see prices on far OTM options that do not follow the theoretical "rules" of options.

Bid-Ask

For a stock investor, the difference between a bid price and an ask price is inconsequential. For option investors, though, it is a factor that must be taken into consideration for reasons that I will detail in subsequent paragraphs. The easiest way to think of the bid-ask spread is to think in terms of buying a new car. If you buy a new car, you pay, let's say, $20,000. This is the ask price. You grab the keys, drive around the block, and return to the showroom offering to sell the car back to the dealership. The dealership buys it for $18,000. This is the bid price. The bid-ask spread is $2,000 in this example.

Bid-ask spreads are proportionally much larger for options than they are for stocks. For example, the options I've highlighted here are on a very large, important, and very liquid stock. The bid-ask spread on the $32-strike call option (which you will learn in the next section is exactly ATM) is $0.02 on a midprice of $1.09. This works out to a percentage bid-ask spread of 1.8 percent. Compare this with the bid-ask spread on Oracle's stock itself, which was $0.01 on a midprice of $31.855—a percentage spread of 0.03 percent.

For smaller, less-liquid stocks, the percentage bid-ask spread is even larger. For instance, here is the option chain for Mueller Water (MWA):

Call						Description	Put						
Last	Change	Bid	Ask	Impl. Bid Vol.	Impl. Ask Vol.	Delta		Last	Change	Bid	Ask	Impl. Bid Vol.	Impl. Ask Vol.	Delta
						▼ AUG 16 '13								
♦ C5.30	♦ 5.20	5.50	N/A	380.099% ♦	2.5		♦ C0.00		0.10	N/A	292.169% ♦	0.0000
♦ C2.80	♦ 2.70	2.95	N/A	142.171% ♦	5		♦ C0.00		0.10	N/A	128.711% ♦	-0.0000
♦ 0.55	0.00	♦ 0.50	0.55	♦ 39.708%	46.039% ♦	7.5		♦ C0.25	♦ 0.20	0.30	♦ 40.733%	53.108% ♦	-0.2779
♦ C0.00		0.10	N/A	76.652% ♦	10		♦ C2.25	♦ 2.10	2.35	N/A	88.008% ♦	-0.8663
						▼ NOV 15 '13								
♦ C5.30	♦ 5.20	5.50	N/A	163.282% ♦	2.5		♦ C0.00		0.05	N/A	117.369% ♦	-0.0616
♦ C2.80	♦ 2.80	3.00	N/A	75.219% ♦	5		♦ C0.00		0.10	N/A	60.675% ♦	-0.1447
♦ 0.85	♦ 0.80	0.90	♦ 36.722%	42.610% ♦	7.5		♦ C0.55	♦ 0.50	0.60	♦ 36.550%	42.413% ♦	-0.3886
♦ C0.10	♦ 0.10	0.20	♦ 36.336%	45.215% ♦	10		♦ C2.35	♦ 2.30	2.40	♦ 35.664%	44.802% ♦	-0.8447
						▼ FEB 21 '14								
♦ C5.30	♦ 5.10	5.50	N/A	122.894% ♦	2.5		♦ C0.00		0.15	N/A	110.810% ♦	-0.0018
♦ 3.00	+0.15	♦ 2.85	3.10	♦ 38.754%	64.543% ♦	5		♦ C0.10	♦ 0.05	0.15	♦ 38.181%	50.757% ♦	-0.0787
♦ C1.10	♦ 1.05	1.15	♦ 38.318%	42.697% ♦	7.5		♦ C0.85	♦ 0.70	0.85	♦ 35.520%	42.074% ♦	-0.3893
♦ C0.35	♦ 0.30	0.40	♦ 39.127%	44.728% ♦	10		♦ C2.55	♦ 2.45	2.60	♦ 35.509%	43.947% ♦	-0.7375
♦ C0.10	♦ 0.05	0.20	♦ 36.347%	50.218% ♦	12.5		♦ C4.80	♦ 4.60	4.90	N/A	49.401% ♦	-0.8913

Looking at the closest to ATM call options for the November expiration— the ones struck at $7.50 and circled in the screenshot—you can see that the bid-ask spread is $0.10 on a midprice of $0.85. This works out to 11.8 percent.

Because the bid-ask spread is so very large on option contracts, *round-tripping*[1] an option contract creates a large hurdle that the returns of the security must get over before the investor makes any money. In the case of Mueller Water, the options one buys would have to change in price by 11.8 percent before the investor starts making any money at all. It is for this reason that I consider day trading in options and/or using complex strategies involving the simultaneous purchase and sale of multiple contracts to be a poor investment strategy.

Implied Bid Volatility/Implied Ask Volatility

Because the price is so different between the bid and the ask, the range of future stock prices implied by the option prices can be thought of as different depending on whether you are buying or selling contracts. Employing the graphic conventions we used earlier in this book, this effect is represented as follows:

Oracle (ORCL)

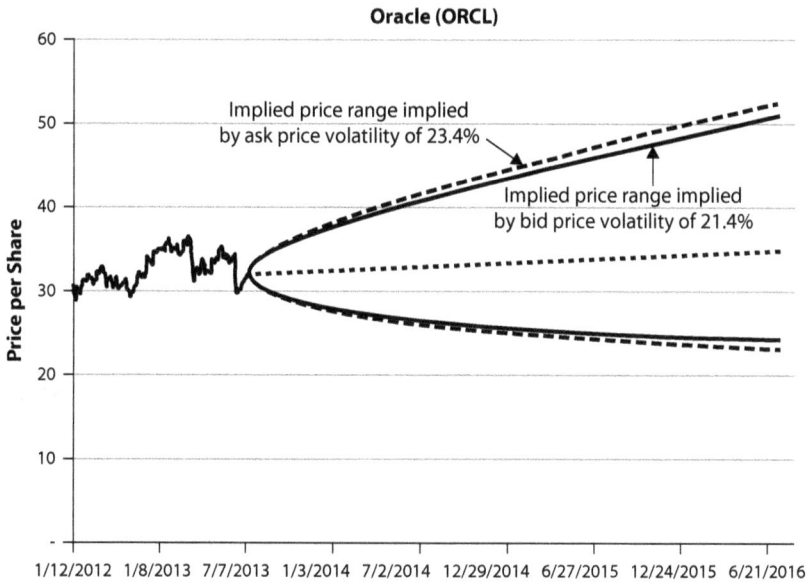

Implied price range implied by ask price volatility of 23.4%

Implied price range implied by bid price volatility of 21.4%

1/12/2012   1/8/2013   7/7/2013   1/3/2014   7/2/2014   12/29/2014   6/27/2015   12/24/2015   6/21/2016

Because Oracle is such a big, liquid company, the difference between the stock prices implied by the different bid-ask implied volatilities is not large, but it can be substantial for smaller, less liquid companies. Looking at the ask implied volatility column, you will notice the huge difference between the far ITM options' implied volatilities and those for ATM and OTM options. The data in the preceding diagram are incomplete, but if you were to graph all the implied volatility data, you would get the following:

Oracle (ORCL) Implied Volatility

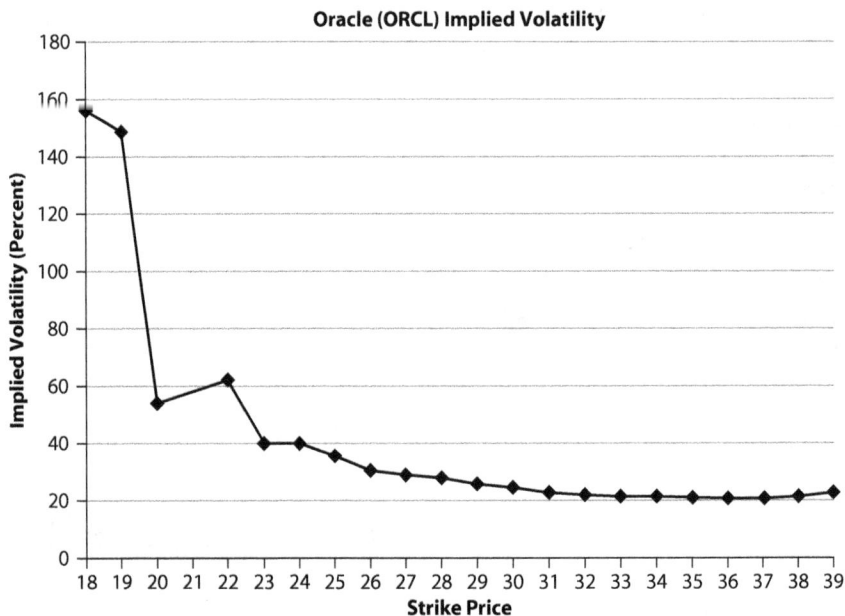

Thinking about what volatility means with regard to future stock prices—namely, that it is a prediction of a range of likely values—it does not make sense that options struck at different prices would predict such radically different stock price ranges. What the market is saying, in effect, is that it expects different things about the likely future range of stock prices depending on what option is selected. Clearly, this does not make much sense.

This "nonsensical" effect is actually proof that practitioners understand that the Black-Scholes-Merton model's (BSM's) assumptions are not correct and specifically that sudden downward jumps in a stock price can and do occur more often than would be predicted if returns followed a normal distribution. This effect does occur and even has a name—the *volatility smile*. Although this effect is extremely noticeable when graphed in this way, it is not particularly important for the intelligent option investing strategies about which I will speak. Probably the most important thing to realize is that the pricing on far OTM and far ITM options is a little more informal and approximate than for ATM options, so if you are thinking about transacting in OTM or ITM options, it is worth looking for the best deal available. For example, notice that in the preceding diagram, the $21-strike implied volatility is actually notably higher than the

$20-strike volatility. If you were interested in buying an ITM call option, you would pay less time value for the $20-strike than for the $21-strike options—essentially the same investment. I will talk more about the volatility smile in the next section when discussing delta.

In a similar way, sometimes the implied volatility for puts is different from the implied volatility for calls struck at the same price. Again, this is one of the market frictions that arises in option markets. This effect also has investing implications that I will discuss in the chapters detailing different option investing strategies.

The last column in this price display is *delta*, a measure that is so important that it deserves its own section—to which we turn now.

Delta: The Most Useful of the Greeks

Someone attempting to find out something about options will almost certainly hear about how the Greeks are so important. In fact, I think that they are so *unimportant* that I will barely discuss them in this book. If you understand how options are priced—and after reading Part I, you do—the Greeks are mostly common sense.

Delta, though, is important enough for intelligent option investors to understand with a bit more detail. Delta is the one number that gives the probability of a stock being above (for calls) or below (for puts) a given strike price at a specific point in time.

Deltas for calls always carry a positive sign, whereas deltas for puts are always negative, so, for instance, a call option on a given stock whose delta is exactly 0.50 will have a put delta of –0.50. The call delta of 0.50 means that there is a 50 percent chance that the stock will expire above that strike, and the put delta of –0.50 means that there is a 50 percent chance that the stock will expire below that strike. In fact, this strike demonstrates the technical definition of ATM—it is the *most likely* future price of the stock according to the BSM.

The reason that delta is so important is that it allows you one way of creating the BSM probability cones that you will need to find option investment opportunities. Recall that the straight dotted line in our BSM cone diagrams meant the statistically most likely future price for the stock. The statistically most likely future price for a stock—assuming that stocks move randomly, which the BSM does—is the price level at which there is an equal chance of the actual future stock price to be above or below. In other words, the 50-delta mark represents the forward price of a stock in our BSM cones.

Recall now also that each line demarcating the cone represents roughly a 16 percent probability of the stock reaching that price at a particular time in the future. This means that if we find the call strike prices that have deltas closest to 0.16 and 0.84 (= 1.00 − 0.16) or the put strike prices that have deltas closest to −0.84 and −0.16 for each expiration, we can sketch out the BSM cone at points in the future (the data I used to derive this graph are listed in tabular format at the end of this section).

Oracle (ORCL)

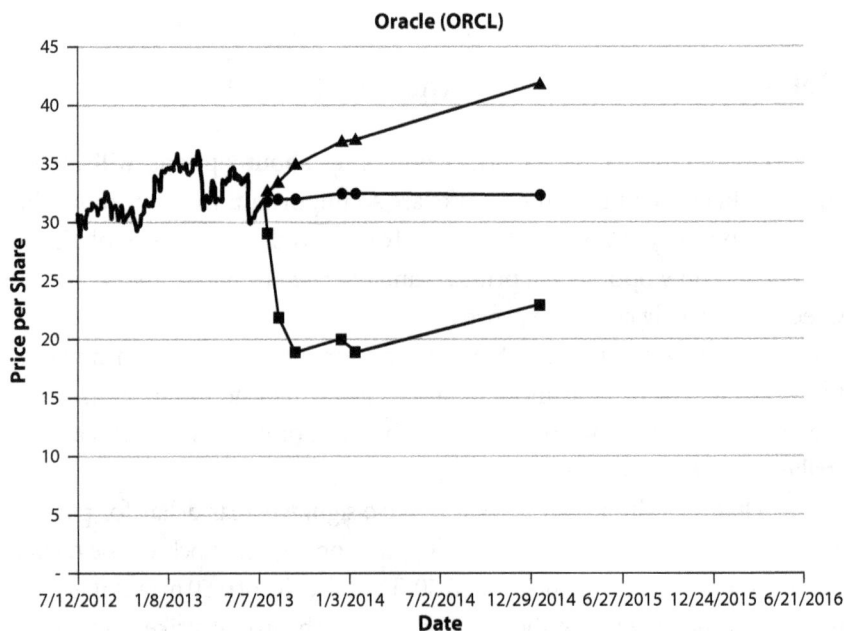

Obviously, the bottom range looks completely distended compared with the nice, smooth BSM cone shown in earlier chapters. This distension is simply another way of viewing the volatility smile. Like the volatility smile, the distended BSM cone represents an attempt by participants in the options market to make the BSM more usable in real situations, where stocks really can and do fall heavily even though the efficient market hypothesis (EMH) says that they should not. The shape is saying,

"We think that these prices far below the current price are much more likely than they would be assuming normal percentage returns." (Or, in a phrase, "We're scared!")

If we compare the delta-derived "cone" with a theoretically derived BSM cone, here is what we would see:

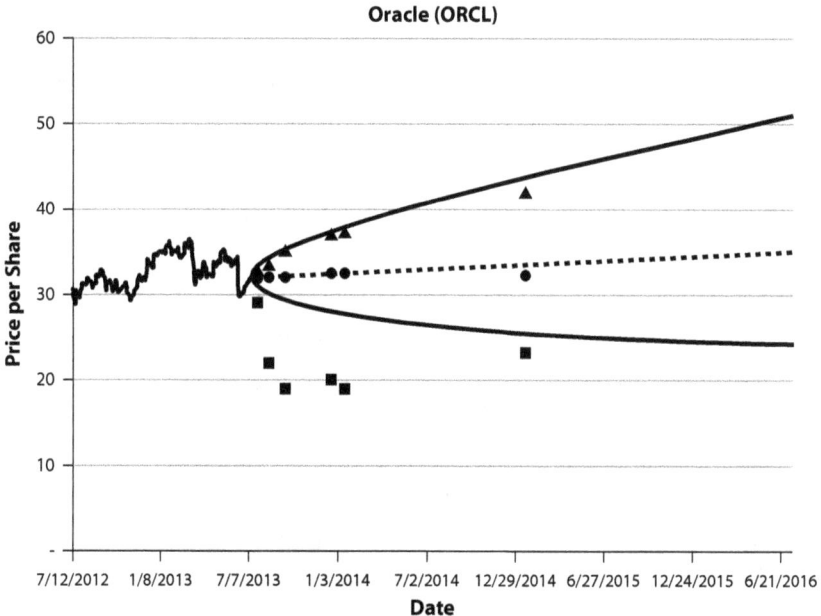

Oracle (ORCL)

Of course, we did not need the BSM cone to tell us that the points associated with the downside strikes look too low. But it is interesting to see that the upside and most likely values are fairly close to what the BSM projects.

Note also that the downside point on the farthest expiration is nearly fairly priced according to the BSM, contrary to the shorter-tenor options. This effect could be because no one is trading the far ITM call long-term equity anticipation securities (LEAPS), so the market maker has simply posted his or her bid and ask prices using the BSM as a base. In the market, this is what usually happens—participants start out with a mechanically generated price (i.e., using the BSM or some other computational option pricing model) and make adjustments based on what feels right, what arbitrage opportunities are available, and so on.

One important thing to note is that although we are using the delta figure to get an idea of the probability that the market is assigning to a certain stock price outcome, we are also using deltas for options that nearly no one ever trades. Most option volume is centered around the 50-delta mark and a 10 to 20 percentage point band around it (i.e., from 30- to 40-delta to 60- to 70-delta). It is doubtful to me that these thinly traded options contain much real information about market projections of future stock prices.

Another problem with using the deltas to get an idea about market projections is that we are limited in the length of time we can project out to only the number of strikes available. For this example, I chose an important tech company with a very liquid stock, so it has plenty of expirations and many strikes available so that we can get a granular look at deltas. However, what if we were looking at Mueller Water's option chain and trying to figure out what the market is saying?

Call							Description
Last	Change	Bid	Ask	Impl. Bid Vol.	Impl. Ask Vol.	Delta	▼ AUG 16 '13
♦ C5.30		♦ 5.70	5.50	N/A	340.099% ♦	0.9978	2.5
♦ C2.80		♦ 2.70	2.95	N/A	142.171% ♦	0.9978	5
♦ 0.55	0.00	♦ 0.50	0.55	♦ 39.708%	46.039% ♦	0.7330	7.5
♦ C0.00			0.10	N/A	76.652% ♦	0.1316	10
							▼ NOV 15 '13
♦ C5.30		♦ 5.20	5.50	N/A	163.282% ♦	0.9347	2.5
♦ C2.80		♦ 2.80	3.00	N/A	75.219% ♦	0.8524	5
♦ C0.85		♦ 0.80	0.90	♦ 36.722%	42.610% ♦	0.6103	7.5
♦ C0.10		♦ 0.10	0.20	♦ 36.336%	45.215% ♦	0.1516	10
							▼ FEB 21 '14
♦ C5.30		♦ 5.10	5.50	N/A	122.894% ♦	0.9933	2.5
♦ 3.00	+0.15	♦ 2.85	3.10	♦ 38.754%	64.543% ♦	0.9190	5
♦ C1.10		♦ 1.05	1.15	♦ 38.318%	42.697% ♦	0.6070	7.5
♦ C0.35		♦ 0.30	0.40	♦ 39.127%	44.728% ♦	0.2566	10
♦ C0.10		♦ 0.05	0.20	♦ 36.347%	50.218% ♦	0.1024	12.5

Here you can see that we only have three expirations: 26, 117, and 215 days from when these data were taken. In addition, there are hardly any strikes that are reasonably close to our crucial 84-delta, 50-delta, and 16-delta strikes, which means that we have to do a lot of extrapolation to try to figure out where the market's idea of the BSM cone lies.

To get a better picture of what the market is saying, I recommend looking at options that are the most heavily traded and assuming that the implied volatility on these strikes gives true information about the market's assumptions about the future price range of a stock. Using the implied volatility on heavily traded contracts as the true forward volatility expected by the market allows us to create a theoretical BSM cone that we can extend indefinitely into the future and that is probably a lot closer to representing actual market expectations for the forward volatility (and, by extension, the range of future prices for a stock). Once we have this BSM cone—with its high-low ranges spelled out for us—we can compare it with the best- and worst-case valuations we derived as part of the company analysis process.

Let's look at this process in the next section, where I spell out, step by step, how to compare an intelligent valuation range with that implied by the option market.

Note: Data used for Oracle graphing example:

Expiration Date	Lower	Middle	Upper
7/25/2013	29.10	31.86	32.75
8/16/2013	22.00	32.00	33.50
9/20/2013	19.00	32.00	35.00
12/20/2013	20.00	32.50	37.00
1/17/2014	19.00	32.50	37.20
1/16/2015	23.00	32.30	42.00

Here I have eyeballed (and sometimes done a quick extrapolation) to try to get the price that is closest to the 84-delta, 50-delta, and 16-delta marks, respectively. Of course, you could calculate these more carefully and get exact numbers, but the point of this is to get a general idea of how likely the market thinks a particular future stock price is going to be.

Comparing an Intelligent Valuation Range with a BSM Range

The point of this book is to teach you how to be an intelligent option investor and not how to do stochastic calculus or how to program a computer to calculate the BSM. As such, I'm not going to explain how to mathematically derive the BSM cone. Instead, on my website I have an application that will allow you to plug in a few numbers and create a graphic representation of a BSM cone and carry out the comparison process described in this section. The only thing you need to know is what numbers to plug into this web application!

I'll break the process into three steps:

1. Create a BSM cone.
2. Overlay your rational valuation range on the BSM cone.
3. Look for discrepancies.

Create a BSM Cone

The heart of a BSM cone is the forward volatility number. As we have seen, as forward volatility increases, the range of future stock prices projected by the BSM (and expected by the market) also increases. However, after having looked at the market pricing of options, we also know that a multitude of volatility numbers is available. Which one should we look at? Each strike price has its own implied volatility number. What strike price's volatility should we use? There are also multiple tenors. What tenor options should we look at? Should we look at implied volatility at the bid price? At the ask price? Perhaps we should take the "kitchen sink" approach and just average all the implied volatilities listed!

The answer is, in fact, easy if you use some simplifying assumptions to pick a single volatility number. I am not an academic, so I don't necessarily care if these simplifying assumptions are congruent with theory. Also, I am not an arbitrageur, so I don't much care about very precise numbers, and this attitude also lends itself well to the use of simplifying assumptions. All we have to make sure of is that the simplifying assumptions don't distort our perception to the degree that we make bad economic choices.

Here are the assumptions that we will make:

1. The implied volatility on a contract one or two months from expiration that is ATM or at least within the 40- to 60-delta band and that is the most heavily traded will contain the market's best idea of the true forward volatility of the stock.
2. If a big announcement is scheduled for the near future, implied volatility numbers may be skewed, so their information might not be reliable. In this case, try to find a heavily traded near ATM strike at an expiry after the announcement will be made. If the announcement will be made in about four months or more, just try

to eyeball the ATM volatility for the one- and two-month contracts.

3. If there is a large bid-ask spread, the relevant forward volatility to use is equal to the implied volatility we want to transact. In other words, use the ask implied volatility if you are thinking about gaining exposure and the bid implied volatility if you are thinking about accepting exposure (the online application shows cones for both the bid implied volatility and the ask implied volatility).

Basically, these rules are just saying, "If you want to know what the option market is expecting the future price range of a stock to be, find a nice, liquid near ATM strike's implied volatility and use that." Most option trading is done in a tight band around the present ATM mark and for expirations from zero to three months out. By looking at the most heavily traded implied volatility numbers, we are using the market's price-discovery function to the fullest. Big announcements sometimes can throw off the true volatility picture, which is why we try to avoid gathering information from options in these cases (e.g., legal decisions, Food and Drug Administration trial decisions, particularly impactful quarterly earnings announcements, and so on).

If I was looking at Oracle, I would probably choose the $32-strike options expiring in September. These are the 50-delta options with 61 days to expiration, and there is not much of a difference between calls and puts or between the bid and ask. The August expiration options look a bit suspicious to me considering that their implied volatility is a couple of percentage points below that of the others. It probably doesn't make a big difference which you use, though. We are trying to find opportunities that are severely mispriced, not trying to split hairs of a couple of percentage points. All things considered, I would probably use a number somewhere around 22 percent for Oracle's forward volatility.

▼ SEP 20 '13

C12.02		11.75	11.90	N/A	55.427% ◆ 0.9897	20	C0.00		0.02	N/A	50.831% ◆ -0.0103
C11.03		10.70	12.35	N/A	123.903% ◆ 0.9869	21	C0.01		0.03	N/A	48.233% ◆ -0.0131
C10.04		9.50	10.10	N/A	64.054% ◆ 0.9834	22	C0.03	0.01	0.05	◆ 37.572%	46.993% ◆ -0.0166
1.65	-9.13	1.65	1.68	◆ 22.720%	23.311% ◆ 0.6325	31	0.84	+0.07	0.80	0.82	◆ 22.989%	23.384% ◆ -0.3679
1.06	-0.12	1.08	1.10	◆ 22.019%	22.407% ◆ 0.4997	32	1.23	+0.05	1.23	1.25	◆ 22.284%	22.672% ◆ -0.5008
0.66	-0.07	0.65	0.67	◆ 21.378%	21.813% ◆ 0.3606	33	1.88	+0.16	1.79	1.82	◆ 21.453%	22.106% ◆ -0.6402
C0.06		0.04	0.05	◆ 20.455%	21.147% ◆ 0.0463	37	C5.03		4.95	5.55	◆ 17.134%	36.111% ◆ -0.9558
0.03	0.00	0.01	0.03	◆ 19.050%	22.144% ◆ 0.0266	38	C6.00		6.15	6.30	◆ 17.134%	30.947% ◆ -0.9757
0.02	+0.01	0.01	0.02	◆ 21.354%	23.409% ◆ 0.0155	39	C6.99		6.85	7.55	N/A	44.342% ◆ -0.9871

For Mueller Water, it's a little trickier:

Call							Description	Put						
Last	Change	Bid	Ask	Impl. Bid Vol.	Impl. Ask Vol.	Delta		Last	Change	Bid	Ask	Impl. Bid Vol.	Impl. Ask Vol.	Delta
							▼ AUG 16 '13							
C0.70	▲5.10	5.50		N/A	140.097%	0.9992	2.5	C0.00			0.10	N/A	292.316%	0.0000
C2.80	▲2.70	2.95		N/A	104.474%		5	C0.00			0.10	N/A	178.011%	
C0.45	0.00 ▲0.50	0.55	▲ 39.708%	46.039%	0.7313	7.5	C0.25	▲0.20	0.30	N/A	33.408%		
C0.00		0.10	N/A	76.652%	0.1316	10	C2.25	▲2.10	2.35	N/A	88.008%	0.8663
							▼ NOV 15 '13							
C5.30	▲5.20	5.50	N/A	163.282%	0.9347	2.5	C0.00			0.05	N/A	117.369%	0.0616
C2.80	▲2.80	3.00	N/A	75.219%	0.8524	5	C0.00			0.10	N/A	60.675%	0.1447
C0.85	▲0.80	0.90	▲36.722%	42.610%	0.6103	7.5	C0.55	▲0.50	0.60	▲36.550%	42.433%	0.3886
C0.10	▲0.10	0.20	▲36.336%	45.215%	0.1516	10	C2.35	▲2.30	2.40	▲35.664%	44.802%	0.8447
							▼ FEB 21 '14							
C5.30	▲5.10	5.50	N/A	122.894%	0.9933	2.5	C0.00			0.15	N/A	110.810%	0.0018
3.00	+0.15 ▲2.85	3.10	▲38.754%	64.543%	0.9190	5	C0.10	▲0.05	0.15	▲38.181%	50.757%	0.0787
C1.10	▲1.05	1.15	▲38.318%	42.692%	0.6070	7.5	C0.85	▲0.70	0.85	▲35.520%	42.074%	0.3890
C0.35	▲0.30	0.40	▲39.127%	44.728%	0.2566	10	C2.55	▲2.45	2.60	▲35.509%	43.947%	0.7375
C0.10	▲0.05	0.20	▲36.347%	50.218%	0.1024	12.5	C4.80	▲4.60	4.90	N/A	49.401%	0.8913

In the end, I would probably end up picking the implied volatility associated with the options struck at $7.50 and expiring in August 2013 (26 days until expiration). I was torn between these and the same strike expiring in November, but the August options are at least being actively traded, and the percentage bid-ask spread on the call side is lower for them than for the November options. Note, though, that the August 2013 put options are so far OTM that the bid-ask spread is very wide. In this case, I would probably look closer at the call options' implied volatilities. In the end, I would have a bid volatility of around 39 percent and an ask volatility of around 46 percent. Because the bid-ask spread is large, I would probably want to see a cone for both the bid and ask.

Plugging in the 22.0/22.5 for Oracle,[2] I would come up with this cone:

Oracle (ORCL)

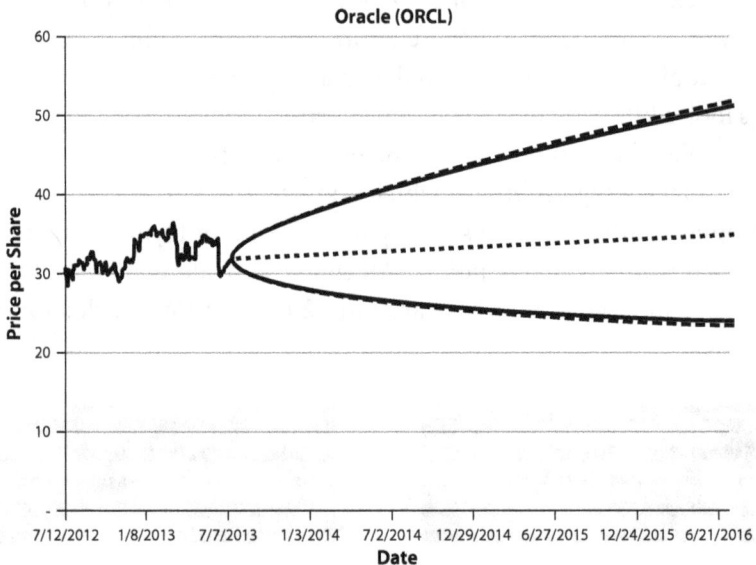

Plugging in the 39/46 for Mueller Water, I would get the following:

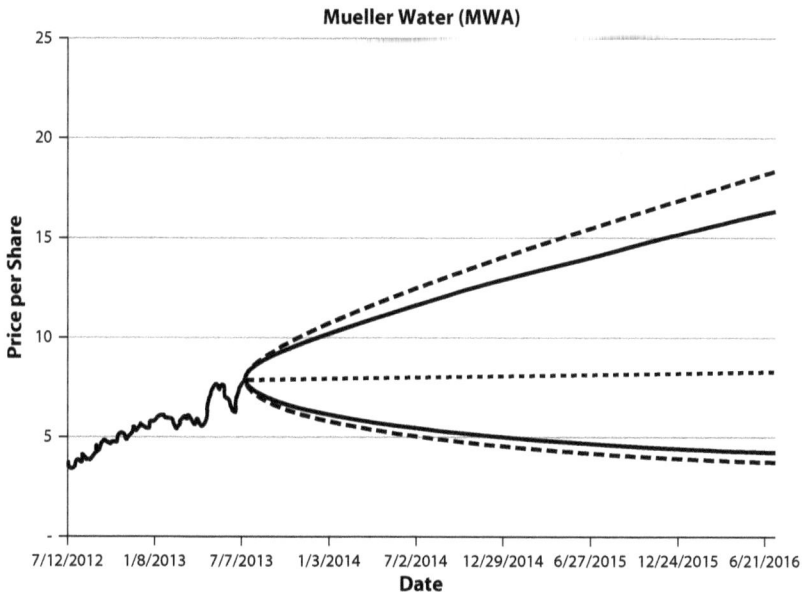

You can see with Mueller Water just how big a 7 percentage point difference can be for the bid and ask implied volatilities in terms of projected outcomes. The 39 percent bid implied volatility generates an upper range at just around $15; the 46 percent ask implied volatility generates an upper range that is 20 percent or so higher than that!

Overlay an Intelligent Valuation Range on the BSM Cone

This is simple and exactly the same for a big company or a small one, so I'll just keep going with the Oracle example. After having done a full valuation as shown in the exam valuation of Oracle on the IOI website, you've got a best-case valuation, a worst-case valuation, and probably an idea about what a likely valuation is. You simply draw those numbers onto a chart like this:

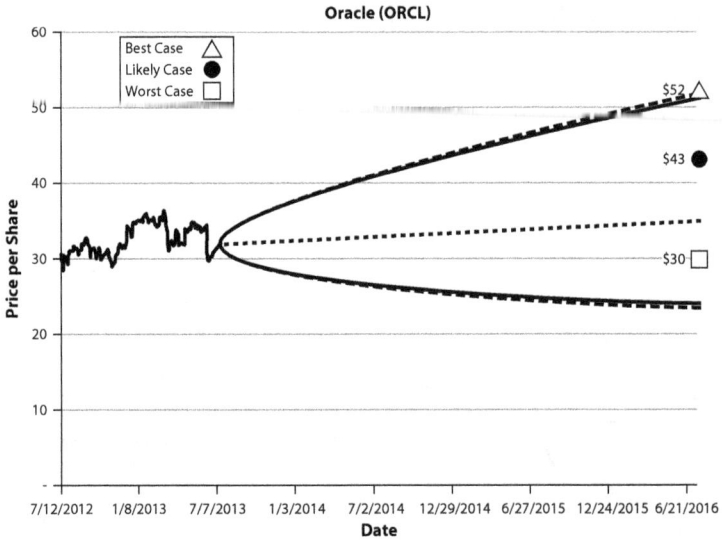

Once this step is done, we are ready to go onto the next and final step.

Look for Discrepancies

The last step is also easy. Because options split a stock's returns into upside and downside exposure, we need to take a look at both the upside and downside to see where our projections differ from those of the market.

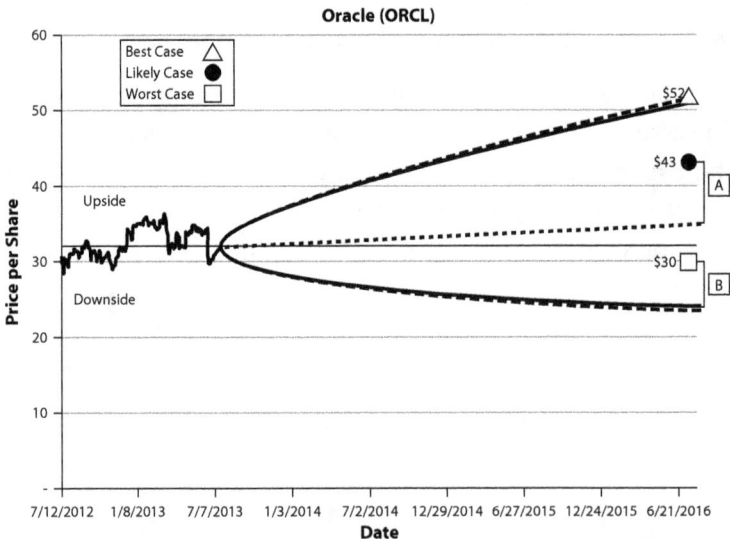

On the upside, we can see that our likely case valuation is $43 per share, whereas the BSM's most likely value is a bit less than $35—a difference of more than 20 percent. This is the area on the graph labeled "A." The BSM prices options based on the likelihood of the stock hitting a certain price level. The BSM considers the $43 price level to be relatively unlikely, whereas I consider it relatively likely. As such, I believe that options that allow me to gain exposure to the upside potential of Oracle—call options—are undervalued. In keeping with the age-old rule of investing to buy low, I will want to gain exposure to Oracle's upside by buying low-priced call options.

On the downside, I notice that there is a fairly large discrepancy between my worst-case valuation ($30) and the lower leg of the BSM cone (approximately $24)—this is the region of the graph labeled "B," and the separation between the two values is again (just by chance) about 20 percent. The BSM is pricing options granting exposure to the downside—put options—struck at $24 as if they were fairly likely to occur; something that is fairly likely to occur will be priced expensively by the BSM. My analysis, on the other hand, makes me think that the BSM's valuation outcome is very unlikely. The discrepancy implies that I believe the put options to be overvalued—the BSM sees a $24 valuation as likely, with expensive options, whereas I see it as unlikely, with nearly valueless options. In this case, we should consider the other half of the age-old investing maxim and sell high.

In a graphic representation, this strategy might look like this:

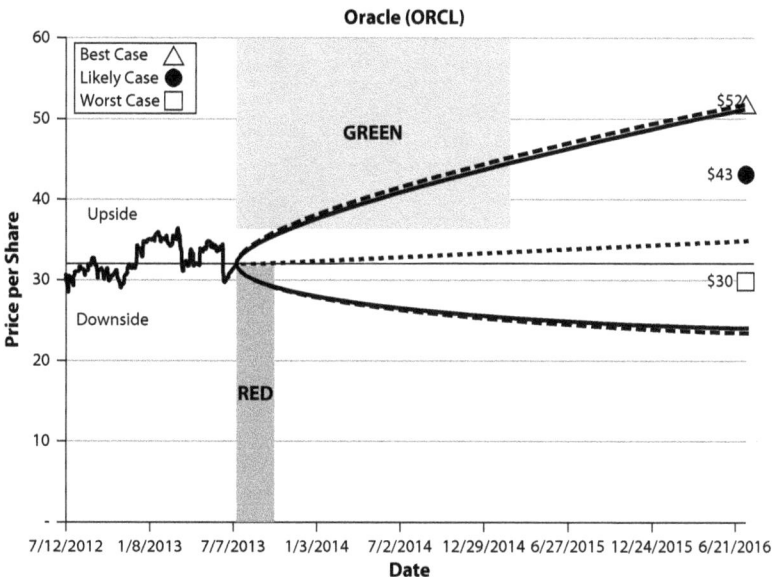

Oracle (ORCL)

Why would I select such a short-term put option to sell? Why would I pick an OTM call option to buy? These are the kinds of questions I will cover in Chapters 9–11, which look at the specifics of different option strategies.

Before we look at strategies, though, an option investor cannot be said to be intelligent without understanding what leverage is and how to use it safely and effectively in a portfolio. We turn to this in Chapter 8.

Chapter 8

UNDERSTANDING AND MANAGING LEVERAGE

In the media, the word *leverage* seems like it usually occurs alongside such words as *dangerous*, *speculative*, or even *irresponsible*, so most people have internalized the message that leverage is morally wrong; options—levered instruments that they are—are, by extension, viewed as morally wrong as well. In fact, nearly everyone uses leverage every day of their lives without incident and presumably without incurring a moral stain. In my opinion, it is not leverage that is the problem but rather an ignorance of how leverage works, coupled with overleverage and the inherent human belief that disasters only happen to someone else, that is the problem.

Leverage is a powerful tool, but like all powerful tools, if used recklessly and without understanding, it can bring its user to unpleasant outcomes. Certainly a discussion of gaining and accepting exposure using option contracts would be incomplete without a good explanation of leverage.

I like to think of leverage coming in three flavors: operational, financial, and investment—the first two of which I mentioned in an earlier chapter and go into more detail in Appendix B. This chapter delves specifically into investment leverage, but to the extent that investment leverage is similar to the other forms of leverage, referring to Appendix B to learn about those forms will help deepen your understanding of investment leverage. In this chapter, I first define investment leverage, discuss how it can be gained by using either debt or options, look at common ways to measure it, and introduce a unique method of measuring and managing leverage in an investment portfolio.

Leverage is not something to be taken lightly. Many very highly trained, well-educated, and well-capitalized investors have gone bankrupt because of their lack of appreciation for the fact that the sword of leverage cuts both ways. Certainly an option investor cannot be considered an intelligent investor without having an understanding and a deep sense of respect for the simultaneous power and danger that leverage conveys.

New jargon introduced in this chapter includes the following:

Lambda
Notional exposure

Investment Leverage

Commit the following definition to memory:

> *Investment leverage* is the boosting of investment returns calculated as a percentage by altering the amount of one's own capital at risk in a single investment.

Investment leverage is inextricably linked to borrowing money—this is what I mean by the phrase "altering the amount of one's own capital at risk." In this way, it is very similar to financial leverage. In fact, in my mind, the difference between financial and investment leverage is that a company uses financial leverage to fund projects that will produce goods or provide services, whereas in the case of investing leverage, it is used not to produce goods or services but to amplify the effects of a speculative position.

Frequently people think of investing leverage as simply borrowing money to invest. However, as I mentioned earlier, you can invest in options for a lifetime and never explicitly borrow money in the process. I believe that the preceding definition is broad enough to handle both the case of investment leverage generated through explicit borrowing and the case of leverage generated by options.

Let's take a look at a few example investments—unlevered, levered using debt, and levered using options.

Unlevered Investment

Let's say that you buy a stock for exactly $50 per share, expecting that its intrinsic value is closer to $85 per share. Over the next year, the stock increases by $5, or 10 percent in value. Your unrealized percentage gain on this investment is obviously 10 percent. If instead the stock declines to $45 per share over that year, you would be sitting on an unrealized percentage loss of 10 percent.

Of course, this is very straightforward. Let's now look at the purchase of a share of common stock using borrowed capital.

Levered Investment Using Debt

Let's say that to buy a $50 share, you borrow $45 from a bank at an interest rate of 5 percent per year, put in $5 of your own cash, and buy that same share of stock. Again, let's assume that the stock increases in value by $5 over one year, closing at $55 per share. At the end of the year, you sell the stock and pay back the bank loan with interest (a total of $47.25). Doing so, you realize gross proceeds of $7.75 on an original investment of $5 of your own capital, which equates to $2.75 in gross profits and implies a percentage investment return of 55 percent.

There are three important things to note by comparing the levered and unlevered examples:

1. The percentage return is much higher for the levered investment (55 versus 10 percent) because you have reduced the amount of your own capital at risk much more than you have reduced the dollar return in the numerator.
2. The actual dollar amount gained is lower in the levered example ($2.75 versus $10). If your investment mandate would have been "Generate at least $10 worth of investment returns," a single unit of the levered investment would have failed to meet this mandate.
3. Obviously, the underlying asset and its returns are the same in both levered and unlevered scenarios—we are changing our profit exposure to the underlying, not altering its volatility or other behavior.

To fully understand leverage's effects, however, we should also consider the loss scenario. Again, let's assume that we borrow $45 and spend $5 of our own money to buy the $50 per share stock. We wake the next morning to news that the company has discovered accounting irregularities in an important foreign subsidiary that has caused it to misstate revenues and profits for the last three years. The shares suddenly fall 10 percent on the news. The unrealized loss is $5—the 10 percent fall in stock value has wiped out 100 percent of our investment capital.

And herein lies the painful lesson learned by many a soul in the financial markets: leverage cuts both ways. The profits happily roll in during the good times, but the losses inexorably crash down during bad times.

Levered Investment Using Options

Discussing option-based investing leverage is much easier if we focus on the perspective of gaining exposure. Because most people are more comfortable thinking about the long side of investing, let's look at an example of gaining upside exposure on a company.

Let's assume we see a $50 per share stock that we believe is worth $85 (in this example, I am assuming that we only have a point estimate of the intrinsic value of the company so as to simplify the following diagram—normally, it is much more helpful to think about fair value ranges, as explained in Part II of this book and demonstrate in the online example). We are willing to buy the share all the way up to a price of $68 (implying a 25 percent return if bought at $68 and sold at $85) and can get call options struck at $65 per share for only $1.50. Graphically, this prospective investment looks like this:

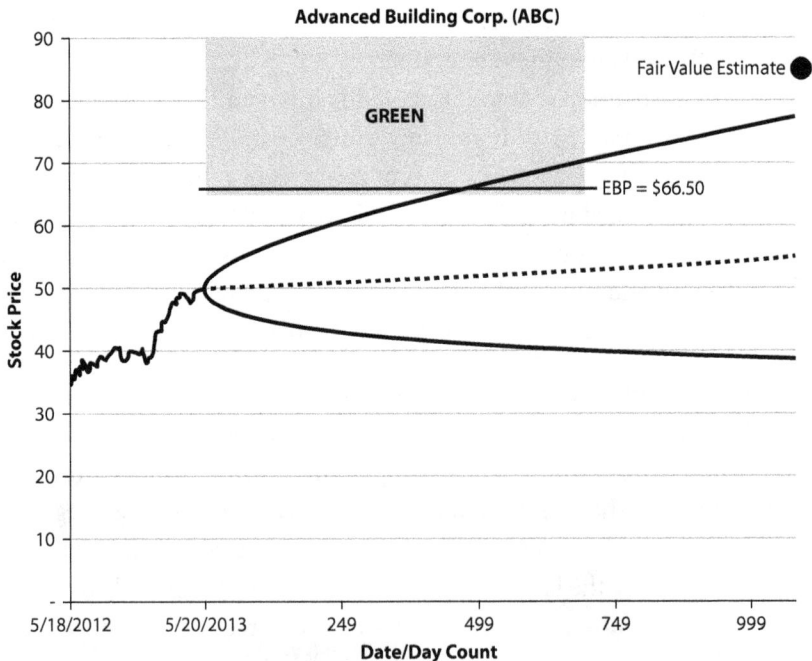

Advanced Building Corp. (ABC)

In two years, you are obligated to pay your counterparty $65 if you want to hold the stock, but the decision as to whether to take possession of the stock in return for payment is solely at your discretion. In essence, then, you can look at buying a call option as a conditional borrowing of funds sometime in the future. Buying the call option, you are saying, "I may want to borrow $65 two years from now. I will pay you some interest up front now, and if I decide to borrow the $65 in two years, I'll pay you that principal then."

In graphic terms, we can think about this transaction like this:

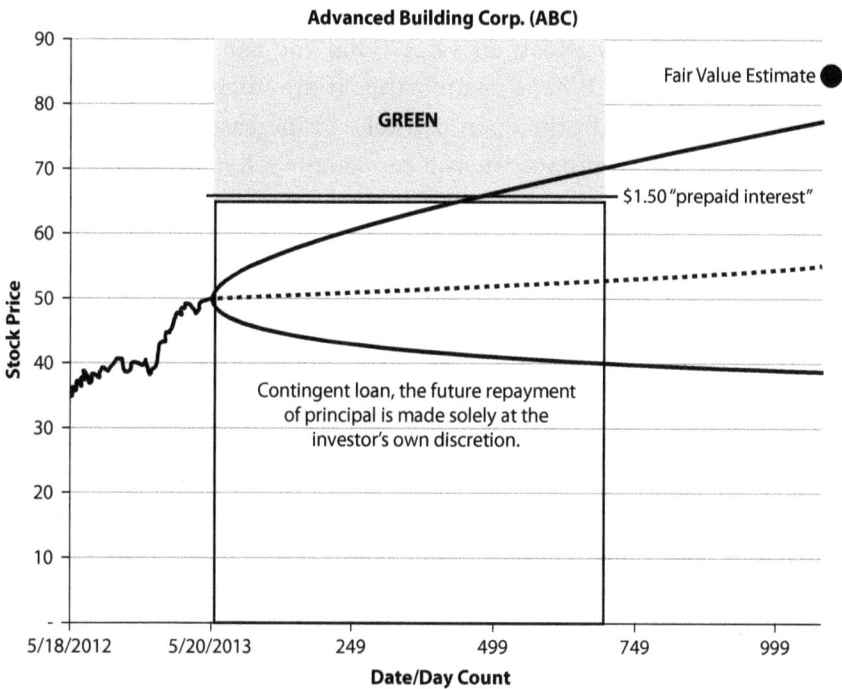

Advanced Building Corp. (ABC)

If the stock does indeed hit the $85 mark just at the time our option expires, we will have realized a gross profit of $20 (= $85 − $65) on an investment of $1.50, for a percentage return of 1,233 percent! Obviously, the call option works very much like a loan in terms of altering the investor's capital at risk and boosting subsequent investment returns. However, although the leverage looks very similar, there are two important differences:

1. As shown and mentioned earlier, when using an option, payment on the *principal* amount of $65 in this case is conditional and completely discretionary. For an option, the *interest* payment is made up front and is a sunk cost.
2. Because repayment is discretionary in the case of an option, you do not have any financial risk over and above the prepayment of *interest* in the form of an option premium. Repayment of a conventional loan is mandatory, so you have a large financial risk if you cannot repay the *principal* at maturity in this case.

Regarding the first difference, not only is the loan conditional and discretionary, the loan also has value and can be transferred to another for a profit. What I mean is this: if the stock rises quickly, the value of that option in the open market will increase, and rather than holding the "loan" to maturity, you can simply sell it with your profits offsetting the original cost of the prepaid interest plus giving you a nice profit.

Regarding the second difference, consider this: if you are using borrowed money to invest and your stock drops heavily, the broker will make a margin call (i.e., ask you to deposit more capital into the account), and if you cannot make the margin call, the broker will liquidate the position (most brokers shoot first and ask questions later, simply closing out the position and selling other assets to cover the loss at the first sign margin requirements will not be met). If this happens, you can be 100 percent correct on your valuation long term but still fail to benefit economically because the position has been forcibly closed. In the case of options, the underlying stock can lose 20 percent in a single day, and the owner of a call option will never receive a margin call. The flip side of this benefit is that although you are not at risk of losing a position to a margin call, option ownership does not guarantee that you will receive an economic reward either.

For example, if the option mentioned in the preceding example expires in two years when the stock is trading at $64.99 and the stock has paid $2.10 in dividends over the previous two years, the option holder ends up with neither the stock nor the dividend check.

Simple Ways of Measuring Option Investment Leverage

There are several single-point, easily calculable numbers to measure option-based investment leverage. There are uses for these simple measures of leverage, but unfortunately, for reasons I will discuss, the simple numbers are not enough to help an investor intelligently manage a portfolio containing option positions.

The two simple measures are lambda and notional exposure. Both are explained in the following sections.

Lambda

The standard measure investors use to determine the leverage in an option position is one called *lambda*. Lambda—sometimes known as *percent delta*—is a derivative of the delta[1] factor we discussed in Chapter 7 and is found using the following equation:

$$\text{Lambda} = \frac{\text{delta} \times \text{stock price}}{\text{option price}}$$

Let's look at an actual example. The other day, I bought a deep in-the-money (ITM) long-tenor call option struck at $20 when the stock was trading at $30.50. The delta of the option at that time was 0.8707, and the price was $11. The leverage in my option position was calculated as follows:

$$\text{Lambda} = \frac{\text{delta} \times \text{stock price}}{\text{option price}} = \frac{0.87 \times 30.50}{11} = 2.40$$

What this figure of 2.4 is telling us is that when I bought that option, if the price of the underlying moved by 1 percent, the value of my position would move by about 2.4 percent. This is not a hard and fast number—a change in price of either the stock or the option (as a result of a change in volatility or time value or whatever) will change the delta, and the lambda will change based on those things.

Because investment leverage comes about by changing the amount of your own capital that is at risk vis-à-vis the total size of the investment, you can imagine that moneyness has a large influence on lambda. Let's take a look at how investment leverage changes for in-the-money (ITM), at-the-money (ATM), and out-of-the-money (OTM) options. The stock underlying the following options was trading at $31.25 when these data were taken, so I'm showing the $29 and $32 strikes as ATM:

Strike Price	K/S Ratio	Call Price	Delta	Lambda	
15.00	0.48	17.30	0.91	1.64	
20.00	0.64	11.50	0.92	2.50	ITM
21.00	0.67	11.30	0.86	2.38	
22.00	0.70	9.60	0.89	2.90	
⋮	⋮	⋮	⋮	⋮	
29.00	0.93	3.40	0.68	6.25	
30.00	0.96	2.74	0.61	6.96	ATM
31.00	0.99	2.16	0.54	7.81	
⋮	⋮	⋮	⋮	⋮	
39.00	1.25	0.18	0.09	15.63	
40.00	1.28	0.13	0.06	14.42	OTM
41.00	1.31	0.09	0.05	17.36	

When an option is deep ITM, as in the case of the $20-strike call, we are making a significant expenditure of our own capital compared with the size of the investment. Buying a call option struck at $20, we are—as explained in the preceding section—effectively borrowing an amount equal to the $20 strike price. In addition to this, we are spending $11.50 in premium. Of this amount, $11.25 is intrinsic value, and $0.25 is time value. We can look at the time value portion as the *prepaid interest* we discussed in the preceding section, and we can even calculate the interest rate implied by this price (this option had 189 days left before expiration, implying an annual interest charge of 2.4 percent, for example). This prepaid interest can be offset partially or fully by profit realized on the position, but it can never be recaptured so must be considered a sunk cost. Time value always decays independent of the price changes of the underlying, so although an upward movement in the stock will offset the money spent on time value, the amount spent on time value is never recoverable.

The remaining $11.25 of the premium paid for a $20-strike call option is *intrinsic value*. Buying intrinsic value means that we are exposing our own capital to the risk of an unrealized loss if the stock falls below $31.25. Lambda is directly related to the amount of capital we are exposing to an unrealized loss versus the size of the "loan" from the option, so because we are risking $11.25 of our own capital and borrowing $20 with the option (a high capital-to-loan proportion), our investment leverage measured by lambda is a relatively low 2.50.

Now direct your attention to a far OTM call option—the one struck at $39. If we invest in the $39-strike option, we are again effectively taking out a $39 contingent loan to buy the shares. Again, we take the time-value portion of the option's price—in this case the entire premium of $1.28—to be the prepaid interest (an implied annualized rate of 6.3 percent) and note that we are exposing none of our own capital to the risk of an unrealized loss. Because we are subjecting none of our own capital in this investment and taking out a large loan, our investment leverage soars to a very high value of 15.63. This implies that a 1 percentage point move in the underlying stock will boost our investment return by over 15 percent!

Obviously, these calculations tell us that our investment returns are going to be much more volatile for small changes in the underlying's price when buying far OTM options than when buying far ITM options. This is fine information for someone interested in more speculative strategies—if a speculator has the sense that a stock will rise quickly, he or she could, rather than buying the stock, buy OTM options, and if the stock went up fast enough and soon enough offset any drop of implied volatility and time decay, he or she would pocket a nice, highly levered profit.

However, there are several factors that limit the usefulness of lambda. First, because delta is not a constant, the leverage factor does not stay put as the stock moves around. For someone who intends to hold a position for a longer time, then, lambda provides little information regarding how the position will perform over their investment horizon.

In addition, reading the preceding descriptions of lambda, it is obvious that this measure deals exclusively with the percentage change in the option's value. Although everyone (especially fly-by-night investment newsletter editors) likes to tout their percentage returns, we know from our earlier investigations of leverage that percentage returns are only part of the story of successful investing. Let's see why using the three investments I mentioned earlier—an ITM call struck at $20, an OTM call struck at $39, and a long stock position at $31.

I believe that there is a good chance that this stock is worth north of $40—in the $43 range, to be precise (my worst-case valuation was $30, and my best-case valuation was in the mid-$50 range). If I am right, and if this stock hits the $43 mark just as my options expire,[2] what do I stand to gain from each of these investments?

Let's take a look.

	Spent	Gross Profit	Net Profit	Percent Profit
$39-strike call	0.18	4.00	3.82	2,122
$20-strike call	11.50	23.00	11.50	100
Shares	31.25	43.00	11.75	38

This table means that in the case of the $20-strike call, we spent $11.50 to win gross proceeds of $23.00 (= $43 − $20) and a profit net of investment of $11.50. Netting $11.50 on an $11.50 investment generates a percentage profit of 100 percent.

Looking at this chart, the first thing you are liable to notice is the "Percent Profit" column. That 2,122 percent return looks like something you might see advertised on an option tout service, doesn't it? Yes, that percentage return is wonderful, until you realize that the absolute value of your dollar winnings will not allow you to buy a latte at Starbuck's. Likewise, the 100 percent return on the $20-strike options looks heads and shoulders better than the measly 38 percent on the shares, until you again realize that the latter is still giving you more money by a quarter.

Recall the definition of leverage as a way of "boosting investment returns calculated as a percentage," and recall that in my previous discussion of financial leverage, I mentioned that the absolute dollar value is always highest in the unlevered case. The fact is that many people get excited about stratospheric percentage returns, but stratospheric percentage returns only matter if a significant chunk of your portfolio is exposed to those returns! Lambda is a good measure to show how sensitive percentage returns are to a move in the stock price, but it is useless when trying to understand what the portfolio effects of those returns will be on an absolute basis.

Notional Exposure

Look back at the preceding table. Let's say that we wanted to make lambda more useful in understanding portfolio effects by seeing how many contracts we would need to buy to match the absolute return of the underlying stock. Because our expected dollar return of one of the $39-strike calls only makes up about a third of the absolute return of the straight stock investment ($3.82 / $11.75 = 32.5% ≈ 1/3), it follows that if we wanted to make the same dollar return by investing in these call options that we expect to make by buying the shares, we would have to buy three of the call options for every share we wanted to buy. Recalling that options are transacted in contract sizes of 100 shares, we know that if we were willing to buy 100 shares of Oracle's stock, we would have to buy options implying control over 300 shares to generate the same absolute profit for our portfolio.

I call this implied control figure *notional exposure*. Continuing with the $39-strike example, we can see that the measure of our leverage on the basis of notional exposure is 3:1. The value of the notional exposure is calculated by multiplying it by the strike; in this case, the notional exposure of 300 shares multiplied by the strike price of $39 gives a notional value for the contracts of $11,700. This value is called the *notional amount* of the option position.

Some people calculate a leverage figure by dividing the notional amount by the total cost of the options. In our example, we would pay $18 per contract for three contracts, so leverage measured in this way would work out to be 217 (= $11,700 ÷ $54). I actually do not believe this last measure of leverage to be very helpful, but notional control will become important when we talk about the leverage of short-call spreads later in this chapter.

These simple methods of measuring leverage have their place in analyzing option investment strategies, but in order to really master leverage, you must understand leverage in the context of portfolio management.

Understanding Leverage's Effects on a Portfolio

Looking at leverage from a lambda or notional control perspective gives some limited information about leverage, but I believe that the best way to think about option-based investment leverage is to think about the effect of leverage on an actual portfolio allocation basis. This gives a richer, more nuanced view of how leverage stands to help or hurt our portfolio and allows us more insight into how we can intelligently structure a mixed option-stock portfolio.

Let's start our discussion of leverage in a portfolio context by thinking about how to select investments into a portfolio. We will assume that we have $100 in cash and want to use some or all of that cash to invest in risky securities. Cash is riskless (other than inflation risk, but let's ignore that for a moment), so the risk we take on in the portfolio will be dampened by keeping cash, and the returns we will win from the portfolio will be similarly dampened.

We have a limited amount of capital and want to allocate that capital to risky investments in proportion to two factors:

1. The amount we think we can gain from the investment
2. Our conviction in the investment, which is a measure of our perception of the riskiness of the investment

We might see a potential investment that would allow us to reap a profit of $9 for every $1 invested (i.e., we would gain a great deal), but if our conviction in that investment is low (i.e., we think the chance of winning $9 for every $1 invested is very low), we would likely not allocate much of our portfolio to it.

In constructing a portfolio, most people set a limit on the proportion of their portfolio they want to allocate to any one investment. I personally favor more concentrated positions, but let's say that you paid better attention to your finance professor in school than I did and figure that you want to limit your risk exposure to any one security to a maximum of $5 of your $100 portfolio.

An unlevered portfolio means that each $5 allocation would be made by spending $5 of your own capital. You would know that if the value of the underlying security decreases by $2.50, the value of the allocation will also fall to $2.50. If, instead, the value of the underlying security increases by $2.50, the value of that allocation will rise to $7.50.

In a levered portfolio, each $5 allocation uses some proportion of capital that is not yours—borrowed in the case of a margin loan and contingently borrowed in the case of an option. This means that for every $1 increase or decrease in the value of the underlying security, the levered allocation increases or decreases by more than $1. Leverage, in this context, represents the rate at which the value of the allocation increases or decreases for every one-unit change in the value of the underlying security.

When thinking about the risk of leverage, we must treat different types of losses differently. A realized loss represents a permanent loss of capital—a sunk cost for which future returns can offset but never undo. An unrealized loss may affect your psychology but not your wealth (unless you need to realize the loss to generate cash flow for something else—I talk about this in Chapter 11 when I address hedging). For this reason, when we measure how much leverage we have when the underlying security declines, we will measure it on the basis of how close we are to suffering a realized loss rather than on the basis of the unrealized value of the loss. Leverage on the profit side will be handled the same way: we will treat our fair value estimate as the price at which we will realize a gain. Because the current market price of a security may not sit exactly between our fair value estimate and the point at which we suffer a realized loss, our upside and downside leverage may be different.

Let's see how this comes together with an actual example. For this example, I looked at the price of Intel's (INTC) shares and options when the former were trading at $22.99. Let's say that we want to commit 5 percent of our portfolio value to an investment in Intel, which we believe is worth $30 per share. For every $100,000 in our portfolio, this would mean buying 217 shares. This purchase would cost us $4,988.83 (neglecting taxes and fees, of course) and would leave us with $11.17 of cash in reserve. After we made the buy, the stock price would fluctuate, and depending on what its price was at the end of 540 days [I'm using as an investment horizon the days to expiration of the longest-tenor long-term equity anticipation securities (LEAPS)], the allocation's profit and loss profile would be represented graphically like this:

Unlevered Investment (Full Allocation)

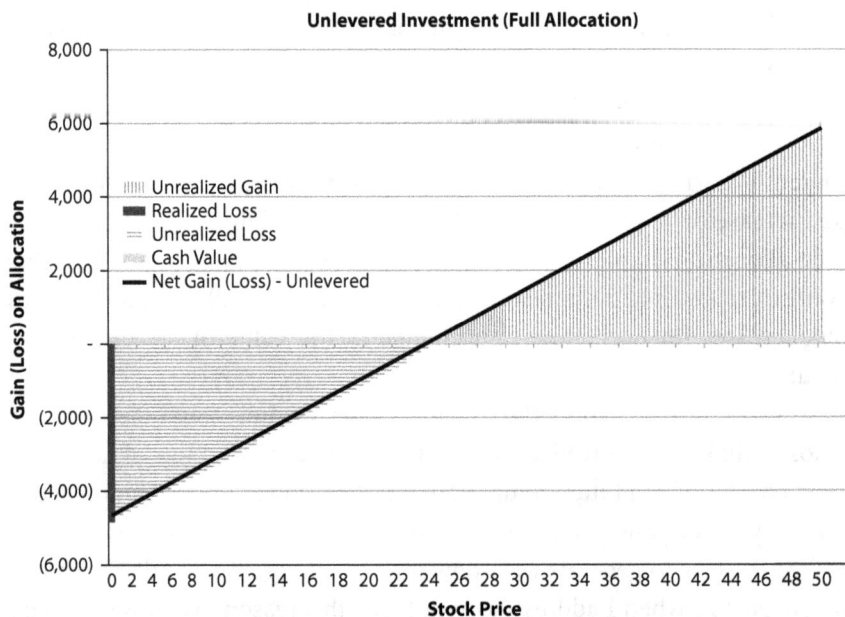

Here the future stock price is listed from 0 to 50 on the horizontal axis, and the net profit or loss to this position is listed on the vertical axis. Obviously, any gain or loss would be unrealized unless Intel's stock price went to zero, at which point the total position would only be worth whatever spare cash we had. The black profit and loss line is straight—the position will lose or gain on a one-for-one basis with the price of the stock, so our leverage is 1.0.

Now that we have a sense of what the graph for a straight stock position looks like, let's take a look at a few different option positions. When I drew the data for this example, the following 540-day expiration call options were available:

Strike Price	Ask Price	Delta
15	8.00	0.79
22	2.63	0.52
25	1.43	0.35

Let's start with the ITM option and construct a simple-minded position that attempts to buy as many of these option contracts as possible with the $5,000 we have reserved for this investment. We will pay $8 per share or $800 per contract, which would allow us to buy six contracts in all for $4,800. There is only $0.01 worth of time value (= $15.00 + $8.00 − $22.99) on these options because they are so far ITM. This means that we are paying $1 per contract worth of time value that is never recoverable, so we shall treat it as a realized loss. If we were to graph our potential profit and loss profile using this option, assuming that we are analyzing the position just as the 540-day options expire, we would get the following[3]:

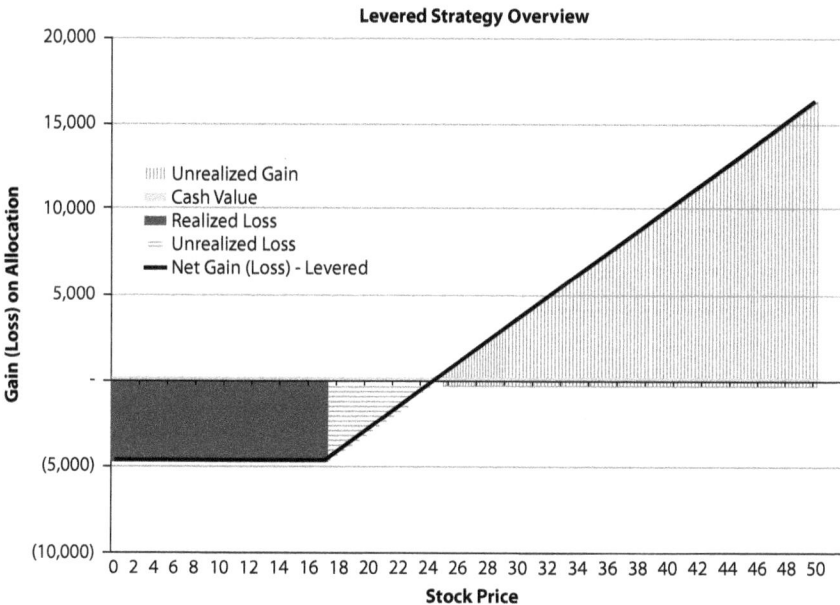

The most obvious differences from the diagram of the unlevered position are (1) that the net gain/loss line is kinked at the strike price and (2) that we will realize a total loss of invested capital—$4,800 in all—if Intel's stock price closes at $15 or below. The kinked line demonstrates the meaning of the first point made earlier regarding option-based investment leverage—an asymmetrical return profile for profits and losses. Note that this kinked line is just the hockey-stick representation of option profit and loss at expiration that one sees in every book about options except this one. Although I don't believe that hockey-stick diagrams are terribly useful for understanding individual option transactions, at a portfolio level, they do represent the effect of leverage very well. This black line represents a levered position, and its slope is much steeper than that of an equivalent line showing net profit and loss on an unlevered position. A comparison of the two net profit lines on the same graph shows this clearly:

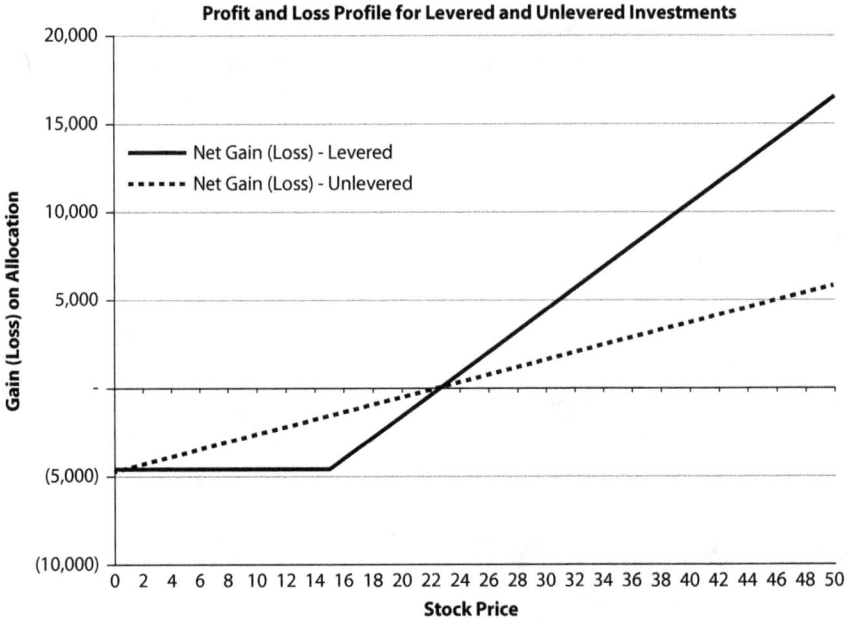

Profit and Loss Profile for Levered and Unlevered Investments

Looking at this diagram, you will notice the following things about the risk and return characteristics of the two positions:

Investment	Maximum Loss Price	Net Profit at Fair Value Estimate
Stock	$0	$1,472
Option	$15 (2.8 × stock loss)	$4,200 (3.0 × stock profit)

The leverage on the stock loss and the leverage on the stock profit are nearly equal in this instance because the point at which we realize a loss ($15) is just about the same distance below the market price as our presumed fair value ($30) is above. The leverage to loss is calculated as

$$\text{Loss leverage} = \frac{\text{realized loss as a percent of allocation}}{\text{percent stock decline to realized loss}}$$

In this example, we suffer a realized loss of 96 percent (= $4,800 ÷ $5,000) if the stock falls 35 percent, so the equation becomes

$$\text{Loss leverage} = \frac{96\%}{-35\%} = -2.8\times$$

(By convention, I'll always write the loss leverage as a negative.) This equation just means that it takes a drop of 35 percent to realize a loss on 96 percent of the allocation.

The profit leverage is simply a ratio of the levered portfolio's net profit to the unlevered portfolio's net profit at the fair value estimate. For this example, we have

$$\text{Profit leverage} = \frac{\$4,200}{\$1,472} = 3.0\times$$

Let's do the same exercise for the ATM and OTM options and see what fully levered portfolios with each of these options would look like from a risk-return perspective. If we bought as many $22-strike options as a $5,000 position size would allow (19 contracts in all), our profit and loss graph and table would look like this:

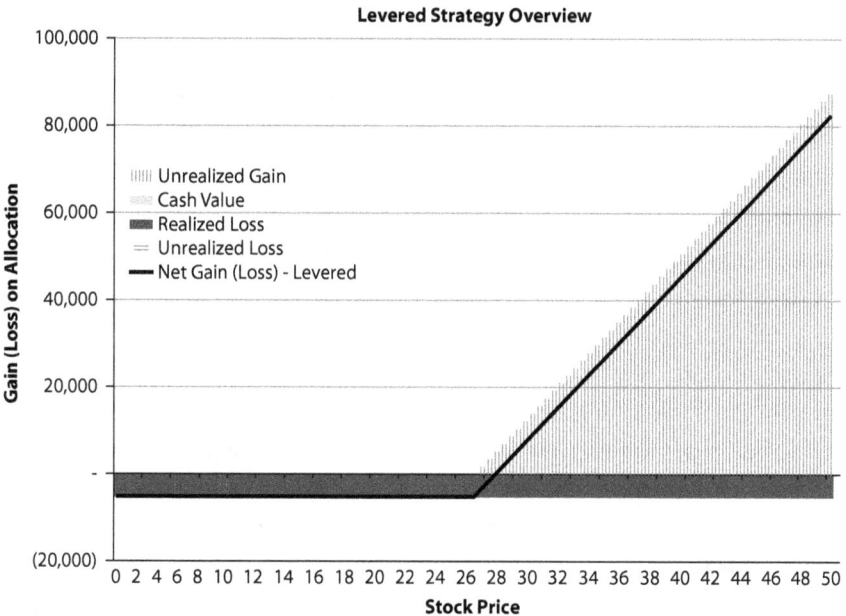

Levered Strategy Overview

Instrument	Maximum-Loss Price	Net Profit at Fair Value Estimate
Stock	$0	$1,472
Option	$22 (23.2 × stock loss)	$10,203 (6.9 × stock profit)

This is quite a handsome potential profit—6.9 times higher than we could earn using a straight stock position—but at an enormous risk. Each $1 drop in the stock price equates to a $23.20 drop in the value of the position. Note that the realized loss shows a step up from $22 to $23. This just shows that above the strike price, our only realized loss is the money we spent on time value.

The last example is that of the fully levered OTM call options. Here is the table illustrating this case:

Instrument	Maximum-Loss Price	Net Profit at Fair Value Estimate
Stock	$0	$1,472
Option	$25 (IRL 5 percent)	$12,495 (8.5 × stock profit)

There is no intrinsic value to this option, so the entire cost of the option is treated as an immediate realized loss (IRL) from inception. The "IRL 5 percent" notation means that there is an immediate realized loss of 5 percent of the total portfolio. The maximum net loss is again at the strike price of $25. The leverage factor at our fair value estimate price is 8.5, but again this leverage comes at the price of having to realize a 5 percent loss on your portfolio—500 basis points of performance—and there is no certainty that you will have enough or any profits to offset this realized loss.

Of course, investing choices are not as black and white as what I have presented here. If you want to commit 5 percent of your portfolio to a straight stock idea, you have to spend 5 percent of your portfolio value on stock, but this is not true for options. For example, I might choose to spend 2.5 percent of my portfolio's worth on ATM calls (nine contracts in this example), considering the position in terms of a 5 percent stock investment, and then leave the rest as cash reserve. Here is what this investment would look like from a leverage perspective:

Levered Strategy Overview

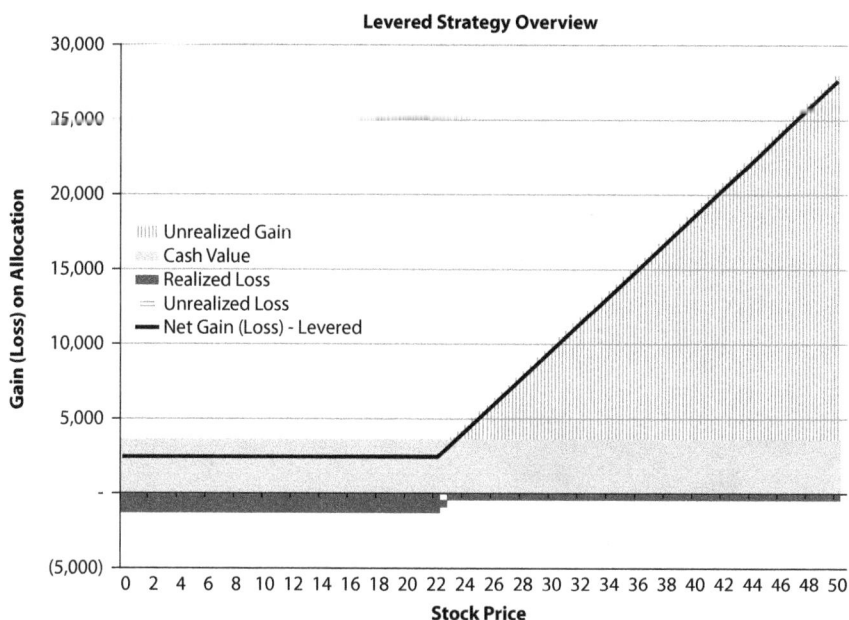

Instrument	Maximum-Loss Price	Net Profit at Fair Value Estimate
Stock	$0	$1,472
Option	$22 (11 × stock loss)	$4,833 (5.1 × stock profit)

The 11 times loss figure was calculated in the following way: there is a total of 47.3 percent of my allocation to this investment that is lost if the price of the stock goes down by 4.3 percent, so −47.3 percent/4.3 percent = −11.0. Obviously, this policy of keeping some cash in reserve represents a sensible approach to portfolio management when leverage is used. An investor in straight stock who makes 20 investments that do not hit his or her expected fair value within the investment horizon might have a few bad years of performance, but an investor who uses maximum option leverage and allocates 5 percent to 20 ideas will end up bankrupt if these don't work out by expiration time!

Similar to setting a cash reserve, you also might decide to make an investment that combines cash, stock, and options. For example, I might buy 100 shares of Intel, three ITM option contracts, and leave the rest of my 5 percent allocation in cash. Here is what that profit and loss profile would look like:

Levered Strategy Overview

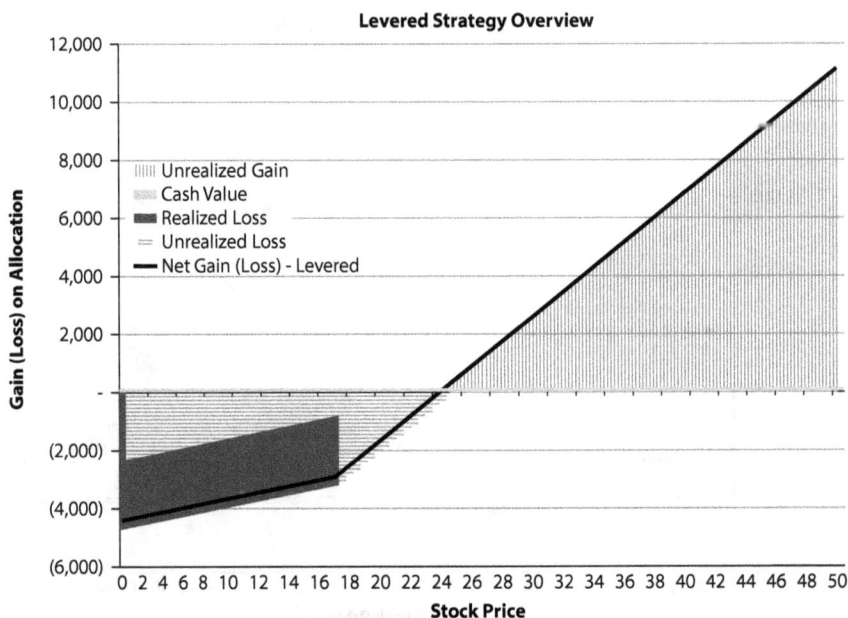

Instrument	Maximum-Loss Price	Net Profit at Fair Value Estimate
Stock	$0	$1,472
Option	$15 (1.4 × stock loss)	$2,801 (1.9 × stock profit)

Three $800 option contracts represent $2,400 of capital or 48 percent of this allocation's capital. Thus 48 percent of the capital was lost with a 34.8 percent move downward in the stock, generating a −1.4 times value for the options, which represents the figure you see on the loss side. Of course, if the option loss is realized, we still own 100 shares, so the maximum loss will not be felt until the shares hit $0, as shown in the preceding diagram.

For the remainder of this book I will describe leverage positions using the two following terms: *loss leverage* and *profit leverage*. I will write these in the following way:

$$\frac{-X.x}{Y.y}$$

where the first number will be the loss leverage ratio, and the second number will be the profit leverage ratio based on the preceding rules that

I've used for calculation. All OTM options will be marked with an IRL followed by the percentage of the total portfolio used in the option purchase (not the percentage of the individual allocation but the total percentage amount of your investment capital). On my website, you'll find an online leverage tool that allows you to calculate these numbers yourself.

Managing Leverage

A realized loss is, to me, serious business. There are times when an investor must take a realized loss—specifically when his or her view of the fair value or fair value range of a company changes materially enough that an investment position becomes unattractive. However, if you find yourself taking realized losses because of material changes in valuation too often, you should either figure out where you are going wrong in the valuation process or just put your money into a low-load mutual fund and spend your time doing something more productive.

The point is that taking a realized loss is not something you have to do too often if you are a good investor, and hopefully, when those losses are taken, they are small. As such, I believe that there are two ways to successfully manage leverage. First is to use leverage sparingly by investing in combinations of ITM options and stocks. ITM option prices mainly represent intrinsic value, and because the time-value component is that which represents a realized loss right out of the gate, buying ITM options means that you are minimizing realized losses.

The second method for managing leverage when you cannot resist taking a higher leverage position is spending as little as possible of your investment capital on it. This means that when you see that there is a company that has a material chance of being worth a lot more or a lot less than it is traded for at present but that material chance is still much less likely than other valuation scenarios, you should invest your capital in the idea sparingly. By making smaller investments with higher leverage, you will not realize a loss on too much of your capital at one time, and if you are right at least some of the time on these low-probability, high-potential-reward bets, you will come out ahead in the end.

Of course, you also can use a combination of these two methods. For example, I have found it helpful to take the main part of a position using a combination of stock and ITM call options but also perhaps buying a few OTM call options as well. As the investment ages and more data about the company's operations come in, if this information leads me to be more bullish about the prospects of the stock, I may again increase my leverage using OTM call options—especially when I see implied volatility trading at a particularly low level or if the stock price itself is depressed because of a generally weak market.

I used to be of the opinion that if you are confident in your valuation and your valuation implies a big enough unlevered return, it is irrational not to get exposure to that investment with as much leverage as possible. A few large and painful losses of capital have convinced me that where-as levering up on high-conviction investments is theoretically a rational investment regime, practically, it is a sucker's game that is more likely to deplete your investment capital than it is to allow you to hit home runs.

Younger investors, who still have a long investing career ahead of them and plenty of time to make up for mistakes early on, probably can feel more comfortable using more leverage, but as you grow closer to the time when you need to use your investments (e.g., paying for retirement, kids' college expenses, or whatever), using lower leverage is better.

Looking back at the preceding tables, one row in one table in particular should stand out to you. This is the last row of the last table, where the leverage is −1.8/2.6. To me, this is a very attractive leverage ratio because of the asymmetry in the risk-reward balance. This position is levered, but the leverage is lopsided in the investor's favor, so the investor stands to win more than he or she loses.

This asymmetry is the key to successful investing—not only from a leverage standpoint but also from an economic standpoint as well. I believe an intelligent, valuation-centric method for investing in companies such as the ones outlined in this book that allow investors an edge up by allowing them to identify cases in which the valuation simply does not line up with the market price. This in itself presents an asymmetrical profit opportunity, and the real job of an intelligent investor is to find as large an asymmetry as possible and courageously invest in that company. If you can also tailor your leverage such that your payout is asymmetrical in your favor as well, this only adds potential for outsized returns, in my opinion.

The other reason that the −1.8/2.6 leverage ratio investment interests me is because of the similarity it has to the portfolio of Warren Buffett's

Berkshire Hathaway (BRK.A). In a recent academic paper written by researchers at AQR Capital titled, "Buffett's Alpha,"[4] the researchers found that a significant proportion of Buffett's legendary returns can be attributed to finding firms that have low valuation risk and investing in them using a leverage ratio of roughly 1.8. The leverage comes from the *float* from his insurance companies (the monies paid in premium by clients over and above that required to pay out claims). As individual investors, we do not have a captive insurance company from which we can receive continual float, but by buying options and using leverage prudently, it is possible to invest in a manner similar to a master investor.

In this section, we have only discussed leverage considerations when we gain exposure by buying options. There is a good reason to ignore the case where we are accepting exposure by selling options that we will discuss when we talk about *margining* in Chapter 10. We now continue with chapters on gaining, accepting, and mixing exposure. In these chapters, we will use all of what we have learned about option pricing, valuation, and leverage to discuss practical option investment strategies.

Chapter 9

GAINING EXPOSURE

This chapter is designed as an encyclopedic listing of the main strategies for gaining exposure (i.e., buying options) that an intelligent option investor should understand. Gaining exposure seems easy in the beginning because it is straightforward—simply pay your premium up front, then if the stock moves into your option's range of exposure by expiration time, you win. However, the more you use these strategies in investing exposure, the more nuances arise.

What tenor should I choose? What strike price should I choose? Should I exercise early if my option is in the money (ITM)? How much capital should I commit to a given trade? If the stock price goes in the opposite direction from my option's range of exposure, should I close my option position? All these questions are examples of why gaining exposure by buying options is not as straightforward a process as it may seem at first and are all the types of questions I will cover in the following pages.

Gaining exposure means buying options, and the one thing that an option buyer must never lose sight of is that time is always working against him or her. Options expire. If your options expire out of the money (OTM), the capital you spent on premiums on those options is a realized loss. No matter how confident you are about your valuation call, you should always keep this immutable truth of option buying in mind. Indeed, there are ways to reduce the risk of this happening or to manage a portfolio in such a way that such a loss of capital becomes just a cost of doing business that will be made up for in another investment down the line.

For each of the strategies mentioned in this chapter, I present a stylized graphic representing the Black-Scholes-Merton model (BSM) cone and the option's range of exposure plus best- and worst-case valuation scenarios. These are two of the required inputs for an intelligent option investing strategy—an intelligently determined valuation range and the mechanically determined BSM forecast range. I will also provide a summary of the relative pricing of upside and downside exposure vis-à-vis an intelligent valuation range (e.g., "Upside exposure is undervalued"), the steps taken to execute the strategy, and its potential risks and return.

After this summary section, I provide textual discussions of tenor selection, strike price selection, portfolio management (i.e., rolling, exercise, etc.), and any miscellaneous items of interest to note. Understanding the strategies well and knowing how to use the tools at your disposal to tilt the balance of risk and reward in your favor are the hallmark and pinnacle of intelligent option investing. Intelligent option investors gain exposure when the market underestimates the likelihood of a valuation that the investor believes is a rational outcome. In graphic terms, this means that either one or both of the investor's best- and worst-case valuation scenarios lie outside the BSM cone.

Simple (one-option) strategies to gain exposure include

- Long calls
- Long puts

Complex (multioption) strategies to gain exposure include

- Long strangles
- Long straddles

Jargon introduced in this chapter includes the following:

Roll
Ratio(ing)

Long Call

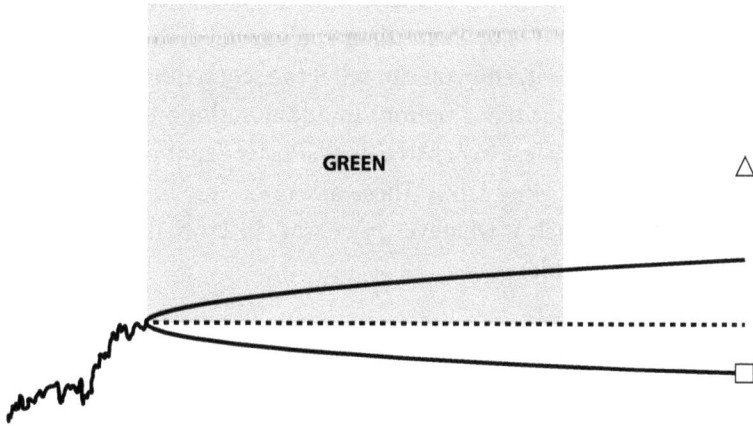

Downside: Fairly priced
Upside: Undervalued
Execute: Buy a call option
Risk: Amount equal to premium paid
Reward: Unlimited less amount of premium paid

The Gist

An investor uses this strategy when he or she believes that there is a material chance that the value of a company is much higher than the present market price. The investor must pay a premium to initiate the position, and the proportion of the premium that represents time value should be recognized as a realized loss because it cannot be recovered. If the stock fails to move into the area of exposure before option expiration, there will be no profit to offset this realized loss.

In economic terms, this transaction allows an investor to go long an undervalued company without accepting an uncertain risk of loss if the stock falls. Instead of the uncertain risk of loss, one must pay the fixed premium. This strategy obeys the same rules of leverage as discussed earlier in this book, with in-the-money (ITM) call options offering less leverage but being much more forgiving regarding timing than are at-the-money (ATM) or especially out-of-the-money (OTM) options.

Tenor Selection

In general, the rule for gaining exposure is to buy as long a tenor as is available. If a stock moves up faster than you expected, the option will still have time value left on it, and you can sell it to recoup the extra money you spent to buy the longer-tenor option. In addition, long-tenor options are usually proportionally less expensive than shorter-tenor ones. You can see this through the following table. These ask prices are for call options on Google (GOOG) struck at whatever price was closest to the 50-delta mark for every tenor available.

Days to Expiration	Ask Price	Marginal Price/Day	Delta
3	6.00	2.00	52
10	10.30	0.61	52
17	12.90	0.37	52
24	15.50	0.37	52
31	17.70	0.31	52
59	22.40	0.17	49
87	34.40	0.43	50
150	42.60	0.13	50
178	47.30	0.17	50
241	56.00	0.14	50
542	86.40	0.10	50

The "Marginal Price/Day" column is simply the extra that you pay to get the extra days on the contract. For example, the contract with three days left is $6.00. For seven more days of exposure, you pay a total of $4.30 extra, which works out to a per-day rate of $0.61. We see blips in the marginal price per day field as we go from 59 to 87 to 150 days, but these are just artifacts of data availability; the closest strikes did not have the same delta for each expiration.

The preceding chart, it turns out, is just the inverse of the rule we already learned in Chapter 3: "time value slips away fastest as we get closer to expiration." If time value slips away more quickly nearer expiration, it must mean that the time value nearer expiration is proportionally worth more than the time value further away from expiration. The preceding table simply illustrates this fact.

Value investors generally like bargains and to buy in bulk, so we should also buy our option time value "in bulk" by buying the longest tenor available and getting the lowest per-day price for it. It follows that if long-term equity anticipation securities (LEAPS) are available on a stock, it is usually best to buy one of those. LEAPS are wonderful tools because, aside from the pricing of time value illustrated in the preceding table, if you find a stock that has undervalued upside potential, you can win from two separate effects:

1. The option market prices options as if underlying stocks were efficiently priced when they may not be (e.g., the market thinks that the stock is worth $50 when it's worth $70). This discrepancy gives rise to the classic value-investor opportunity.
2. As long as interest rates are low, the *drift* term understates the actual, probable drift of the stock market of around 10 percent per year. This effect tends to work for the benefit of a long-tenor call option whether or not the pricing discrepancy is as profound as originally thought.

There are a couple of special cases in which this "buy the longest tenor possible" rule of thumb should not be used. First, if you believe that a company may be acquired, it is best to spend as little on time value as possible. I will discuss this case again when I discuss selecting strike prices, but when a company agrees to be acquired by another (and the market does not think there will be another offer and regulatory approvals will go through), the time value of an option drops suddenly because the expected life of the stock as an independent entity has been shortened by the acquiring company. This situation can get complicated for stock-based acquisitions (i.e., those that use stocks as the currency of acquisition either partly or completely) because owners of the acquiree's options receive a stake in the acquirer's options with strike price adjusted in proportion to the acquisition terms. In this case, the time value on your acquiree options would not disappear after the acquisition but be transferred to the acquirer's company's options. The real point is that it is impossible, as far as I know, to guess whether an acquisition will be made in cash or in shares, so the rule of thumb to buy as little time value as possible still holds.

In general, attempting to profit from potential mergers is difficult using options because you have to get both the timing of the suspected transaction and the acquisition price correct. I will discuss a possible solution to this situation in the next section about picking strike prices.

The second case in which it is not necessary to buy as long a tenor as possible is when you are trading in expectation of a particular company announcement. In general, this game of anticipating stock price movements is a hard one to win and one that value investors usually steer clear of, but if you are sure that some announcement scheduled for a particular day or week is likely to occur but do not want to make a long-term investment on the company, you can buy a shorter-tenor option that obviously must include the anticipated announcement date. It is probably not a bad idea to build in a little cushion between your expiration and the anticipated date of the announcement because sometimes announcements are pushed back and rescheduled.

Strike Price Selection

From the discussion regarding leverage in the preceding section, it is clear that selecting strike prices has a lot to do with selecting what level of leverage you have on any given bet. Ultimately, then, strike selection—the management of leverage, in other words—is intimately tied to your own risk profile and the degree to which you are risk averse or risk seeking.

My approach, which I will talk more about in the following section on portfolio management, may be too conservative for others, but I put it forward as one alternative among many that I have found over time to be sensible. Any investment has risk to the extent that there is never perfect certainty regarding a company's valuation. Some companies have a fairly tight valuation range—meaning that the confluence of their revenue stream, profit stream, and investment efficacy does not vary a great deal from best to worst case. Other companies' valuation ranges are wide, with a few clumps of valuation scenarios far apart or with just one or two outlying valuation scenarios that, although not the most likely, are still materially probable.

On the rare occasion in which we find a company that has a valuation range that is far different from the present market price (either tight or wide), I would rather commit more capital to the idea, and for me, committing more capital to a single idea means using less leverage. In other words, I would prefer to buy an ITM call and lever at a reasonable rate (e.g., the $-1.8 \times /2.6 \times$ level we saw in the Intel example earlier). Graphically, my approach would look like this:

Advanced Building Corp. (ABC)

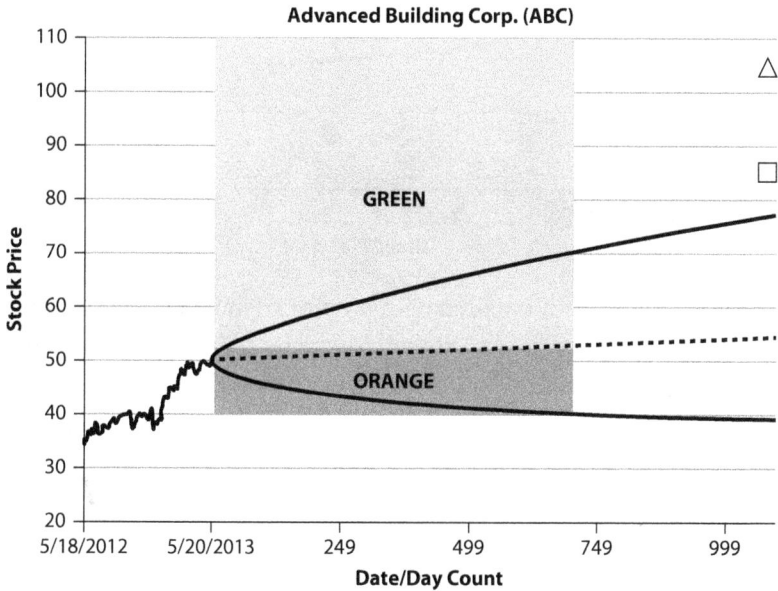

Here I have bought a deep ITM call option LEAPS that gives me leverage of about $-1.5/2.0$. I have maximized my tenor and minimized my leverage ratio with the ITM call. This structure will allow me to profit as long as the stock goes up by the time my option expires, even if the stock price does not hit a certain OTM strike price.

In the more common situation, in which we find a company that is probably about fairly valued in most scenarios but that has an outlying valuation scenario or two that doesn't seem to be priced in properly by the market, I will commit less capital to the idea but use more leverage. Graphically, my approach would look more like this:

Advanced Building Corp. (ABC)

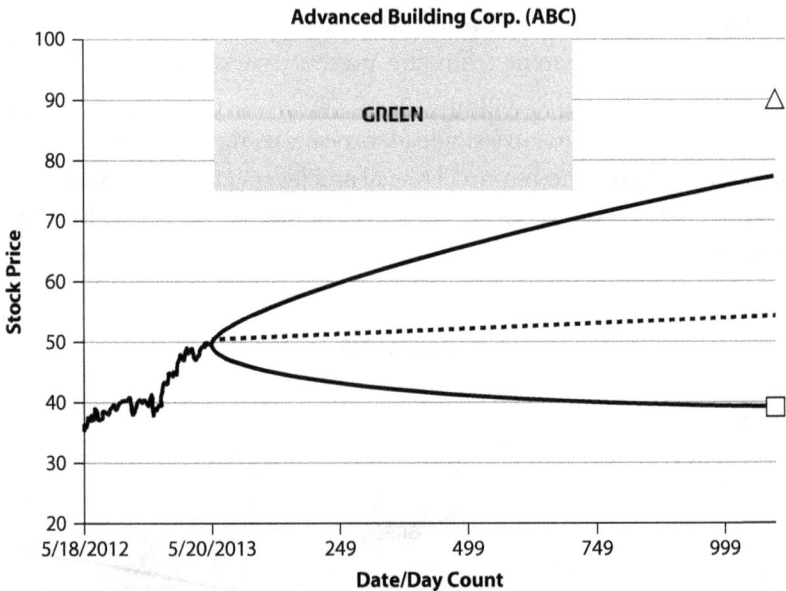

Here I have again maximized my tenor by buying LEAPS, but this time I increase my leverage to something like an "IRL/10.0" level in case the stars align and the stock price sales to my outlier valuation.

Some people would say that the IIM approach is absolutely the opposite of a rational one. If you are—the counterargument goes—confident in your valuation range, you should try to get as much leverage on that idea as possible; buying an ITM option is stupid because you are not using the leverage of options to their fullest potential. This counterargument has its point, but I find that there is just too much uncertainty in the markets to be too bold with the use of leverage.

Options are time-dependent instruments, and if your option expires worthless, you have realized a loss on whatever time value you originally spent on it. Economies, now deeply intertwined all over the globe, are phenomenally complex things, so it is the height of hubris to claim that I can perfectly know what the future value of a firm is and how long it will take for the market price to reflect that value. In addition, I as a human decision maker am analyzing the world and investments through a congenital filter based on behavioral biases.

Retaining my humility in light of the enormous complexity of the marketplace and my ingrained human failings and expressing this humility by using relatively less leverage when I want to commit a significant amount of capital to an idea constitute, I have found, given my risk tolerance and experience, the best path for me for a general investment.

In contrast, we all have special investment loves or wild hares or whatever, and sometimes we must express ourselves with a commitment of capital. For example, "If XYZ really can pull it off and come up with a cure for AIDS, its stock will soar." In instances such as these, I would rather commit less capital and express my doubt in the outcome with a smaller but more highly levered bet. If, on average, my investment wild hares come true every once in a while and, when they do, the options I've bought on them pay off big enough to more than cover my realized losses on all those that did not, I am net further ahead in the end.

These rules of thumb are my own for general investments. In the special situation of investing in a possible takeover target, there are a few extra considerations. A company is likely to be acquired in one of two situations: (1) it is a sound business with customers, product lines, or geographic exposure that another company wants, or (2) it is a bad business, either because of management incompetence, a secular decline in the business, or something else, but it has some valuable asset(s) such as intellectual property that a company might want to have.

If you think that a company of the first sort may be acquired, I believe that it is best to buy ITM call options to attempt to minimize the time value spent on the investment (you could also sell puts, and I will discuss this approach in Chapter 10). In this case, you want to minimize the time value spent because you know that the time value you buy will drain away when a takeover is announced and accepted. By buying an ITM contract, you are mainly buying intrinsic value, so you lose little time value if and when the takeover goes through. If you think that a company of the second sort (a bad company in decline) may be acquired, I believe that it is best to minimize the time value spent on the investment by not buying a lot of call contracts and by buying them OTM. In this case, you want to minimize the time value spent using OTM options by limiting the number of contracts bought because you do not want to get stuck losing too much capital if and when the bad company's stock loses value while you are holding the options. Typical buyout premiums are in the 30 percent range, so buying call options 20 percent OTM or so should generate a decent profit if the company is taken out. Just keep in mind that the buyout premium is 30 percent over the last price, not 30 percent over the price at which you decided to make your investment. If you buy 20 percent OTM call options and the stock decreases by 10 percent before a 30 percent premium buyout is announced, you will end up with nothing, as shown in the following timeline:

$12-Strike Options Bought When the Stock Is Trading for $10

- Stock falls to $9.
- Buyout is announced at 30 percent above last price—$11.70.
- 12-strike call owner's profit = $0.

However, there is absolutely no assurance that an acguirer will pay something for a prospective acguiree. Depending on how keen the acquirer is to get its hands on the assets of the target, it may actually allow the target company to go bankrupt and then buy its assets at $0.30 on the dollar or whatever. It is precisely this uncertainty that makes it unwise to commit too much capital to an idea involving a bad company—even if you think it may be taken out.

Portfolio Management

I like to think of intelligent option investing as a meal. In our investment meal, the underlying instrument—the stock—should, in most cases, form the main course.

People have different ideas about diversification in a securities portfolio and about the maximum percentage of a portfolio that should be allocated to a specific idea. Clearly, most people are more comfortable allocating a greater percentage of their portfolio to higher-confidence ideas, but this is normally framed in terms of relative levels (i.e., for some people, a high-conviction idea will make up 5 percent of their portfolio and a lower-conviction one 2.5 percent; for others, a high-conviction idea will make up 20 percent of their portfolio and a lower-conviction one 5 percent). Rather than addressing what size of investment meal is best to eat, let's think about the meal's composition.

Considering the underlying stock as the main course, I consider the leverage as sauces and side dishes. ITM options positions are the main sauce to make the main course more interesting and flavorful. You can layer ITM options onto the stock to increase leverage to a level with which you feel comfortable. This does not have to be Buffett's 1.8:1 leverage of course. Levering more lightly will provide less of a kick when a company performs according to your best-case scenario, but also carries less risk of a severe loss if the company's performance is mediocre or worse. OTM option positions (and "long diagonals" to be discussed in Chapter 11) can be thought of as a spicy side dish to the main meal. They can be added opportunistically (when and if the firm in which you are investing has a bad quarter and its stock price drops for temporary reasons involving sentiment rather than substance) for extra flavor. OTM options can also be used as a snack to be nibbled on between proper meals. Snack, in this case, means a smaller sized position in firms that have a small but real upside potential but a greater chance that it is fairly valued as is, or in a company in which you don't have the conviction in its ability to create much value for you, the owner.

Another consideration regarding the appropriate level of investment leverage one should apply to a given position is how much operational and financial leverage (both are discussed in detail in Appendix B) a firm has. A firm that is highly levered will have a much wider valuation range and will be much more likely to be affected by macroeconomic considerations that are out of the control of the management team and inscrutable to the investor. In these cases, I think the best response is to adjust one's investment leverage according to the principles of "margin of safety" and contrarianism.

By creating a valuation range, rather than thinking only of a single point-estimate for the value of the firm, we have unwittingly allowed ourselves to become very skillful at picking appropriate margins of safety. For example, I recently looked at the value of a company whose stock was trading for around $16 per share. The company had very high operational and financial leverage, so my valuation range was also very large—from around $6 per share worst case to around $37 per share best case with a most likely value of around $25 per share. The margin of safety is 36 percent (= ($25 − $16)/$25). While some might think this is a reasonable margin of safety to take a bold, concentrated position, I elected instead to take a small, unlevered one because to me, the $9 margin of safety for this stock is still not wide enough. The best time to take a larger position and to use more leverage is when the market is pricing a stock as if it were *almost certain* that a company will face a worst-case future when you consider this worst-case scenario to be relatively unlikely. In this illustration, if the stock price were to fall by 50 percent—to the $8 per share level—while my assessment of the value of the company remained unchanged (worst, likely, and best case of $6, $25, and $37, respectively), I would think I had the margin of safety necessary to commit a larger proportion of my portfolio to the investment and add more investment leverage. With the stock sitting at $8 per share, my risk ($8 − $6 = $2) is low and unlikely to be realized while my potential return is large and much closer to being assured. With the stock's present price of $16 per share, my risk ($16 − $6 = $10) is large and when bad-case scenarios are factored in along with the worst-case scenario, more likely to occur.

Thinking of margins of safety from this perspective, it is obvious that one should not frame them in terms of arbitrary levels (e.g., "I have a rule to only buy stocks that are 30% or lower than my fair value estimate."), but rather in terms informed by an intelligent valuation range. In this example, a 36 percent margin of safety is sufficient for me to commit a small proportion of my portfolio to an unlevered investment, but not to go "all in." For a concentrated, levered position in this investment, I would need a margin of safety approaching 76 percent (= ($25 − $6)/$25) and at least over 60 percent (= ($25 − $10)/$25).

When might such a large margin of safety present itself? Just when the market has lost all hope and is pricing in disaster for the company. This is where the contrarianism comes into play. The best time to make a levered investment in a company with high levels of operational leverage is when the rest of the market is mainly concerned about the possible negative effects of that operational leverage. For example, during a recession, consumer demand drops and idle time at factories increases. This has a quick and often very negative effect on profitability for companies that own the idle factories, and if conditions are bad enough or look to have no near-term (i.e., within about six months) resolution, the price of those companies' stocks can plummet. Market prices often fall so low as to imply, from a valuation perspective, that the factories are likely to remain idled forever. In these cases, I believe that *not using* investment leverage in this case may carry with it more real risk than *using* investment leverage (see my discussion of risk in Chapter 12 after reading the paragraphs below about financial leverage).

In boom times, just the opposite is true. Factories are nearing full capacity and demand is strong. Most of the market is thinking only of the extra percentage points of profit that can be squeezed out of the operations when continuing strong demand pushes factory capacity even higher. As every contrarian knows, this is precisely the wrong time to fall in love with the stock of an operationally levered company; it is also precisely the wrong time to use investment leverage to gain exposure to the stock of an operationally levered company.

Financial leverage is more dangerous and requires a much more careful consideration of valuation scenarios, especially if the economy is in or is going into recession. In recessions, consumer demand for products slows, but banks' and bondholders' demand for interest and principal payments continues unabated. If demand is so low that a company is not generating enough cash flow to pay interest on its debt, or if it can pay interest on its debt but does not have enough cash on hand to pay an entire principal payment (and banks refuse to finance that payment), the equity of the company will be worth nothing. As Buffett has so eloquently wrote in the 2010 annual letter to Berkshire Hathaway shareholders, "[A]ny series of positive numbers, however impressive the numbers may be, evaporates when multiplied by a single zero." It doesn't matter how great a given business may be during boom times; if its equity value falls to zero during bad times, the owner of the company's stock will lose his or her entire investment.

One sad fact of life is that in many cases, companies with great operational leverage (e.g., those that own factories) have funded this leverage through the issuance of debt—hereby layering financial leverage onto operational leverage. Because financial leverage represents such a severe risk to equity investors during bust times, and because it is devilishly hard to know when the next bust time might come, I personally think that using less investment leverage on companies fitting this profile is generally prudent.

Let us assume that you have decided on the composition of an investment meal and dug in using your chosen allocation size and leverage level. How do you know when to stop "eating" and close all or part of your position? Or conversely, what should you do when you realize that the meal is more delicious than you had originally imagined? These are natural questions to ask.

After you enter a position and some time passes, it becomes clearer what valuation scenario the company is tending toward. In some cases, a bit of information will come out that is critical to your valuation of the company on which other market participants may not be focused. Obviously, if a bit of information comes out that has a big, positive or negative impact on your assessment of the company's value, you should adjust your position size accordingly. If you believe the impact is positive, it makes sense to build to a position by increasing your shares owned and/or by adding "spice" to that meal by adjusting your target leverage level. If the impact is negative, it makes sense to start by reducing leverage (or you can think of it as increasing the proportion of cash supporting a particular position), even if this reduction means realizing a loss. If the impact of the news is so negative that the investment is no longer attractive from a risk-reward perspective, I believe that it should be closed and the lumps taken sooner rather than later. Considering what we know about prospect theory, this is psychologically a difficult thing to do, but in my experience, waiting to close a position in which you no longer have confidence seldom does you any good.

Obviously, the risk/reward equation of an investment is also influenced by a stock's market price. If the market price starts scraping against the upper edge of your valuation range, again, it is time to reduce leverage and/or close the position.

If your options are in danger of expiring before a stock has reached your fair value estimate, you may *roll* your position by selling your option position and using the proceeds to buy another option position at a more distant tenor. At this time, you must again think about your target leverage and adjust the strikes of your options accordingly. If the price of the stock has decreased over the life of the option contract, this will mean that you realize a loss, which is not an easy thing to do psychologically, but considering the limitations imposed by time for all option investments, this is an unavoidable situation in this case.

One of the reasons I dislike investing in non-LEAPS call options is that rolling means that not only do we have to pay another set of broker and exchange fees, but we also must pay both sides of the bid-ask spread. Keeping in mind how wide the bid-ask spread can be with options and what an enormous drag this can be on returns, you should carefully consider whether the prospective returns justify entering a long call position that will likely have to be rolled multiple times before the stock hits your fair value estimate.

By the way, it goes without saying that to the extent that an option you want to roll has a significant amount of time value on it, it is better to roll before time decay starts to become extreme. This usually occurs at around three months before expiration. It turns out that option liquidity increases in the last three months before expiration, and rolling is made easier with the greater liquidity.

Having discussed gaining bullish exposure with this section about long calls, let's now turn to gaining bearish exposure in the following section on long puts.

Long Put

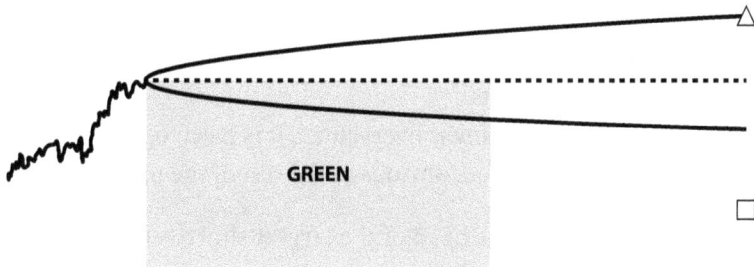

Downside: Undervalued
Upside: Fairly priced
Execute: Buy a put option
Risk: Amount of premium paid
Reward: Amount equal to strike price—premium

The Gist

An investor uses this strategy when he or she believes that it is very likely that the value of a company is much lower than the present market price. The investor must pay a premium to initiate the position, and the proportion of the premium that represents time value should be recognized as a realized loss because it cannot be recovered. If the stock fails to move into the area of exposure before option expiration, there will be no profit to offset this realized loss.

In economic terms, this transaction allows an investor to sell short an overvalued company without accepting an uncertain risk of loss if the stock rises. Instead of the uncertain risk of loss, the investor must pay the fixed premium. This strategy obeys the same rules of leverage as discussed earlier in this book, with ITM put options offering less leverage but a greater cushion before realizing a loss than do ATM or OTM put options.

Tenor Selection

Shorting stocks, which is what you are doing when you buy put options, is hard work, not for the faint of heart. There are a couple of reasons for this:

1. Markets generally go up, and for better or worse, a rising tide usually does lift all boats.
2. Even when a company is overvalued, it is hard to know what catalyst will make that fact obvious to the rest of the market and when.

In the words of Jim Chanos, head of the largest short-selling hedge fund in the world, the market is a "giant positive reinforcement machine."[1] It is psychologically difficult to hold a bearish position when it seems like the whole world disagrees with you. All these difficulties in taking bearish positions are amplified by options because options are levered instruments, and losses feel all the more acute when they occur on a levered position.

My rule for gaining bullish exposure is to pick the longest-tenor option possible. I made the point that by buying LEAPS, you can enjoy a likely upward drift that exceeds the drift assumed by option pricing. When buying puts, you are on the opposite side of this drift factor (i.e., the "rising tide lifts all boats" factor), and every day that the stock does not fall is another day of time value that has decayed without you enjoying a profit. On the other hand, if you decide not to spend as much on time value and buy a shorter-tenor put option, unless the market realizes that the stock is overvalued and it drops before the shorter option expires, you must pay the entire bid-ask spread and the broker and exchange fees again when you roll your put option.

The moral of the story is that when selecting tenors for puts, you need to balance the existence of upward market drift (which lends weight to the argument for choosing shorter tenors) with bid-ask spreads and other fees (which lends weight to the argument for longer tenors). If you can identify a catalyst, you can plan the tenor of the option investment based on the expected catalyst. However, it's unfortunate but mysteriously true that bearish catalysts have a tendency to be ignored by the market's "happy machine" until the instant when suddenly they are not and the shares collapse. The key for a short seller is to be in the game when the market realizes the stock's overvaluation.

Strike Price Selection

When it comes to strike prices, short sellers find themselves fighting drift in much the same way as they did when selecting tenors. A short seller with a position in stocks can be successful if the shares he or she is short go up less than other stocks in the market. The short exposure acts as a hedge to the portfolio as a whole, and if it loses less money than the rest of the portfolio gains, it can be thought of as a successful investment.

However, the definition for success is different for buyers of a put option, who must not only see their bearish bets not go up by much but rather must see their bearish bets fall if they are to enjoy a profit. If the investor wanting bearish exposure decides to gain it by buying OTM puts, he or she must—as we learned in the section about leverage—accept a realized loss as soon as the put is purchased. If, on the other hand, the investor wants to minimize the realized loss accepted up front, he or she must accept that he or she is in a levered bearish position so that every 1 percent move to the upside for the stock generates a loss larger than 1 percent for the position.

There is another bearish strategy that you can use by accepting exposure that I will discuss in the next section, but for investors who are gaining bearish exposure, there is no way to work around the dilemma of the option-based short seller just mentioned.

Portfolio Management

There is certainly no way around the tradeoff between OTM and ITM risk—the rules of leverage are immutable whether in a bullish or a bearish investment—but there are some ways of framing the investment that will allow intelligent investors to feel more comfortable with making these types of bearish bets. First, I believe that losses associated with a bearish position are treated differently within our own minds than those associated with bullish positions. The reason for this might be the fact that if you decide to proactively invest in the market, you must buy securities, but you need not sell shares short. The fact that you are losing when you are engaged in an act that you perceive as unnecessary just adds to a sense of regret and self-doubt that is necessarily part of the investing process.

In addition, investors seem to be able to accept underperforming bullish investments in a portfolio context (e.g., "XYZ is losing, but it's only 5 percent of my holdings, and the rest of my portfolio is up, so it's okay") but look at underperforming bearish investments as if they were the only investments they held (e.g., "I'm losing 5 percent on that damned short. Why did I ever short that stock in the first place?"). In general, people have a hard time looking at investments in a portfolio context (I will discuss this more when I talk about hedging in Chapter 11), but this problem seems to be orders of magnitude worse in the case of a bearish position.

My solution to this dilemma—perhaps not the best or most rational from a performance standpoint but most manageable to me from a psychological one—is to buy OTM puts with much smaller position sizes than I might for bullish bets with the same conviction level. This means that I have smaller, more highly levered positions. The reason this works for me is that once I spend the premium on the put option, I consider the money gone—a sunk cost—and do not even bother to look at the mark-to-market value of the option after that unless there is a large drop in the stock price. Somehow this acknowledgment of a realized loss up front is easier to handle psychologically than watching my ITM put position suffer unrealized losses of 1.5 times the rise of the stock every day.

This strategy may well be proof that I simply am not a natural-born short seller, and you are encouraged, now that you understand the issues involved, to devise a method for gaining bearish exposure that fits your own risk profile.

Strangle

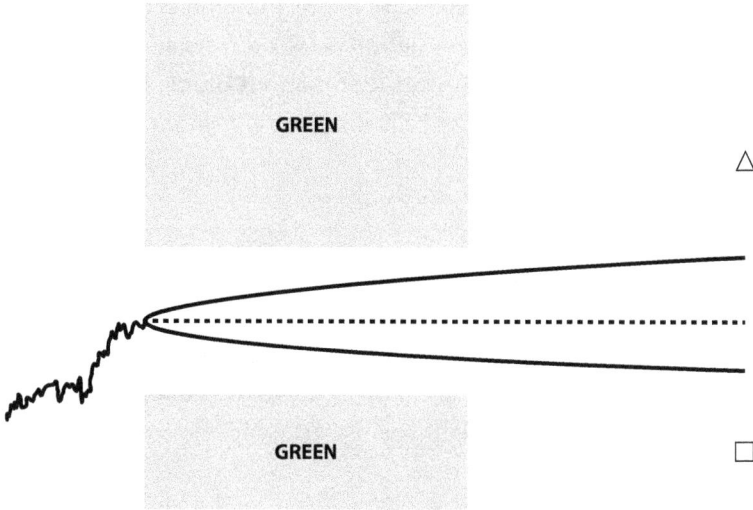

Downside: Undervalued
Upside: Undervalued
Execute: Buy an OTM call option simultaneously with buying an OTM put option
Risk: Amount of premium paid
Reward: Unlimited on upside, limited to strike less total (two-leg) premium on the downside

The Gist

The strangle is used when the market is undervaluing the likelihood that a stock's value is significantly above or below the present market price. It is a more speculative position and, because both legs are OTM, a highly leveraged one. It can sometimes be useful for companies such as smaller drug companies whose value hinges on the success or failure of a particular drug or for companies that have a material chance of bankruptcy but if they can avoid this extreme downside are worth much more than they are presently trading at.

The entire premium paid must be treated as a realized loss because it can never be recovered. If the stock fails to move into one of the areas of exposure before option expiration, there will be no profit to offset this realized loss.

There is no reason why you have to buy puts and calls in equal numbers. If you believe that both upside and downside scenarios are materially possible but believe that the downside scenario is more plausible, you can buy more puts than calls. This is called *ratioing* a position.

Tenor Selection

Because the strangle is a combination of two strategies we have already discussed, the considerations regarding tenor are the same as for each of the components—that is, using the drift advantage in long-term equity anticipating securities (LEAPS) and buying them or the longest-tenor calls available and balancing the fight against drift and the cost of rolling and buying perhaps shorter-tenor puts.

Strike Price Selection

A strangle is slightly different in nature from its two components—long calls and long puts. A strangle is an option investor's way of expressing the belief that the market in general has underestimated the intrinsic uncertainty in the valuation of a firm. Options are directional instruments, but a strangle is a strategy that acknowledges that the investor has no clear idea of which direction a stock will move but only that its future value under different scenarios is different from its present market price.

Because both purchased options are OTM ones, this implies, in my mind, a more speculative investment and one that lends itself to taking profit on it before expiration. Nonetheless, my conservatism forces me to select strike prices that would allow a profit on the entire position if the stock price is at one of the two strikes at expiration. Because I am buying exposure to both the upside and the downside, I always like to make sure that if the option expires when the stock price is at either edge of my valuation range, it is far enough in-the-money to pay me back for both legs of the investment (plus an attractive return).

Portfolio Management

As mentioned earlier, this is naturally a more speculative style of option investment, and it may well be more beneficial to close the successful leg of the strategy before expiration than to hold the position to expiration. Compared with the next strategy presented here (the straddle), the strangle actually generates worse returns if held to expiration, so if you are happy with your returns midway through the investment, you should close the position rather than waiting for expiration. The exception to this rule is that if news comes out that convinces you that the value of the firm is materially higher or lower than what you had originally forecast and uncertainty in the other direction has been removed, you should assess the possibility of making a more substantial investment in the company.

One common problem with investors—even experienced and sophisticated ones—is that they check the past price history of a stock and decide whether the stock has "more room" to move in a particular direction. The most important two things to know when considering an investment are its value and the uncertainty surrounding that value. Whether the stock was cheaper three years ago or much more expensive does not matter—these are backward-looking measures, and you cannot invest with a rear-view mirror.

One final note regarding this strategy is what to do with the unused leg. If the stock moves up strongly and you take profits on the call, what should you do with the put, in other words. Unfortunately, the unused leg is almost always worthless, and often it will cost more than it's worth to close it. I usually keep this leg open because you never know what may happen, and perhaps before it expires, you will be able to close it at a better price.

This is a speculative strategy—a bit of spice or an after-dinner mint in the meal of investing. Don't expect to get rich using it (if you do get rich using it, it means that you were lucky because you would have had to have used a lot of leverage in the process), but you may be pleasantly surprised with the boost you get from these every once in a while.

Let's now turn briefly to a related strategy—the straddle.

Straddle

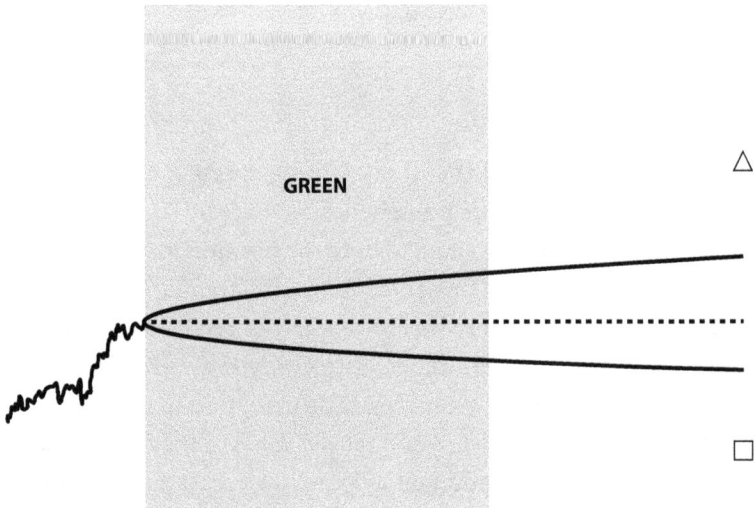

Downside: Undervalued
Upside: Undervalued
Execute: Simultaneously buy an ATM put and an ATM call
Risk: Amount of premium paid
Reward: Unlimited?

The Gist

I include the straddle here for completeness sake. I have not included a lot of the fancier multioption strategies in this book because I have found them to be more expensive than they are worth, especially for someone with a definite directional view on a security. However, the straddle is referred to commonly and is deceptively attractive, so I include it here to warn investors against its use, if for no other reason.

The straddle shares many similarities with the strangle, of course, but straddles are enormously expensive because you are paying for every possible price the stock will move to over the term of the options. For example, I just looked up option prices for BlackBerry (BBRY), whose stock was trading at $9.00. For the 86 days to expiry, $9-strike calls (delta = 0.56) and $9-strike puts (delta = –0.44) were priced at $1.03 and $1.13, respectively.

The total premium of $2.16 represents 24 percent of the stock's price, which means that if the implied volatility (around 60 percent) remains constant, the stock would have to move 24 percent before an investor even breaks even. It is true that during sudden downward stock price moves, implied volatility usually rises, so it might take a little less of a stock price movement to the downside to break even. However, during sudden upside moves, implied volatility often drops, which would make it more difficult to break even to the upside.

Despite this expense, a straddle will still give an investor a lower breakeven point than a strangle on the same stock if held to expiration. The key is that a strangle will almost always generate a higher profit than a straddle if it is closed before expiration simply because the initial cost of the strangle is lower and the relative leverage of each of its legs is higher. This is yet another reason to consider closing a *strangle* early if and when you are pleased with the profits made.

If you do not know whether a stock will move up or down, the best you can hope for is to make a speculative bet on the company. When you make speculative bets, it is best to reduce the amount spent on it or you will whittle down all your capital on what amounts to a roulette wheel. Reducing the amount spent on a single bet is the reason an intelligent investor should stay away from straddles.

With all the main strategies for gaining exposure covered, let's now turn to accepting exposure by selling options.

Chapter 10

ACCEPTING EXPOSURE

Brokerages and exchanges treat the acceptance of exposure by counterparties in a very different way from counterparties who want to gain exposure. There is a good reason for this: although an investor gaining exposure has an *option* to transact in the future, his or her counterparty—an investor accepting exposure—has a *commitment* to transact in the future at the sole discretion of the option buyer. If the investor accepting exposure does not have the financial wherewithal to carry out the committed transaction, the broker or exchange is on the hook for the liability.[1]

For example, an investor selling a put option struck at $50 per share is committing to buy the stock in question for $50 a share at some point in the future—this is the essence of accepting exposure. If, however, the investor does not have enough money to buy the stock at $50 at some point in the future, the investor's commitment to buy the shares is economically worthless.

To guard against this eventuality, brokers require exposure-accepting investors to post a security deposit called *margin* that will fully cover the financial obligation to which the investor is committing. In the preceding example, for instance, the investor would have to keep $5,000 (= $50 per share × 100 shares/contract) in reserve and would not be able to spend those reserved funds for stock or option purchases until the contract has expired worthless.

Because of this margin requirement, it turns out that one of our strategies for accepting leverage—short puts—always carries with it a loss leverage of –1.0—exactly the same as the loss leverage of a stock. Think about it this way: what difference is there between using $50 to buy a stock and setting $50 aside in an escrow account you can't touch and promising that you will buy the stock with the escrow funds in the future if requested to do so? From a risk perspective, "very little" is the answer.

Short calls are more complicated, but I will discuss the leverage carried by them using elements of the structure I set forth in Chapter 8. In the following overviews, I add one new line item to the tables that details the margin requirements of the positions.

Intelligent option investors accept exposure when the market overestimates the likelihood of a valuation that the investor believes is not a rational outcome. In graphic terms, this means that either one or both of the investor's best- and worst-case valuation scenarios lie well within the Black-Scholes-Merton model (BSM) cone.

Simple (one-option) strategies to accept exposure include

1. Short put
2. Short call (call spread)

Complex (multioption) strategies to accept exposure include the following:

1. Short straddle
2. Short strangle

Jargon introduced in this chapter includes the following:

Margin   Put-call parity
Early exercise   Cover (a position)
Writing (an option)

Short Put

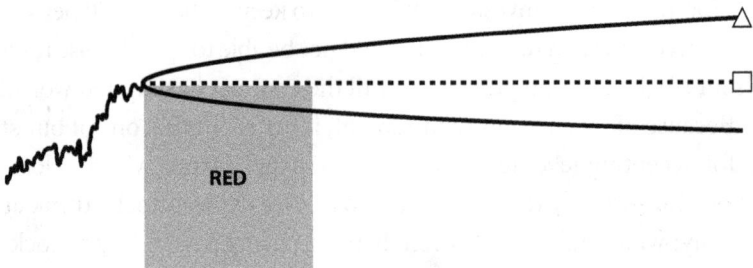

RED

Downside: Overvalued
  Upside: Fairly valued
   Execute: Sell a put contract
    Risk: Strike price minus premium received [same as stock inves-
      tor at the effective buy price (EBP)]
   Reward: Limited to premium received
   Margin: Notional amount of position

The Gist

The market is pricing in a relatively high probability that the stock price will fall. An investor, from a longer investment time frame perspective, believes that the value of the stock is likely worth at least the present market value and perhaps more. The investor agrees to accept the downside risk perceived by the market and, in return, receives a premium for doing so. The premium cannot be fully realized unless the option expires out-of-the money (OTM). If the option expires in-the-money (ITM), the investor pays an amount equal to the strike price for the stock but can partially offset the cost of the stock by the premium received. The investor thus promises to buy the stock in question at a price of the strike price of the option less the premium received—what I call the *effective buy price.*

    I think of the short-put strategy as being very similar to buying corporate bonds and believe that the two investment strategies share many similarities. A bond investor is essentially looking to receive a specific monetary return (in the form of interest) in exchange for accepting the risk of the business failing. The only time a bond investor owns a company's assets is after the value of the firm's equity drops to zero, and the assets revert to the control of the creditors. Similarly, a short-put investor is looking to receive a specific monetary return (in the form of an option premium) in exchange for accepting the risk that the company's stock will decrease in value. The only time a short-put investor owns a company's shares is after the market value of the shares expires below the preagreed strike price.

    Because the strategies are conceptually similar, I usually think of short-put exposure in similar terms and compare the "yield" I am generating from a portfolio of short puts with the yield I might generate from a corporate bond portfolio. With this consideration, and keeping in mind that these investments are unlevered,[2] the name of the game is to generate as high a percentage return as possible over the investing time horizon while minimizing the amount of real downside risk you are accepting.

Tenor Selection

To maximize percentage return, in general, it is better to sell options with relatively short-term expirations (usually tenors of from three to nine months before expiration). This is just the other side of the coin of the rule to buy long-tenor options: the longer the time to expiration, the less time value there is on a per-day basis. The rule to sell shorter-tenor options implies that you will make a higher absolute return by chaining together two back-to-back 6-month short puts than you would by selling a single 12-month option at the beginning of the period.

During normal market conditions, selling shorter-tenor options is the best tactical choice, but during large market downdrafts, when there is terror in the marketplace and implied volatilities increase enormously for options on all companies, you might be able to make more by selling a longer-tenor option than by chaining together a series of shorter-tenor ones (because, presumably, the implied volatilities of options will drop as the market stabilizes, and this drop means that you will make less money on subsequent put sales). At these times of extreme market stress, there are situations where you can find short-put opportunities on long-tenor options that defy economic logic and should be invested in opportunistically.

For example, during the terrible market drops in 2009, I found a company whose slightly ITM put long-term equity anticipation securities (LEAPS) were trading at such a high price that the effective buy price of the stock was less than the amount of cash the firm had on its balance sheet. Obviously, for a firm producing positive cash flows, the stock should not trade at less than the value of cash presently on the balance sheet! I effectively got the chance to buy a firm with $6 of cash on the balance sheet and the near certainty of generating about $2 more over the economic life of the options for $5.50. The opportunity to buy $6–$8 worth of cash for

$5.50 does not come along very often, so you should take advantage of it when you see it.

Of course, the absolute value of premium you will receive by *writing* (jargon that means selling an option) a short-term put is less than the absolute value of the premium you will receive by writing a long-term one.[3] As such, an investor must balance the effective buy price of the stock (the strike price of the option less the amount of premium to be received) in which he or she is investing in the short-put strategy with the percentage return he or she will receive if the put expires OTM.

I will talk more about effective buy price in the next section, but keep in mind that we would like to generate the highest percentage return possible and that this usually means choosing shorter-tenor options.

Strike Price Selection

In general, the best policy is to sell options at as close to the 50-delta [at-the-money (ATM)] mark as one can because that is where time value for any option is at its absolute maximum. Our expectation is that the option's time value will be worthless at expiration, and if that is indeed the case, we will be selling time value at its maximum and "closing" our time value position at zero—its minimum. In this way, we are obeying (in reverse order) the old investing maxim "Buy low, sell high." Selling ATM puts means that our effective buy price will be the strike price at which we sold less the amount of the premium we received. It goes without saying that an intelligent investor would not agree to accept the downside exposure to a stock if he or she were not prepared to buy the stock at the effective buy price.

Some people want to sell OTM puts, thereby making the effective buy price much lower than the present market price. This is an understandable impulse, but simply attempting to minimize the effective buy price means that you must ignore the other element of a successful short put strategy: maximizing the return generated. There are times when you might like to sell puts on a company but only at a lower strike price. Rather than accepting a lower return for accepting that risk, I find that the best strategy is simply to wait awhile until the markets make a hiccup and knock down the price of the stock to your desired strike price.

Portfolio Management

As we have discussed, the best percentage returns on short-put investments come from the sale of short-tenor ATM options. I find that each quarter there are excellent opportunities to find a fairly constant stream of this type of short-term bet that, when strung together in a portfolio, can generate annualized returns in the high-single-digit to low-teens percentage range. This level of returns—twice or more the yield recently found on a high-quality corporate bond portfolio and closer to the bond yield on highly speculative small companies with low credit ratings—is possible by investing in strong, high-quality blue chip stocks. In my mind, it is difficult to allocate much money to corporate bonds when this type of alternative is available.

Some investors prefer to sell puts on stocks that are not very volatile or that have had a significant run-up in price,[4] but if you think about how options are priced, it is clear that finding stocks that the market perceives as more volatile will allow you to generate higher returns. You can confirm this by looking at the diagrams of a short-put investment given two different volatility scenarios. First, a diagram in which implied volatility is low:

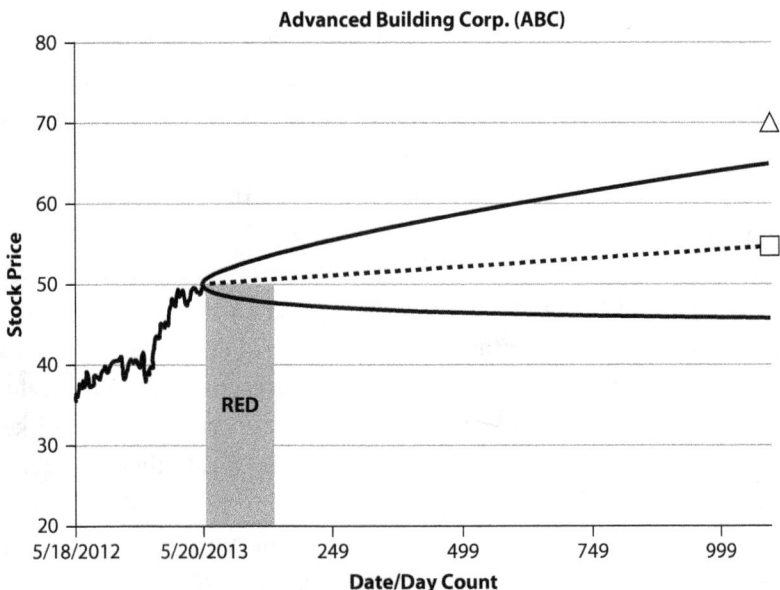

Advanced Building Corp. (ABC)

Now a diagram when implied volatility is higher:

Advanced Building Corp. (ABC)

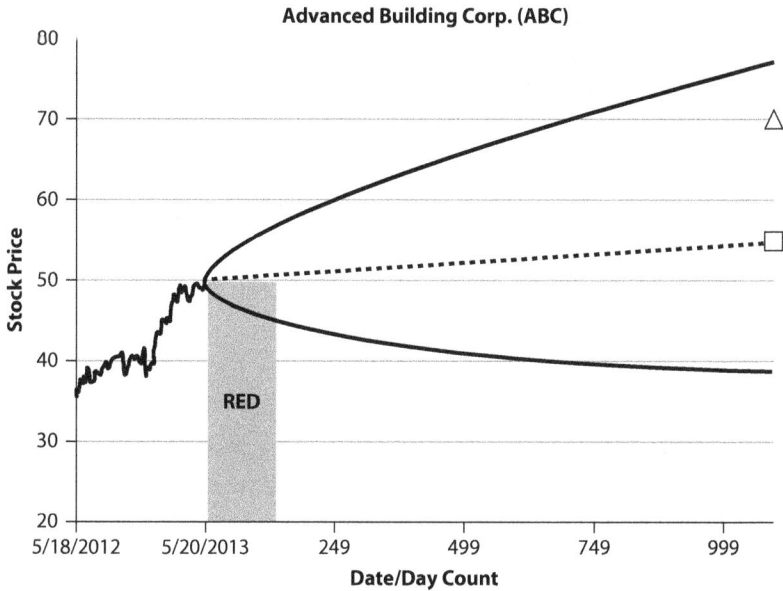

Obviously, there is much more of the put option's range of exposure bounded by the BSM cone in the second, high-volatility scenario, and this means that the price received for accepting the same downside risk will be substantially higher when implied volatility is elevated.

The key to setting up a successful allocation of short puts is to find companies that have relatively low downside valuation risk but that also have a significant amount of perceived price risk (as seen by the market)— even if this risk is only temporary in nature. Quarterly earnings seasons are nearly custom made for this purpose. Sell-side analysts (and the market in general) mainly use multiples of reported earnings to generate a target price for a stock. As such, a small shortfall in reported earnings as a result of a transitory and/or nonmaterial accounting technicality can cause sell-side analysts and other market participants to bring down their short-term target price estimates sharply and can cause stock prices to drop sharply as well.[5]

These times, when a high-quality company drops sharply as a result of perceived risk by other investors, are a wonderful time to replenish a portfolio of short puts. If you time the tenors well, your short-put investment will be expiring just about the time another short-put invest-ment is becoming attractive, so you can use the margin that has until re-cently been used to support the first position to support the new one.

Obviously, this strategy only works when markets are generally trend-ing upward or at least sideways over the investment horizon of your short puts. If the market is falling, short-put positions expire ITM, so you are left with a position in the underlying stocks. For an option trader (i.e., a short-term speculator), being put a stock is a nightmare because he or she has no concept of the underlying value of the firm. However, for an intelligent option investor, being put a stock simply means the opportunity to receive a dividend and enjoy capital appreciation in a strong stock with very little downside valuation risk.

The biggest problem arises when an investor sells a put and then re-vises down his or her lowest-case valuation scenario at a later time. For in-stance, the preceding diagram shows a worst-case scenario of $55 per share. What if new material information became known to you that changed your lower valuation range to $45 per share just as the market price for the stock dropped, as in the following diagram?

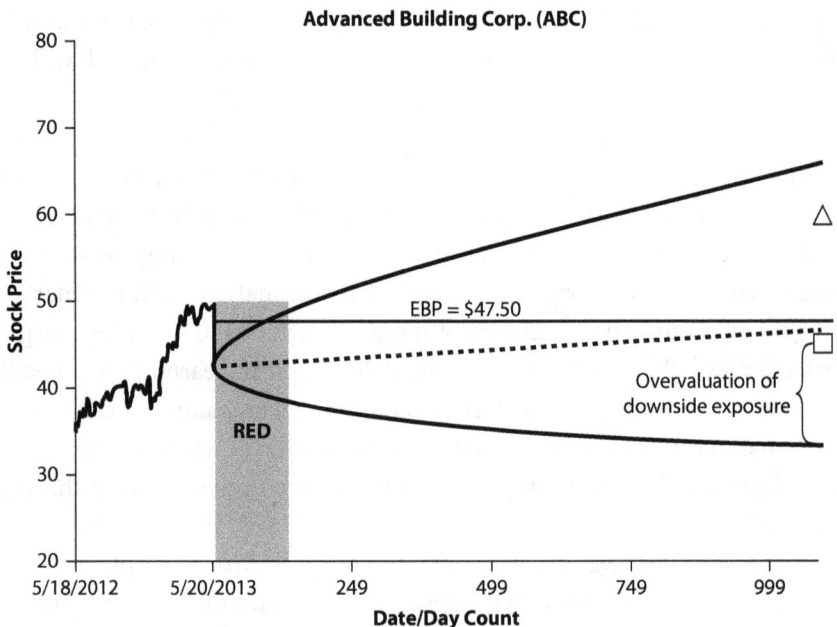

Looking at this diagram closely, you should be able to see several things:

1. The investor who is short this put certainly has a notable unrealized loss on his or her position. You can tell this because the put the investor sold is now much more valuable than at the time of the original sale (more of the range of exposure is carved out by the BSM cone now). When you sell something at one price and the value of that thing goes up in the future, you suffer an opportunity loss on your original sale.
2. With the drop in price and the cut in fair value, the downside exposure on this stock still looks overvalued.
3. If the company were to perform so that its share price eventually hit the new, reduced best-case valuation mark, the original short-put position would generate a profit—albeit a smaller profit than the one originally envisioned.

At this point, there are a couple of choices open to the investor:

1. Convert the unrealized loss on the short-put position to a realized one by buying $50-strike puts to close the position (a.k.a. *cover the position*).
2. Leave the position open and manage it in the same way that the investor would manage a struggling stock position.

It is rarely a sound idea to close a short put immediately after the release of information that drives down the stock price (the first choice above, in other words). At these times, investors are generally panicked, and this panic will cause the price of the option you buy to cover to be more expensive than justified. Waiting a few days or weeks for the fear to drain out of the option prices (i.e., for the BSM cone to narrow) and for the stock price to stabilize some will usually allow you to close the option position at a more favorable price. There is one exception to this rule: if your new valuation suggests a fair value at or below the present market price, it is better to close the position immediately and realize those losses. If you do not close the position, you are simply gambling (as opposed to investing) because you no longer have a better than even chance of making money on the investment.

The decision to leave the position open must depend on what other potential investments you are able to make and how the stock position that will likely be put to you at expiration of the option contract stacks up on a relative basis. For instance, let's assume that you had received a premium of $2.50 for writing the puts struck at $50. This gives you an effective buy price of $47.50. The stock is now trading at $43 per share, so you can think of your position as an unlevered, unrealized loss of $4.50, or a little under 10 percent of your EBP. Your new worst-case valuation is $55 per share, which implies a gain of about 15 percent on your EBP; your new best-case valuation is $65 per share, which implies a gain of 37 percent.

How do these numbers compare with other investments in your portfolio? How much spare capacity does your portfolio have for additional investments? (That is, do you have enough spare cash to increase the size of this investment by selling more puts at the new market price or buying shares of stock? And if so, would your portfolio be weighted too heavily on a single industry or sector?) By answering these questions and understanding how this presently losing investment compares with other existing or potential investments should govern your portfolio management of the position.

An investor cannot change the price at which he or she transacted in a security. The best he or she can do is to develop a rational view of the value of a security and judge that security by its relative merit versus other possible investments. Whether you ever make an option transaction, this is a good rule to keep in mind.

Let us now take a look at short calls and short-call spreads—the strategy used for accepting upside exposure.

Short Call (Call Spread)

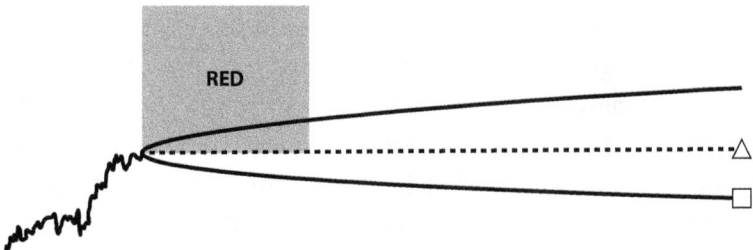

Downside: Fairly valued
  Upside: Overvalued
  Execute: Sell a call contract (short call); sell a call contract while simultaneously buying a call contract at a higher strike price (short-call spread)
    Risk: Unlimited for short call; difference between strike prices and premium received (short-call spread)
  Reward: Limited to the amount of premium received
  Margin: Variable for a short call; dollar amount equal to the difference between strike prices for a short-call spread

The Gist

The market overestimates the likelihood that the value of a firm is above its present market price. An investor accepts the overvalued upside exposure in return for a fixed payment of premium. The full amount of the premium will only flow through to the investor if the price of the stock falls and the option expires OTM.

There are two variations of this investment—the short call and the short-call spread. This book touches on the former but mainly addresses the latter. A short call opens up the investor to potentially unlimited capital losses (because stocks theoretically do not have an upper bound for their price), and a broker will not allow you to invest using this strategy except for the following conditions:

1. You are a hedge fund manager and have the ability to borrow stocks through your broker and sell them short.
2. You are short calls not on a stock but on a diversified index (such as the Dow Jones Industrial Index or the Standard and Poor's 500 Index) through an exchange-traded fund (ETF) or a futures contract and hold a diversified stock portfolio.

For investors fitting the first condition, short calls are margined in the same way as the rest of your short portfolio. That is, you must deposit initial margin on the initiation of the investment, and if the stock price goes up, you must pay in variance margin to support the position. Obviously, as the stock price falls, this margin account is settled in your favor. For investors fitting the second condition, when you originally sell the call option, your broker should indicate on your statements that a certain proportion of your account effectively will be treated as margin. This means that you stand to receive the economic benefit from your diversified portfolio of securities but will not be able to liquidate all of it. If the market climbs higher, a larger proportion of your portfolio will be considered as margin; if it falls lower, a smaller proportion of your portfolio will be considered as margin. Basically, a proportion of any gains from your diversified stock portfolio will be reapportioned to serve as collateral for your short call when the market is rising, and a proportion of any losses from your diversified stock portfolio will be offset by a freeing of margin related to your profits on the short call when the market is falling.

Most brokers restrict the ability of individual investors to write uncovered calls on individual stocks, so the rest of this discussion will cover the short-call spread strategy for individual stocks.

Tenor Selection

Tenors for short-call spreads should be fairly short under the same reasoning as that for short puts—one receives more time value per day for shorter-tenor options. Look for calls in the three- to nine-month tenor range. The tenor of the purchased call (at the higher strike price) should be the same as the tenor of the sold calls (at the lower strike price). Theoretically, the bought calls could be longer, but it is hard to think of a valuation justification for such a structure. By buying a longer-tenor call for the upside leg of the investment, you are expressing an investment opinion that the stock will likely rise over the long term—this exactly contradicts the purpose of this strategy: expressing a bearish investment opinion.

Strike Price Selection

Theoretically, you can choose any two strike prices, sell the call at the lower price, and buy the call at the higher price and execute this investment. If you sold an ITM call, you would receive premium that consists of both time and intrinsic value. If the stock fell by expiration, you would realize all the wasted time value plus the difference between the intrinsic value at initiation and the intrinsic value at expiration.

Despite the theory, however, in practice, the lower strike option is usually sold ATM or OTM because of the threat of *assignment*. Assignment is the process the exchange goes through when investors choose to exercise the option they own rather than trade them away for a profit. Recall from Chapter 2 that experienced option investors do not do this most of the time; they know that because of the existence of time value, it is usually more beneficial for them to sell their option in the market and use the proceeds to buy the stock if they want to hold the underlying. Inexperienced investors, however, often are not conscious of the time-value nuance and sometimes elect to exercise their option. In this case, the exchange randomly pairs the option holders who wish to exercise with an option seller who has promised to sell at that exercise price.

There is one case in which a sophisticated investor might chose to exercise an ITM call option early, related to a principle in option pricing called *put-call parity*. This rule, which was used to price options before advent of the BSM, simply states that a certain relationship must exist between the price of a put at one strike price, the price of a call at that same strike price, and the market price of the underlying stock. Put-call parity is discussed in Appendix C. In this appendix, you can learn what the exact put-call parity rule is (it is ridiculously simple) and then see how it can be used to determine when it is best to exercise early in case you are long a call and when your short-call (spread) position is in danger of *early exercise* because of a trading strategy known as *dividend arbitrage*.

The assignment process is random, but obviously, the more contracts you sell, the better the chance is that you will be assigned on some part or all of your sold contracts. Even if you hold until expiration, there is still a chance that you may be assigned to fulfill a contract that was exercised on settlement.

Clearly, from the standpoint of option sale efficiency, an ATM call is the most sensible to sell for the same reason that a short put also was most efficient ATM. As such, the discussion that follows assumes that you are selling the ATM strike and buying back a higher strike to cover.

In a call-spread strategy, the capital you have at risk is the difference between the two strike prices—this is the amount that must be deposited into margin. Depending on which strike price you use to cover, the net premium received differs because the cost of the covering call is cheaper the further OTM you cover. As the covering call becomes more and more OTM, the ratio of premium received to capital at risk changes. Put in these terms, it seems that the short-call spread is a levered strategy because leverage has to do with altering the capital at risk in order to change the percentage return. This contrasts with the short-call spread's mirror strategy on the put side—short puts— in that the short-put strategy is unlevered.

For instance, here are data from ATM and OTM call options on IBM (IBM) expiring in 80 days. I took these data when IBM's shares were trading at $196.80 per share.

Sell a Call at 195

Cover at ($)	Net Premium Received ($)	Percent Return	Capital at Risk ($)
200	2.40	48	5
205	4.26	43	10
210	5.47	36	15
215	6.17	31	20
220	6.51	26	25
225	6.70	22	30
230	6.91	20	35
235	6.90	17	40
240	6.96	15	45

In this table, net premium received was calculated by selling at the $195 strike's bid price and buying at each of the listed strike price's ask prices. Percent return is the proportion of net premium received as a percentage of the capital at risk—the width of the spread. This table clearly shows that accepting exposure with a call spread is a levered strategy. The potential return on a percentage basis can be raised simply by lowering the amount of capital at risk.

However, although accepting exposure with a call spread is undeniably levered from this perspective, there is one large difference: unlike the leverage discussed earlier in this book for a purchase of call options—in which your returns were potentially unlimited—the short-call spread investor receives premium up front that represents the maximum return possible on the investment. As such, in the sense of the investor's potential gains being limited, the short-call spread position appears to be an unlevered investment.

Considering the dual nature of a short-call spread, it is most helpful to think about managing these positions using a two-step process with both tactical and strategic aspects. We will investigate the tactical aspect of leverage in the remainder of this section and the strategic aspect in the portfolio management section.

Tactically, once an investor has decided to accept exposure to a stock's upside potential using a call spread, he or she has a relatively limited choice of investments. Let's assume that we sell the ATM strike; in the IBM example shown earlier, there is a choice of nine strike prices at which we can cover. The highest dollar amount of premium we can receive—what I will call the *maximum return*—is received by covering at the most distant strike. Every strike between the ATM and the most distant strike will at most generate some percentage of this maximum return.

Now let's look at the risk side. Let's say that we sell the $195-strike call and cover using the $210-strike call. Now assume that some bit of good news about IBM comes out, and the stock suddenly moves to exactly $210. If the option expires when IBM is trading at $210, we will have lost the entire amount of margin we posted to support this investment—$15 in all. This $15 loss will be offset by the amount of premium we received from selling the call spread—$5.47 in the IBM example—generating a net loss of $9.53 (= $5.47 − $15). Compare this with the loss that we would suffer if we had covered using the most distant call strike. In this case, we would have received $6.96 in premium, so if the option expires when IBM is trading at the same $210 level as earlier, our net loss would be $8.04 (= $6.96 − $15). Because our maximum return is generated with the widest spread, it follows that our minimum loss for the stock going to any intermediate strike price also will be generated with the widest spread.

At the same time, if we always select the widest spread, we face an entirely different problem. That is, the widest spread exposes us to the greatest potential loss. If the stock goes only to $210, it is true that the widest spread will generate a smaller loss than the $195–$210 spread. However, in the extreme, if the stock moves up strongly to $240, we would lose the $45 gross amount supporting the margin account and a net amount of $38.04 (= $45 − $6.96). Contrast this with a net loss of $9.53 for the $195–$210 spread. Put simply, if the stock moves up only a bit, we will do better with the wider spread; if it moves up a lot, it is better to choose a narrower spread.

In short, when thinking about call spreads, we must balance our amount of total exposure against the exposure we would have for an intermediate outcome against the total amount of premium we are receiving. If we are too protective and initiate the smallest spread possible, our chance of losing the entire margin amount is higher, but the margin amount lost is smaller. On the other hand, if we attempt to maximize our winnings and initiate the widest spread possible, our total exposure is greatest, even though the chance of losing all of it is lower.

Plotting these three variables on a graph, here is what we get:

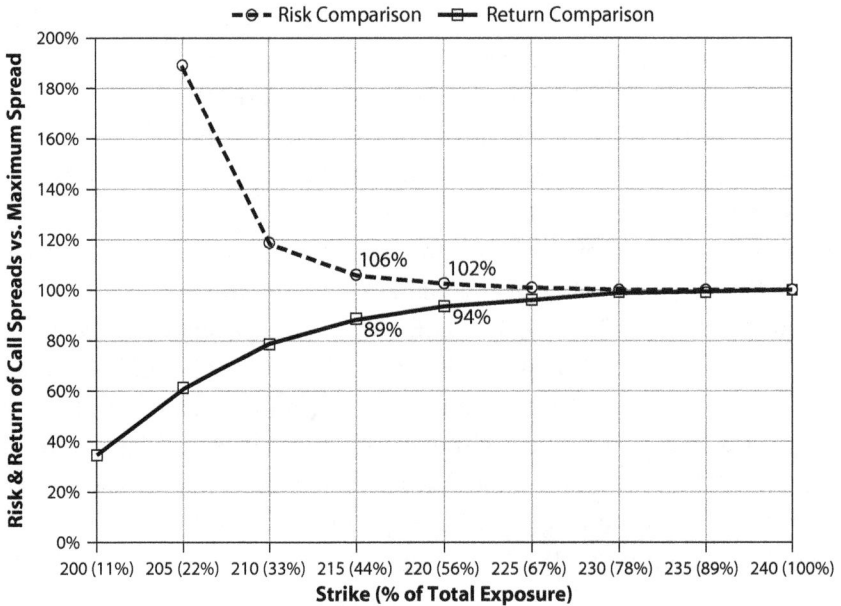

Here, on the horizontal axis, we have the value of the covering strike and the size of the corresponding spread as a percentage of the widest spread. This shows how much proportional capital is at risk (e.g., at the $215-strike, we are risking a total of $20 of margin; $20 is 44 percent of total exposure of $45 if we covered at the $240-strike level). The top line shows how much greater the loss would be if we used that strike to cover rather than the maximum strike and the option expired at that strike price (e.g., if we cover at the $215-strike and the option expires when the stock is trading at $215, our loss would be 6 percent greater than the loss we would suffer if we covered at the $240-strike). The bottom line shows the premium we will realize as income if the stock price declines as a percentage of the total premium possible if we covered at the maximum strike price. Here are the values from the graph in tabular format so that you can see the numbers used:

Strike Price	Dollar Spread	Percent of Maximum Spread (a)	Bid Price	Ask Price	Covering at Strike		Covering at Maximum Strike			Risk Comparison (%) (b)	Return Comparison (%) (c)
					Potential Gain	Worst-Case (Loss)	Potential Gain	Worst-Case Gain (Loss)	Difference		
195	—	—	7.05	7.10	—	—	—	—	—	—	—
200	5	11	4.55	4.65	2.40	(2.60)	6.96	1.96	(3.55)	N.C.	34
205	10	22	2.75	2.79	4.26	(5.74)	6.96	(3.04)	2.29	189	61
210	15	33	1.54	1.58	5.47	(9.53)	6.96	(8.04)	0.87	119	79
215	20	44	0.84	0.88	6.17	(13.83)	6.96	(13.04)	0.53	106	89
220	25	56	0.38	0.54	6.51	(18.49)	6.96	(18.04)	0.39	102	94
225	30	67	0.12	0.35	6.70	(23.30)	6.96	(23.04)	0.30	101	96
230	35	78	0.11	0.14	6.91	(28.09)	6.96	(28.04)	0.25	100	99
235	40	89	0.03	0.15	6.90	(33.10)	6.96	(33.04)	0.21	100	99
240	45	100	0.02	0.09	6.96	(38.04)	6.96	(38.04)	0.18	100	100

With a table like this, you can balance, on the one hand, the degree you are reducing your overall exposure in a worst-case scenario (by looking at column a) against how much risk you are taking on for a bad-case (intermediary upward move of the stock) scenario (by looking at column b) against how much less premium you stand to earn if the stock does go down as expected (by looking at column c).

There are no hard and fast rules for which is the correct covering strike to select—that will depend on your confidence in the valuation and timing, your risk profile, and the position size—but looking at the table, I tend to be drawn to the $215 and $220 strikes. With both of those strikes, you are reducing your worst-case exposure by about half, increasing your bad-case exposure just marginally, and taking only a small haircut on the premium you are receiving.[6]

Now that we have an idea of how to think about the potential risk and return on a per-contract basis, let's turn to leverage in the strategic sense—figuring out how much capital to commit to a given bearish idea.

Portfolio Management

When we thought about leverage from a call buyer's perspective, we thought about how large of an allocation we wanted to make to the idea itself and changed our leverage within that allocation to modify the profits we stood to make. Let's do this again with IBM—again assuming that we are willing to allocate 5 percent of our portfolio to an investment in the view that this company's stock price will not go higher. At a price of $196.80, a 5 percent allocation would mean controlling a little more than 25 shares for every $100,000 of portfolio value.[7] Because options have a contract size of 100 shares, an unlevered 5 percent allocation to this investment would require a portfolio size of $400,000.

The equation to calculate the leverage ratio on the basis of notional exposure is

$$\frac{\text{Notional value of one contract}}{\text{Dollar value of allocation}} \times \text{number of contracts} = \text{leverage ratio}$$

So, for instance, if we had a $100,000 portfolio of which we were willing to commit 5 percent to this short-call spread on IBM, our position would have a leverage ratio of

$$\frac{\$19,500}{\$5,000} \times 1 = 3.9 \approx 4:1 \, \text{leverage}$$

Selling the $195/$220 call spread will generate $651 worth of premium income and put at risk $2,500 worth of capital. Nothing can change these two numbers—in this sense, the short-call spread has no leverage. The 4:1 leverage figure merely means that the *percentage* return will appear nearly four times as large on a given allocation as a 1:1 allocation would appear. The following table—assuming the sale of one contract of the $195/$220 call spread—shows this in detail:

			Winning Case		Losing Case		
Premium Received ($)	Target Allocation ($)	Leverage	Stock Move ($)	Percent Return on Allocation	Stock Move ($)	Dollar Return	Percent Return on Allocation
651	20,000	1:1	−2	3.3	+25	−1,849	−9.2
651	10,000	2:1	−2	6.5	+25	−1,849	−18.5
651	5,000	4:1	−2	13.0	+25	−1,849	−37.0

Note: The dollar return in the losing case is calculated as the loss of the $2,500 of margin per contract less than the premium received of $651.

Notice that the premium received never changes, nor does the worst-case return. Only the perception of the loss changes with the size of our target allocation.

Now that we have a sense of how to calculate what strategic leverage we are using, let's think about how to size the position and about how much risk we are willing to take. When we are selling a call or call spread, we are committing to sell a stock at the strike price. If we were actually selling the stock at that price rather than committing to do so, where would we put our *stop loss*—in other words, when would we close the position, assuming that our valuation or our timing was not correct?

Let's say that for this stock, if the price rose to $250, you would be willing to admit that you were wrong and would realize a loss of $55 per share, or $5,500 per hundred shares. This figure—the $5,500 per hundred shares you would be willing to lose in an unlevered short stock position—can be used as a guide to select the size of your levered short-call spread.

In this case, you might choose to sell a single \$195–\$240 call spread, in which case your maximum exposure would be \$4,500 [= 1 × (240 − 195) × 100] at the widest spread. This investment would have a leverage ratio of approximately 1:1. Alternatively, you could choose to sell two \$195–\$220 spreads, in which case your maximum exposure would be \$5,000 [= 2 × (220 − 195) × 100], with a leverage ratio of approximately 2:1. Which choice you select will depend on your assessment of the valuation of the stock, your risk tolerance, and the composition of your portfolio (i.e., how much of your portfolio is allocated to the tech sector, in this example of an investment in IBM). Because the monetary returns from a short-call or call-spread strategy are fixed and the potential for losses are rather high, I prefer to execute bearish investments using the long-put strategy discussed in the "Gaining Exposure" section.

With this explanation of the short-call spread complete, we have all the building blocks necessary to understand all the other strategies mentioned in this book. Let's now turn to two nonrecommended complex strategies for accepting exposure—the short straddle and the short strangle—both of which are included not because they are good strategies but rather for the sake of completeness.

Short Straddle/Short Strangle

Short Straddle

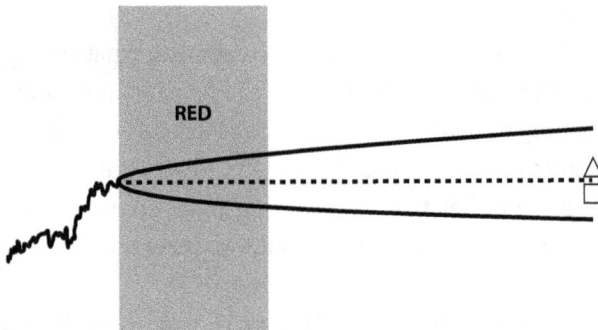

Downside: Overvalued
Upside: Overvalued
Execute: Sell an ATM put; simultaneously sell an ATM call spread

> *Risk:* Amount equal to upper strike price minus premium received
> *Reward:* Limited to premium received
> *Margin:* Dollar amount equal to upper strike price

Short Strangle

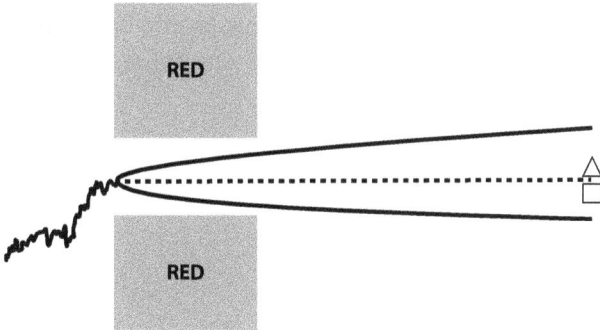

> *Downside:* Overvalued
> *Upside:* Overvalued
> *Execute:* Sell an OTM put; simultaneously sell an OTM call spread
> *Risk:* Call-spread leg: Amount equal to difference between strikes and premium received. Put leg: Amount equal to strike price minus premium received. Total exposure is the sum of both legs.
> *Reward:* Limited to premium received
> *Margin:* Call-spread leg: Amount equal to difference between strikes. Put leg: Amount equal to strike price. Total margin is the sum of both legs.

The Gist

In my opinion, these are short-term trades rather than investments. Even though a short put uses a short-tenor option, the perspective of the investor is that he or she is buying shares. These strategies are a way to express the belief that the underlying stock price will not move over a short time. In my experience, there is simply no way to develop a rational view of how a single stock will move over a short time frame. In the short term, markets fluctuate based on animal spirits, fads, and various other insanities. Why subject yourself to the torture of trying to figure out these insanities and profit from them when there are easier, more intelligent ways of doing so?

Of the two strategies, the short straddle is preferable because it yields the greatest amount of premium. Use this strategy at your own peril, however.

Let's turn now to a discussion of how to mix exposure—simultaneously gaining and accepting exposure and overlaying options on stock positions.

Chapter 11

MIXING EXPOSURE

Mixing exposure uses combinations of gaining and accepting exposure, employing strategies that we already discussed to create what amounts to sort of a short-term synthetic position in a stock (either long or short). These strategies, nicknamed "diagonals" can be extremely attractive and extremely financially rewarding in cases where stocks are significantly mispriced (in which case, exposure to one direction is overvalued, whereas the other is extremely undervalued).

Frequently, using one of these strategies, an investor can enter a position in a levered out-of-the-money (OTM) option for what, over time, becomes zero cost (or can even net a cash inflow) and zero downside exposure. This is possible because the investor uses the sale of one shorter-tenor at-the-money (ATM) option to subsidize the purchase of another longer-tenor OTM one. Once the sold option expires, another can be sold again, and whatever profit is realized from that sale goes to further subsidize the position.

This strategy works well because of a couple of rules of option pricing that we have already discussed:

1. ATM options are more expensive than OTM options of the same tenor.
2. Short-tenor options are worth less than long-tenor options, but the value per day is higher for the short-tenor options.

I provide actual market examples of these strategies in this chapter and will point out the effect of both these points in those examples.

Because these strategies are a mix of exposures, it makes sense that they are just complex (i.e., multioption) positions. I will discuss the following:

1. Long diagonal
2. Short diagonal

Note that the nomenclature I use here is a bit different from what others in the market may use. What I term a diagonal in this book is what others might call a "spit-strike synthetic stock." Since Bernie Madoff's infamous "split-strike conversion" fraud, this term doesn't have a very good ring to it. For other market participants, a diagonal means simultaneously buying and selling options of the same type (i.e calls or puts). In this book, it means selling an option of one kind and buying the other kind.

I will also talk about what is known in the options world as *overlays*. One of the most useful things about options is the way that they can be grafted or overlain onto an existing common stock position in a way that alters the portfolio's overall risk-reward profile. The strategies I will review here are as follows:

1. Covered calls
2. Protective puts
3. Collars

These strategies are popular but often misunderstood ways to alter your portfolio's risk-reward profile.

Coming this far in this book, you already have a good understanding about how options work, so the concepts presented here will not be difficult, but I will discuss some nuances that will help you to evaluate investment choices and make sound decisions regarding the use of these strategies. I will refer to strike selection and tenor selection in the following pages, but for these, along with "The Gist" section, I'll include an "Execution" section and a "Common Pitfalls" section.

Covered calls are an easy strategy to understand once you understand short puts, so I will discuss those first. Protective puts share a lot of similarities with in-the-money (ITM) call options, and I will discuss those next.

Collars are just a combination of the other two overlay strategies and so are easiest left to the end.

Long Diagonal

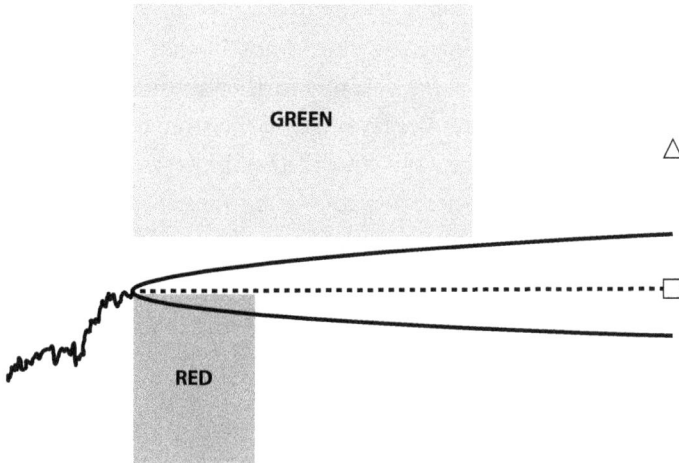

Downside: Overvalued
Upside: Undervalued
Execute: Sell an ATM put option (short put) and simultaneously buy an OTM call option (long call)
Risk: Sum of put's strike price and net premium paid for call
Reward: Unlimited
Margin: Amount equal to put's strike price

The Gist

Other than the blank space in the middle of the diagram and the disparity between the lengths of the tenors, the preceding diagram looks very much like the risk-return profile diagram for a long stock—accepting downside exposure in return for gaining upside exposure. As you can see from the diagram, the range of exposure for the short put lies well within the Black-Scholes-Merton model (BSM) cone, but the range of exposure for the long call is well outside the cone. It is often possible to find short-put–long-call combinations that allow for an immediate net credit when setting up this investment.

Because we must fully margin a short-put investment, that leg of the long diagonal carries with it a loss leverage ratio of –1.0. However, the OTM call leg represents an immediate realized loss coupled with a very high lambda value for gains. As such, if the put option expires ITM, the long diagonal is simply a levered strategy; if the put option expires OTM, the investment is a very highly levered one because the unlevered put ceases to influence the leverage equation. Another short put may be written after the previous short put expires; this further subsidizes the cost of the calls and so greatly increases the leverage on the strategy.

If the stock moves quickly toward the upper valuation range, this structure becomes extremely profitable on an unrealized basis. If the put option expires ITM, the investor is left with a levered long investment in the stock in addition to the long position in the OTM. As in any other complex structure, the investment may be ratioed—for instance, by buying one call for every two puts sold or vice versa.

Strike Price Selection

The put should be sold ATM or close to ATM in order to maximize the time value sold, as explained earlier in the short-put summary. The call strike may be bought at any level depending on the investor's appetite for leverage but is usually purchased OTM. The following table shows the net debit or credit associated with the long diagonal between the ATM put ($55 strike price, delta of –0.42, priced at the bid price) with an expiration of 79 days and each call strike (at the ask price) listed, all of which are long-term equity anticipated securities (LEAPS) having expirations in 534 days. The lambda figure for the OTM calls is also given to provide an idea of the comparative leverage of each call option. For this example, I am using JP Morgan Chase (JPM) when its stock was trading for $56.25.

Strike	Delta	(Debit) Credit	Call Lambda (%)
57.50	0.43	(2.52)	5.6
60.00	0.37	(1.57)	6.1
62.50	0.31	(0.76)	6.7
65.00	0.26	(0.25)	7.0
70.00	0.16	0.78	8.4
75.00	0.10	1.28	9.5
80.00	0.06	1.56	10.5

Here we can see that for a long diagonal using 79-day ATM puts and 594-day LEAPS that are OTM by just over 15 percent, we are paying a net of only $25 per contract for notional control of 100 shares. On a per-contract basis, at the following settlement prices, we would generate the following profits (or losses, in the case of the first row):

Settlement Price ($)	Dollar Profit per Contract	Percentage Return on Original Investment (%)
65	0	−100
66	100	300
67	200	700
68	300	1,100
69	400	1,500
70	500	1,900
71	600	2,300
72	700	2,700
73	800	3,100
74	900	3,500
75	1,000	3,900

If the stock price moves up very quickly, it might be more beneficial to close the position or some portion of the position before expiration. Let's say that my upper-range estimate for this stock was $75. From the preceding table, I can see that my profit per contract if the stock settles at my fair value range is $1,000. If there is enough time value on a contract when the stock is trading in the upper $60 range to generate a realized profit of $1,000, I am likely to take at least some profits at that time rather than waiting for the calls to expire.

In Chapter 9, I discussed portfolio composition and likened the use of leverage as a side dish to a main course. This is an excellent side dish that can be entered into when we see a chance to supplement the main meal of a long stock–ITM call option position with a bit more spice. Let's now turn to its bearish mirror—the short diagonal.

Short Diagonal

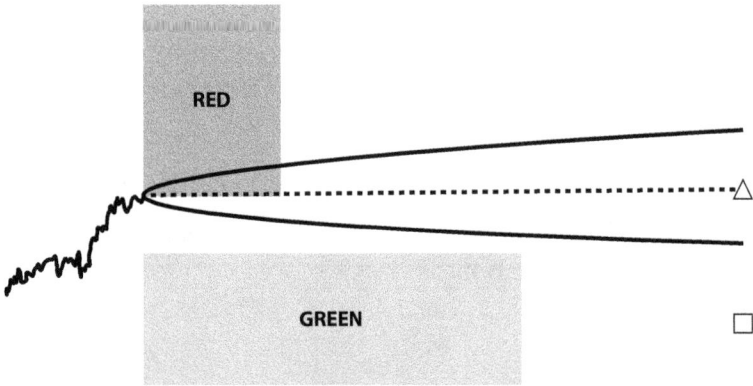

Downside: Undervalued
Upside: Overvalued
Execute: Sell an ATM call option while buying one to cover at a higher price (short-call spread) and simultaneously buy an OTM put option (long put)
Risk: Sum of put's strike price and net premium paid for call
Reward: Amount equal to the put's strike price minus any net premium paid for it
Margin: Amount equal to spread between call options

The Gist

The diagram for a short diagonal is just the inverse of the long diagonal and, of course, looks very similar to the risk-return profile diagram for a short stock—accepting upside exposure in return for gaining downside exposure. The gist of this strategy is simply the short-exposure equivalent to the long diagonal, so the comments about the long diagonal are applicable to this strategy as well. The one difference is that because you must spend money to cover the short call on the upside, the subsidy that the option sale leg provides to the option purchase leg is less than in the case of the long diagonal. Also, of course, a stock price cannot turn negative, so your profit upside is capped at an amount equal to the effective sell price. This investment also may be ratioed (e.g., by using one short-call spread to subsidize two long puts).

Strike Price Selection

Strike price selection for a short diagonal is more difficult because there are three strikes to price this time. Looking at the current pricing for a call spread with the short call struck at $55, I get the following selection of credits:

Upper Call Strike ($)	Call Spread Net Credit ($)	Percent Total Risk	Percent Total Return
57.50	1.27	17	49
60.00	2.14	33	83
62.50	2.44	50	94
65.00	2.51	67	97
70.00	2.59	100	100

Looking at this, let's say we decide to go with the $55.00/$62.50 call spread. Doing so, we would receive a net credit of $2.44. Now selecting the put to purchase is a matter of figuring out the leverage of the position with which you are comfortable.

Strike ($)	Delta	(Debit) Credit ($)	Put Lambda (%)
20.00	−0.02	2.20	−4.5
23.00	−0.02	2.11	−4.6
25.00	−0.03	2.05	−4.6
28.00	−0.04	1.91	−4.8
30.00	−0.05	1.78	−4.8
33.00	−0.07	1.57	−4.8
35.00	−0.09	1.38	−4.8
38.00	−0.12	0.99	−4.8
40.00	−0.15	0.67	−4.7
42.00	−0.17	0.30	−4.7
45.00	−0.23	(0.43)	−4.5
47.00	−0.26	(1.01)	−4.4
50.00	−0.33	(1.91)	−4.4
52.50	−0.39	(3.11)	−4.0

Notice that there is much less leverage on the long-put side than on the long-call side. This is a function of the volatility smile and the abnormally high pricing on the far OTM put side. It turns out that the $20-strike puts have an implied volatility of 43.3 percent compared to an ATM implied volatility of 22.0 percent.

Obviously, the lower level of leverage will make closing before expiration less attractive, so it is important to select a put strike price between the present market price and your worst-case fair value estimate. In this way, if the option does expire when the stock is at that level, you will at least be able to realize the profit of the intrinsic value.

With these explanations of the primary mixed-exposure strategies, now let's turn to overlays—where an option position is added to a stock position to alter the risk-return characteristics of the investor's portfolio.

Covered Call

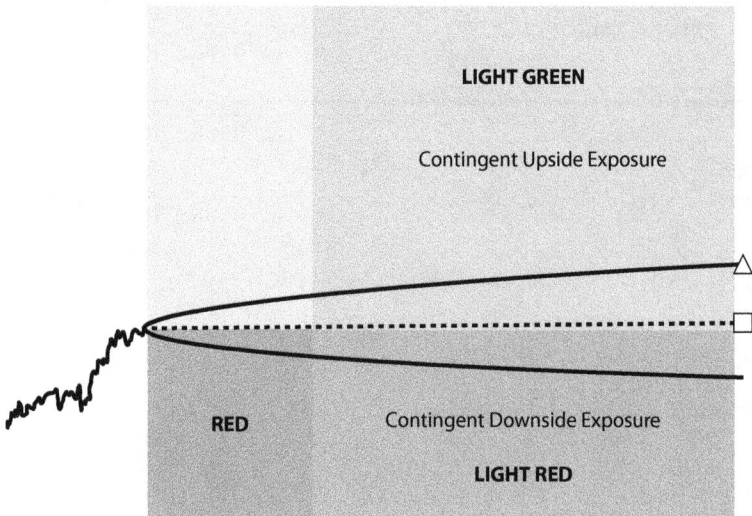

Downside: Overvalued
Upside: Fairly valued or undervalued

Execute: Buy common stock and simultaneously sell a call option

 Risk: Strike price minus premium received

Reward: Limited to premium and, as long as the shares are not called, the dividends received during the tenor of the option

Margin: None as long as stock and option positions are evenly matched—long stock position serves as collateral for the sold call

The Gist

If you look just as far as the option tenor lasts on the preceding diagram, you will see that the risk-return profile is identical to that of a short put. As evidence, please compare the following two diagrams:

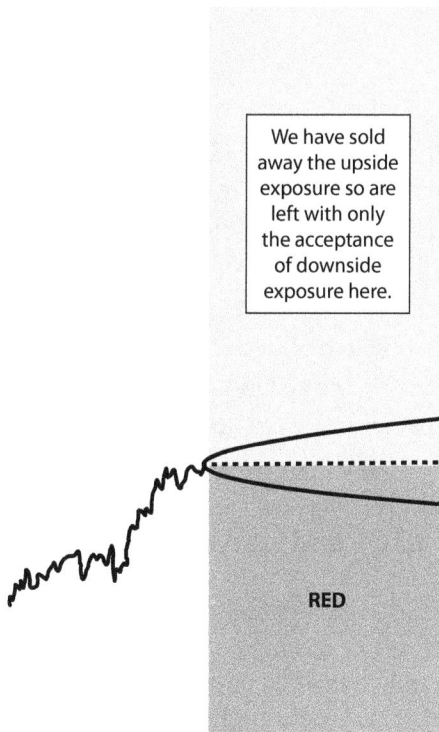

We have sold away the upside exposure so are left with only the acceptance of downside exposure here.

RED

Covered call

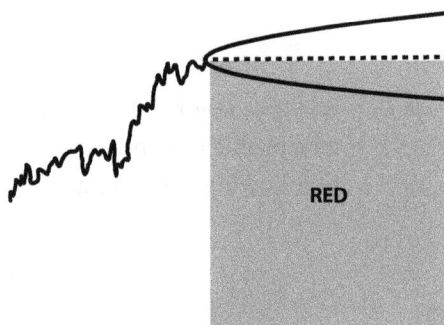

We accepted downside exposure when we sold this put, so have no exposure to the upside here.

RED

Short put

The top of the "Covered call" diagram is grayed out because we have sold away the upside exposure to the stock by selling the call option, and we are left only with the acceptance of the stock's downside exposure. The pictures are slightly different, but the economic impact is the same.

The other difference you will notice is that after the option expires, in the case of the covered call, we have represented the graphic as though there is some residual exposure. This is represented in this way because if the option expires ITM, you will have to deliver your stock to the counterparty who bought your call options. As such, your future exposure to the stock is contingent on another investor's actions and the price movement of the stock. This is an important point to keep in mind, and I will discuss it more in the "Common Pitfalls" section.

Execution

Because this strategy is identical from a risk-reward perspective to short puts, the execution details should be the same as well. Indeed, covered calls should—like short puts—be executed ATM to get the most time value possible and preferably should be done on a stock that has had a recent fall and whose implied volatility has spiked. However, these theoretical points ignore the fact that most people simply want to generate a bit of extra income out of the holdings they already have and so are psychologically resistant to both selling ATM (because this makes it more likely for their shares to be called away) and selling at a time when the stock price suddenly drop (because they want to reap the benefit of the shares recovering).

Although I understand these sentiments, it is important to realize that options are financial instruments and not magical ones. It would be nice if we could simply find an investment tool that we could bolt onto our present stock holdings that would increase the dividend a nice amount but that wouldn't put us at risk of having to deliver our beloved stocks to a complete stranger; unfortunately, this is not the case for options.

For example, let's say that you own stock in a company that is paying out a very nice dividend yield of 5 percent at present prices. This is a mature firm that has tons of cash flow but few opportunities for growth, so management has made the welcome choice to return cash to shareholders. The stock is trading at $50 per share, but because the dividend is attractive to you, you are loathe to part with the stock. As such, you would prefer to write the covered call at a $55 or even a $60 strike price. A quick look at the BSM cone tells us why you should not be expecting a big boost in yield from selling the covered calls:

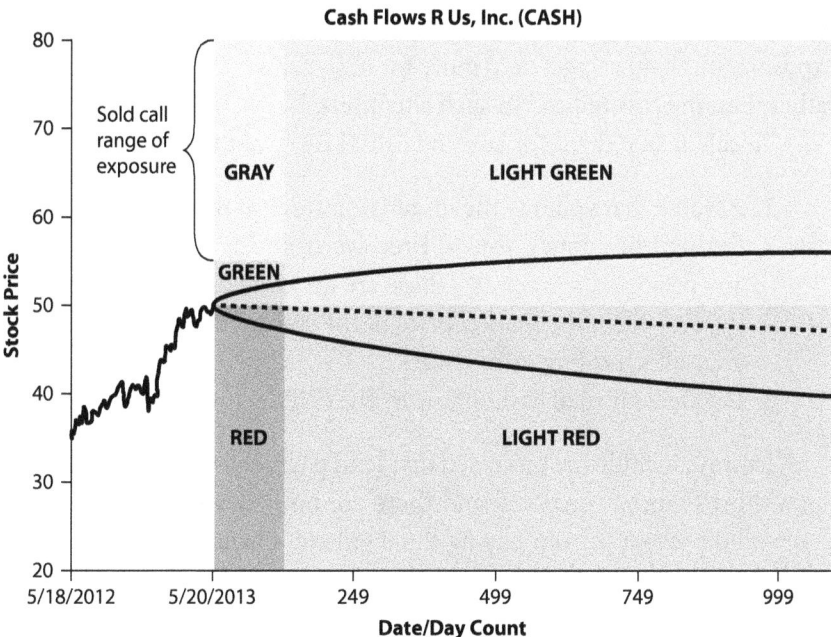

Cash Flows R Us, Inc. (CASH)

Clearly, the range of exposure for the $55-strike call is well above the BSM cone. The BSM cone is pointing downward because the dividend rate is 5 percent—higher than the risk-free rate. This means that BSM drift will be lower. In addition, because this is an old, mature, steady-eddy kind of company, the expected forward volatility is low. Basically, this is a perfect storm for a low option price.

My suggestion is to either write calls on stocks you don't mind delivering to someone else—stocks for which you are very confident in the valuation range and are now at or above the upper bound—or simply to look for a portfolio of short-put/covered-call investments and treat it like a high-yield bond portfolio, as I described in Chapter 10 when explaining short puts. It goes without saying that if you think that a stock has a lot of unappreciated upside potential, it's not a good idea to sell that exposure away!

One other note about execution: as I have said, short puts and covered calls are the same thing, but a good many investors do not realize this fact or their brokerages prevent them from placing any trade other than a covered call. This leads to a situation in which there is a tremendous supply of calls. Any time there is a lot of supply, the price goes down, and you will indeed find covered calls on some companies paying a lot less than the equivalent short put. Because you will be accepting the same downside exposure, it is better to get paid more for it, so my advice is to write the put rather than the covered call in such situations.

To calculate returns for covered calls, I carry out the following steps:

1. Assume that you buy the underlying stock at the market price.
2. Deduct the money you will receive from the call sale as well as any projected dividends—these are the two elements of your cash inflow—from the market price of the stock. The resulting figure is your effective buy price (EBP).
3. Divide your total cash inflow by the EBP.

I always include the projected dividend payment as long as I am writing a short-tenor covered call and there are no issues with the company that would prevent it from paying the dividend. Owners of record have a right to receive dividends, even after they have written a covered call on the stock, so it makes sense to count the dividend inflow as one element that reduces your EBP. In formula form, this turns out to be

$$\text{Covered call return} = \frac{\text{premium received from call} + \text{projected dividends}}{\text{stock price} - \text{premium from call} - \text{projected dividends}}$$

For a short put, you have no right to receive the dividend, so I find the return using the following formula:

$$\text{Short put return} = \frac{\text{premium received from short put}}{\text{strike price} - \text{premium from short put}}$$

Common Pitfalls

Taking Profit

One mistake I hear people make all the time is saying that they are going to "take profit" using a covered call. Writing a covered call is taking profit in the sense that you no longer enjoy capital gains from the stock's appreciation, but it is certainly not taking profit in the sense of being immune to falls in the market price of the stock. The call premium you receive will cushion a stock price drop, but it will certainly not shield you from it. If you want to take profits on a successful stock trade, hit the "Sell" button.

Locking in a Loss

A person sent me an e-mail telling me that she had bought a stock at $17, sold covered calls on it when it got to $20 (in order to "take profits"), and now that the stock was trading for $11, she wanted to know how she could "repair" her position using options. Unfortunately, options are not magical tools and cannot make up for a prior decision to buy a stock at $17 and ride it down to $11.

If you are in such a position, don't panic. It will be tempting to write a new call at the lower ATM price ($11 in this example) because the cash inflow from that covered call will be the most. Don't do it. By writing a covered call at the lower price, you are—if the shares are called away—locking in a realized loss on the position. You can see this clearly if you list each transaction in the example separately.

No.	Buy/Sell	Instrument	Price of Instrument	Effective Buy (Sell) Price of Stock	Note
1	Buy	Stock	$17/share	$17/share	Original purchase
2	Sell	Call option	$1/share	$16/share	Selling a covered call to take profits when stock reaches $20/share leaves the investor with down-side exposure and $1 in premium income.
3	Sell	Call option	$0.75	($11.75/share)	Stock falls to $11, and investor sells another covered call to generate income to ameliorate the loss.

In transaction 1, the investor buys the shares for $17. In transaction 2, when the stock hits $20 per share, the investor sells a covered call and receives $1 in premium. This reduces the effective buy price to $16 per share and means that the investor will have to deliver the shares if the stock is trading at $20 or above at expiration. When the stock instead falls to $11, the investor—wanting to cushion the pain of the loss—sells another ATM covered call for $0.75. This covered call commits the investor to sell the shares for $11.75. No matter how you look at it, buying at $16 per share and selling at $11.75 per share is not a recipe for investing success.

The first step in such a situation as this—when the price of a stock on which you have accepted downside exposure falls—is to look back to your valuation. If the value of the firm has indeed dropped because of some material negative news and the position no longer makes sense from an economic perspective, just sell the shares and take the lumps. If, however, the stock price has dropped but the valuation still makes for a compelling investment, stay in the position; if the investment is compelling enough, this is the time to figure out a clever way to get more exposure to it.

You can write calls as long as they are at least at the same strike price as your previous purchase price or EBP; this just means that you are buying at $16 and agreeing to sell at at least $16, in other words. Also keep in mind that any dividend payment you receive you can also think of as a reduction of your EBP—that cash inflow is offsetting the cost of the shares. Factoring in dividends and the (very small) cash inflow associated with writing far OTM calls will, as long as you are right about the valuation, eventually reduce your EBP enough so that you can make a profit on the investment.

Over-/Underexposure

Options are transacted in contract sizes of 100 shares. If you hold a number of shares that is not evenly divisible by 100, you must decide whether you are going to sell the next number down of contracts or the next number up. For example, let's say that you own 250 shares of ABC. You can either choose to sell two call contracts (in which case you will not be receiving yield on 50 of your shares) or sell three call contracts (in which case you will be effectively shorting 50 shares). My preference is to sell fewer contracts controlling fewer shares than I hold, and in fact, your broker may or may not insist that you do so as well. If not, it is an unpleasant feeling to get a call from a broker saying that you have a margin call on a position that you didn't know you had.

Getting Assigned

If you write covered calls, you live with the risk that you will have to deliver your beloved shares to a stranger. You can deliver your shares and use the proceeds from that sale (the broker will deposit an amount equal to the strike price times the contract multiplier into your account, and you get to keep the premium you originally received) to buy the shares again, but there is no way around delivering the shares if assigned.

Now that you understand covered calls, let's turn to protective puts.

Protective Puts

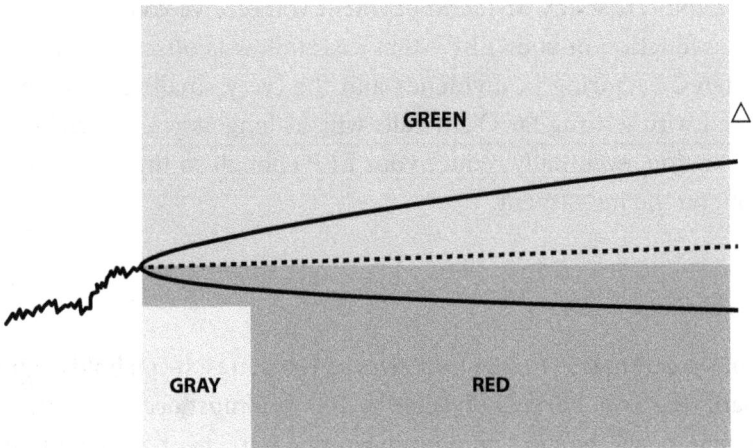

Downside: Irrelevant
  Upside: Undervalued
 Execute: Buy common stock and simultaneously buy a put option (the diagram shows the purchase of an OTM put option)
    Risk: Purchase price of stock minus strike price of put option minus premium paid
 Reward: Unlimited, less premium paid for put option, which cannot be recovered
  Margin: None because this is a purchase of an option

The Gist

If you look just as far as the option tenor lasts in the preceding diagram, you will see that the risk-return profile is identical to that of an ITM call. As evidence, please compare the following two diagrams:

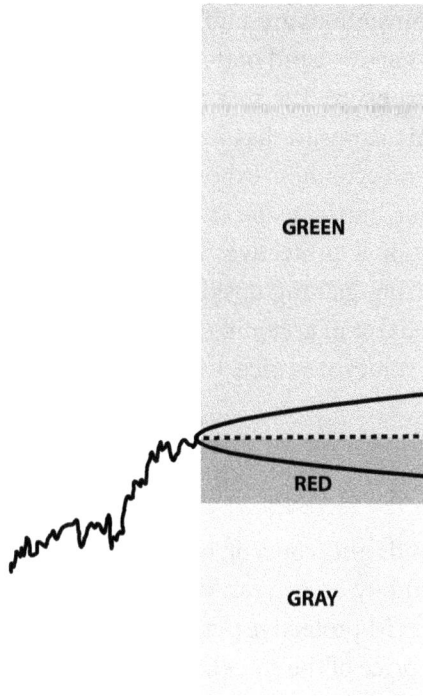

Protective put

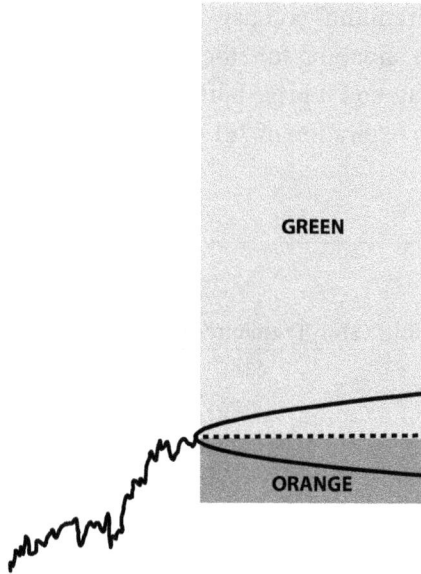

ITM call

The graphic conventions are a little different, but both diagrams show the acceptance of a narrow band of downside exposure offset by a boundless gain of upside exposure. The area below the protective put's strike price shows that economic exposure has been neutralized, and the area below the ITM call shows no economic exposure. The pictures are slightly different, but the economic impact is the same.

The objective of a protective put is obvious—allow yourself the economic benefits from gaining upside exposure while shielding yourself from the economic harm of accepting downside exposure. The problem is that this protection comes at a price. I will provide more infromation about this in the next section.

Execution

Everyone understands the concept of protective puts—it's just like the home insurance you buy every year to insure your property against damage. If you buy an OTM protective put (let's say one struck at 90 percent of the current market price of the stock), the exposed amount from the stock price down to the put strike can be thought of as your "deductible" on your home insurance policy. The premium you pay for your put option can be thought of as the "premium" you pay on your home insurance policy.

Okay—let's go shopping for stock insurance. Apple (AAPL) is trading for $452.53 today, so I'll price both ATM and OTM put insurance for these shares with an expiration of 261 days in the future. I'll also annualize that rate.

Strike ($)	"Deductible" ($)	"Premium" ($)	Premium as Percent of Stock Price	Annualized Premium (%)
450	2.53	40.95	9.1	12.9
405	47.53	20.70	4.6	6.5
360	92.53	8.80	1.9	2.7

Now, given these rates and assuming that you are insuring a $500,000 house, the following table shows what equivalent deductibles, annual premiums, and total liability to a home owner would be for deductibles equivalent to the strike prices I've picked for Apple:

Equivalent AAPL Strike ($)	Deductible ($)	Annual Premium ($)	Total Liability to Home Owner ($)
450	2,795	64,500	67,295
405	52,516	32,500	85,016
360	102,236	13,500	115,736

I know that I would not be insuring my house at these rates and under those conditions! In light of these prices, the first thing you must consider is whether protecting a particular asset from unrealized price declines is worth the huge realized losses you must take to buy put premium. Buying ATM put protection on AAPL is setting up a 12.9 percent hurdle rate that the stock must surpass in one year just for you to start making a profit on the position, and 13 percent per year is quite a hurdle rate!

If there is some reason why you believe that you need to pay for insurance, a better option—cheaper from a realized loss perspective—would be to sell the shares and use part of the proceeds to buy call options as an option-based replacement for the stock position. This approach has a few benefits:

1. The risk-reward profile is exactly the same between the two structures.
2. Any ATM or ITM call will be more lightly levered than any OTM put, meaning a lower realized loss on initiation.
3. For dividend-paying stocks, call owners do not have the right to receive dividends, but the amount of the projected dividend is deducted from the premium (as part of the drift calculation shown in the section on covered calls). As such, although not being paid dividends over time, you are getting what amounts to a one-time upfront dividend payment.
4. If you do not like the thought of leverage in your portfolio, you can self-margin the position (i.e., keep enough cash in reserve such that you are not "borrowing" any money through the call purchase).

I do not hedge individual positions, but I do like the ITM call option as an alternative for people who feel the need to do so. For hedging of a general portfolio, rather than hedging of a particular holding in a portfolio, options on sector or index exchange-traded funds (ETFs) are more reasonably priced. Here are the ask prices for put options on the SPX

ETF [tracking the Standard and Poor's 500 Index (S&P 500), which closed at 1,685.73 when these data were retrieved] expiring in about 10 months:

Strike/Stock ($)	Ask Price ($)	Premium as Percent of Stock Price
0.99	106.60	6.3
0.89	50.90	3.0
0.80	25.80	1.5

This is still a hefty chunk of change to pay for protection on an index but much less than the price of protection on individual stocks.[1]

Common Pitfalls

Hedge Timing

Assume that you had talked to me a year ago and decided to take my advice and avoid buying protective puts on single-name options. Instead, you took a protective put position on the S&P 500. Good for you.

Setting aside for a moment how much of your portfolio to hedge, let's take a look at what happened since you bought the downside protection:

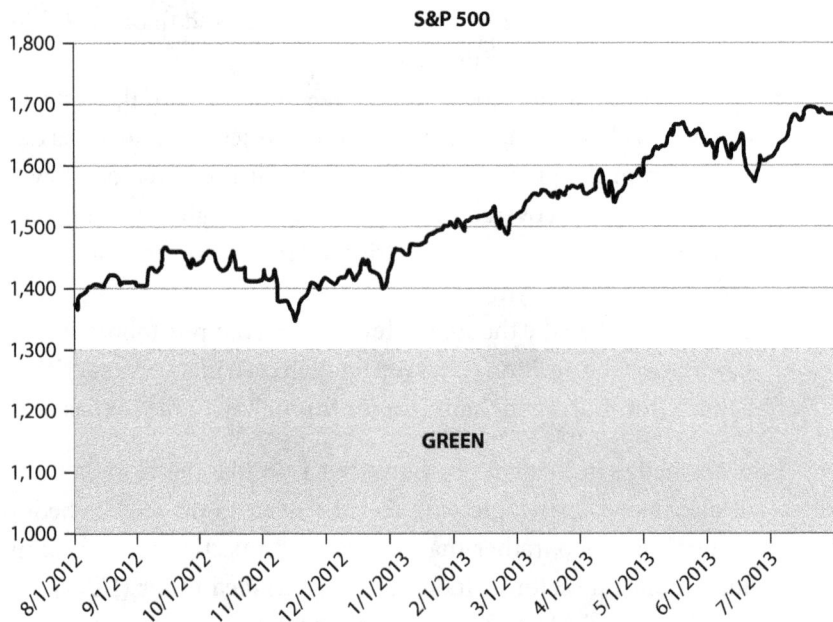

S&P 500

When you bought the protection, the index was trading at 1,375, so you bought one-year puts about 5 percent OTM at $1,300. If the market had fallen heavily or even moderately during the first five months of the contract, your puts would have served you very well. However, now the puts are not 5 percent OTM anymore but 23 percent OTM, and it would take another Lehman shock for the market to make it down to your put strike.

Keeping in mind that buying longer-tenor options gives you a better annualized cost than shorter-tenor options, you should be leery of entering into a hedging strategy such as the one pictured here:

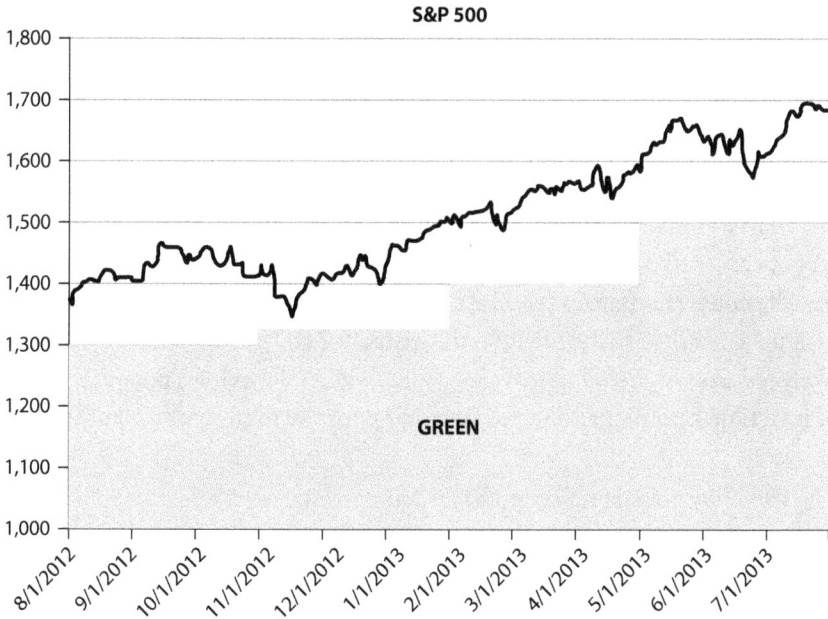

Buying short-tenor puts helps in terms of providing nearer to ATM protection, but the cost is higher, and it gets irritating to keep buying expensive options and never benefiting from them (funny—no one ever says this about home insurance). Although there are no perfect solutions to this quandary, I believe the following approach has merit:

S&P 500

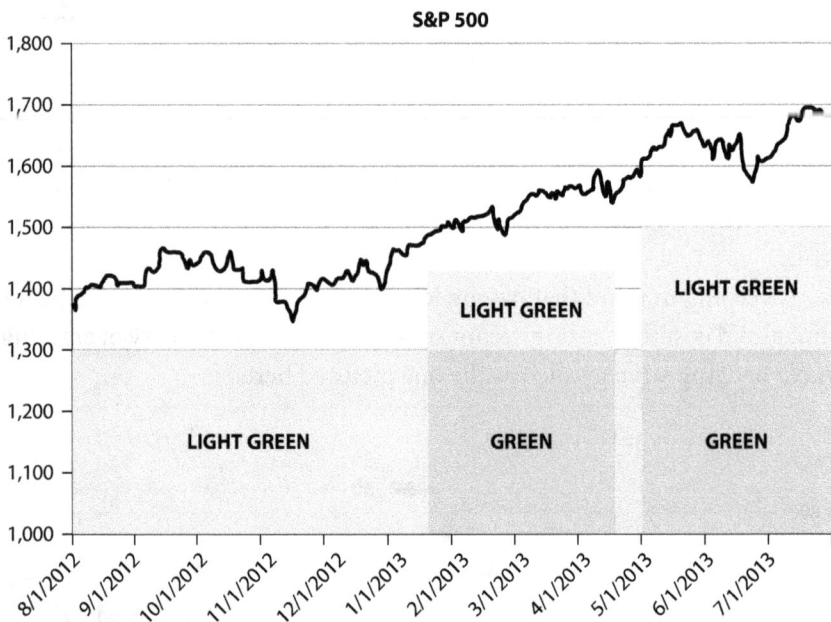

Here I bought fewer long-term put contracts at the outset and then added put contracts at higher strikes opportunistically as time passed. I have left myself somewhat more exposed at certain times, and my protection doesn't all pick up at a single strike price, so the insurance coverage is spotty, but I have likely reduced my hedging cost a great deal while still having a potential source of investible cash on hand in the form of options with time value on them.

The Unhappy Case of a Successful Hedge

Markets are down across the board. Your brokerage screen is awash in red. The only bright spot is the two or three lines of your screen showing your S&P 500 puts, which are strongly positive. You bought your protection when the market was going up, so it was very cheap to purchase. Now, with the market in a terror, the implied volatilities have shot up, and you are sitting on a huge positive unrealized value.

Now what?

The psychological urge to keep that hedge on will be strong. Such a position is safe after all, and with the rest of the world falling apart, it feels nice to have somewhere safe to go. What should you do with this unrealized profit?

Step one is always assessing the value of securities in your portfolio and securities that might be on your watch list. Does the news driving the markets down have a material effect on the value of any of your holdings? Certainly, if the market believes that the economy is going into a recession, the next few years' worth of revenue growth and profits may be those that you projected for your explicit-period worst-case scenarios, but that will likely be offset by faster medium-term growth as the economy bounces back. Think about the valuations you have for your holdings objectively and with as little passion as possible. It's better not to have your brokerage screen or a price chart of the financial markets or whatever up while you do this.

Are there securities whose present prices are significantly different from your worst-case valuation range? Do the prices imply an unlevered return of 30, 40, or 50 percent or more? Is there a stock that has been on your watch list for a long time but until now has never been at a price at which you wanted to buy it?

This is where you must resist the urge to take the safe path and close the hedge and then turn around the cash and increase your position size on your best investments or on investments that you have always wanted to make but haven't had the chance. This will be a hard thing to do psychologically. The world is telling you to run and hide. This is the time to remember the maxim, "Be bold when others are scared and scared when others are bold." Times of stress are those that set great investors apart from the rest of the crowd.

Not Having a Plan

Finally, we get to the question of how to size our hedge. If we look at the indicative prices for S&P 500 puts shown earlier, we can see that if we choose to hedge the entire amount of our portfolio, we set up at least a 6 percentage point drag on our portfolio every 10 months or so, and that is a lot of potentially dead weight to be carrying around.

In daily life, I believe that people are prone to overinsure (e.g., extended warrantees for consumer electronic items and so on), and this is a good habit to keep away from in investing. Risk is not a temporary unrealized loss caused by market panic. Usually risk is not the inability to invest more capital when you want to invest more capital (unless by not investing it you will have a shortfall in capital in the future). Risk is usually not any of the things TV pundits talk about as being risk.

I will discuss risk in greater detail in Chapter 12, but a sensible definition of risk is not having the capital resources to pay for something when you need to pay for it. In this sense, risk can be talked about in terms of liquidity—a short-term lack of spending power—and solvency—a fundamental lack of capital assets. For example, let's say that you have committed to pay a restaurant and entertainers the remainder of their $50,000 fee for your son's bar mitzvah or your daughter's wedding, and you only have $20,000 in net worth. You are in a position of risk because of problems of solvency but not necessarily liquidity (i.e., you could borrow the money to pay for these things). However, if you have a net worth of $3 million—all of it unrealized gains on real estate holdings—and you have the same $50,000 bill to pay, you may be in a position of risk because of problems in liquidity but not solvency.

Risk that stems from issues of liquidity usually can be controlled through intelligent asset allocation. For example, the millionaire father in the preceding bar mitzvah/wedding example can realize $50,000 worth of his unrealized investment gains to meet his immediate cash need. A 79-year-old with 85 percent of her net worth of $2.5 million invested in tech sector initial public offerings (IPOs) or companies in the Chinese infrastructure supply chain can ameliorate her risk of not being able to pay for necessary healthcare and living expenses by shifting more of her assets into bonds and CDs. Usually, in cases such as this—which, I believe, make up the majority of cases people are trying to "hedge"—there are much better ways of controlling risk than buying puts on the S&P 500 or the Russell 2000!

However, there is a more subtle instance of risk—not maximizing returns on one's invested capital and, because of this, not having the capital adequacy to meet unforeseen cash-flow needs in the future. This instance of risk deals with solvency, rather than liquidity.

This type of risk cannot be ameliorated through a defensive strategy but must be controlled through an offensive one. Setting aside savings, investing those savings wisely and consistently in good times, and having the courage to invest when it is hardest to do so (i.e., when the market is crashing) are all elements of this risk-control strategy. Put options can only help with the third case here—investing when it is hardest to do so—but they cannot help without the put owner's input of personal courage.

This topic brings us back to the last section—investing the proceeds in a successful hedge in undervalued assets. I believe that portfolio hedges should be set up with a particular cost and investing goal in mind. For example, "I am willing to allocate as much as 1 percentage point of my investment performance this year to have an extra 5 percent of cash on hand to invest in case the market drops by 10 to 20 percent." This is the rough outline of a hedging plan. It specifies the maximum you are willing to spend and a target for how much cash you want in case of a certain market downdraft.

This plan does not mean that you always have to spend 1 percent of your net worth on hedges. There are times when it is more sensible to spend more on hedges—because of building macroeconomic uncertainty or whatever—and other times when it is more sensible to spend less—when the economy is just coming out of a recession for instance.

Also note that the plan specifies a cash level. If you are not fully invested in your securities portfolio, you are already hedged to the degree that your cash assets are not subject to direct security price risk (cash is subject to inflation risk, but this is another topic). The cash you have on reserve will allow you to purchase if and when the market falls. As such, I don't believe that people holding a significant allocation of cash should think about hedging per se. You may believe that the market is ready to fall, in which case, you can make a bearish bet on the level of the index using a long put, a short-call spread, or a short diagonal, but this is a proactive investment that expresses your opinion about the level of the market vis-à-vis the state of the economy.

What it does not specify is what you will spend the cash on. This is where an understanding of the value of the companies in your portfolio or on your watch list comes into play. If you had an extra 5 percent (or $50,000 or however you want to think about it) in cash, in what securities would you invest? Of course, the answer will change depending on the price of the securities vis-à-vis what you know to be a sensible valuation range because the expected returns on the investments will change with the market price.

So this is the last step in a sensible hedging plan—having an idea of what companies you would want to invest in were you to have the extra capital and if you could be reasonably assured of a good return. Having a plan like this in place will allow you to size and time your hedges appropriately and will help you to make the most out of whatever temporary crisis might come your way.[2]

Now that you have a good understanding of protective puts and hedging, let's turn to the last overlay strategy—the collar.

Collar

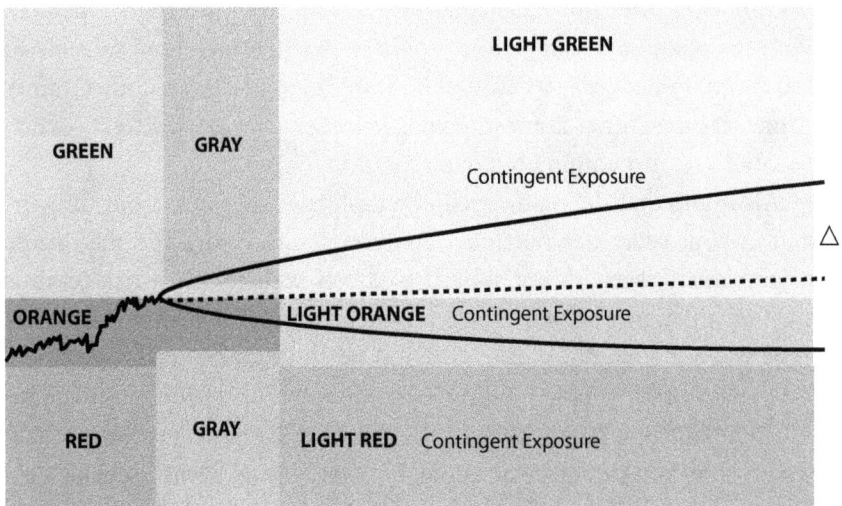

Downside: Irrelevant
Upside: Overvalued
Execute: Sell a call option on a stock or index that you own and on which you have a gain, and use the proceeds from the call sale to buy an OTM put
Risk: Flexible, depending on selection of strikes
Reward: Limited to level of sold call strike
Margin: None because the long position in the hedged security serves as collateral for the sold call option, and the OTM put option is purchased, so it does not require margining

The Gist

This structure is really much simpler and has a much more straightforward investment purpose than it may seem when you look at the preceding diagram. When people talk about "taking profits" using a covered call, the collar is actually the strategy they should be using.

Imagine that you bought a stock some time ago and have a nice unrealized gain on it. The stock is about where you think its likely fair value is, but you do not want to sell it for whatever reason (e.g., it is paying a nice dividend or you bought it less than a year ago and do not want to be taxed on short-term capital gains or whatever). Although you do not want to sell it, you would like to protect yourself from downside exposure.

You can do this cheaply using a collar. The collar is a covered call, which we have already discussed, whose income subsidizes the purchase of a protective put at some level that will allow you to keep some of the unrealized gains on your securities position. The band labeled "Orange" on the diagram shows an unrealized gain (or, conversely, a potential unrealized loss). If you buy a put that is within this orange band or above, you will be guaranteed of making at least some realized profit on your original stock or index investment. Depending on how much you receive for the covered call and what strike you select for the protective put, this collar may represent completely "free" downside protection or you might even be able to realize a net credit.

Execution

The execution of this strategy depends a great deal on personal preference and on the individual investor's situation. For example, an investor can sell a short-tenor covered call and use those proceeds to buy a longer-tenor protective put. He or she can sell the covered call ATM and buy a protective put that is close to ATM; this means the maximum and minimum potential return on the previous security purchase is in a fairly tight band. Conversely, the investor might sell an OTM covered call and buy a protective put that is also OTM. This would lock in a wider range of guaranteed profits over the life of the option.

I show a couple of examples below that give you the flavor of the possibilities of the collar strategy. With these examples, you can experiment yourself with a structure that fits your particular needs. Look on my website for a collar scenario calculator that will allow you to visualize the collar and understand the payoff structure given different conditions. For these examples, I am assuming that I bought Qualcomm stock at $55 per share. Qualcomm is now trading for $64.71—an unrealized gain of 17.7 percent.

Collar 1: 169 Days to Expiration

	Strike Price ($)	Bid (Ask) Price ($)
Sold call	65.00	3.40
Purchased put	60.00	(2.14)
Net credit		$1.26

This collar yields the following best- and worst-case effective sell prices (ESPs) and corresponding returns (assuming a $55 buy price):

	ESP ($)	Return (%)
Best case	66.26	20.5
Worst case	61.26	11.4

Here we sold the $65-strike calls for $3.40 and used those proceeds to buy the $60-strike put options at $2.14. This gave us a net credit of $1.26, which we simply add to both strike prices to calculate our ESP. We add the net credit to the call strike because if the stock moves above the call strike, we will end up delivering the stock at the strike price while still keeping the net credit. We add the net credit to the put strike because if the stock closes below the put strike, we have the right to sell the shares at the strike price and still keep the net credit. The return numbers are calculated on the basis of a $55 purchase price and the ESPs listed. Thus, by setting up this collar in this way, we have locked in a worst possible gain of 11.4 percent and a best possible gain of 20.5 percent for the next five and a half months.

Let's look at another collar with a different profit and loss profile:

Collar 2: 78 Days to Expiration

	Strike Price ($)	Bid (Ask) Price ($)
Sold call	70	0.52
Purchased put	62.50	(1.55)
Net debit		(1.03)

This collar yields the following best- and worst-case ESPs and corresponding returns (assuming a $55 buy price):

	ESP ($)	Return (%)
Best case	68.97	25.4
Worst case	61.47	11.8

This shows a shorter-tenor collar—about two and a half months before expiration—that allows for more room for capital gains. This might be the strategy of a hedge fund manager who is long the stock and uncertain about the next quarterly earnings report. For his or her own business reasons, the manager does not want to show an unrealized loss in case Qualcomm's report is not good, but he or she also doesn't want to restrict the potential capital gains much either.

Calculating the ESPs and the returns in the same way as described here, we get a guaranteed profit range from around 12 to over 25 percent. One thing to note as well is that the protection is provided by a put, and a put option can be sold any time before expiry to generate a cash inflow from time value. Let's say then that when Qualcomm reports its quarterly earnings, the stock price drops to $61—a mild drop that the hedge fund manager considers a positive sign. Now that the manager is less worried about the downside exposure, he or she can sell the put for a profit.

The cash inflow from selling the put for a profit may even change the net debit on the collar to a net credit, or the manager can use some of the cash flow to buy back the sold call option if he or she is worried about the upside being limited.

These are just two examples, but they show the kind of flexibility that makes collars very useful investing instruments. With this chapter complete, you have all the tools required to be an intelligent option investor. Let's finish with an important discussion—an investigation of risk and intelligent option investing. This is the topic of Chapter 12.

Chapter 12

RISK AND THE INTELLIGENT OPTION INVESTOR

The preceding 11 chapters have given you a great deal of information about the mechanics of option investing and stock valuation. In this last chapter, let's look at a subject that I have mentioned throughout this book—risk—and see how an intelligent option investor conceives of it.

There are many forms of risk—some of which we discussed earlier (e.g., the career risk of an investment business agent, solvency risk of a retiree looking to maintain a good quality of life, and liquidity risk of a parent needing to make a big payment for a child's wedding). The two risks I discuss here are those that are most applicable to an owner of capital making potentially levered investments in complex, uncertain assets such as stocks. These two risks are *market risk* and *valuation risk*.

Market Risk

Market risk is unavoidable for anyone investing capital. Markets fluctuate, and in the short term, these fluctuations often have little to do with the long-term value of a given stock. *Short term*, it must be noted, is also relative. In words attributed to John Maynard Keynes, but which is more likely an anonymous aphorism, "The market can remain irrational longer than you can remain solvent." Indeed, it is this observation and my own painful experience of the truth of it that has brought me to my appreciation for in-the-money (ITM) options as a way to preserve my capital and cushion the blow of timing uncertainty.

Market risk is a factor that investors in levered instruments must always keep in mind. Even an ITM call long-term equity anticipated security (LEAPS) in the summer of 2007 might have become a short-tenor out-of-the-money (OTM) call by the fall of 2008 after the Lehman shock because of the sharp decline in stock prices in the interim. Unexpected things can and do happen. A portfolio constructed oblivious to this fact is a dangerous thing.

As long as market fluctuations only cause unrealized losses, market risk is manageable. But if a levered loss must be realized, either because of an option expiration or in order to fund another position, it has the potential to materially reduce your available investment capital. You cannot materially reduce your investment capital too many times before running out.

A Lehman shock is a worst-case scenario, and some investors live their entire lives without experiencing such severe and material market risk. In most cases, rather than representing a material threat, market risk represents a wonderful opportunity to an intelligent investor.

Most human decision makers in the market are looking at either technical indicators—which are short term by nature—or some sort of multiple value (e.g., price-to-something ratio). These kinds of measures are wonderful for brokers because they encourage brokerage clients to make frequent trades and thus pay the brokerages frequent fees.

The reaction of short-term traders is also wonderful for intelligent investors. This is so because a market reaction that might look sensible or rational to someone with an investment time horizon measured in days or months will often look completely ridiculous to an investor with a longer-term perspective. For example, let's say that a company announces that its earnings will be lower next quarter because of a delay in the release of a new product. Investors who are estimating a short-term value for the stock based on an earnings multiple will sell the stock when they see that earnings will likely fall. Technical traders see that the stock has broken through some line of "resistance" or that one moving average has crossed another moving average, so they sell it as well. Perhaps an algorithmic trading engine recognizes the sharp drop and places a series of sell orders that are covered almost as soon as they are filled. In the meantime, someone who has held the stock for a while and has a gain on it gets protective of this gain and decides to buy a put option to protect his or her gains.

For an intelligent option investor who has a long-term worst-case valuation that is now 20 percent higher than the market price, there is a wonderful opportunity to sell a put and receive a fat premium (with the possibility of owning the stock at an attractive discount to the likely fair value), sell a put and use the proceeds to buy an OTM call LEAPS, or simply buy the stock to open a position.

Indeed, this strategy is perfectly in keeping with the dictum, "Be fearful when others are greedy and greedy when others are fearful." This strategy is also perfectly reasonable but obviously rests on the ability of the investor to accurately estimate the actual intrinsic value of a stock. This brings us to the next form of risk—valuation risk.

Valuation Risk

Although valuation is not a difficult process, it is one that necessarily includes unknowable elements. In our own best- and worst-case valuation methodology, we have allowed for these unknowns by focusing on plausible ranges rather than precise point estimates. Of course, our best- or worst-case estimates might be wrong. This could be due to our misunderstanding of the economic dynamics of the business in which we have invested or may even come about because of the way we originally framed the problem. Thinking back to how we defined our ranges, recall that we were focusing on one-standard-deviation probabilities—in other words, scenarios that might plausibly be expected to materialize two times out of three. Obviously, even if we understand the dynamics of the business very well, one time out of three, our valuation process will generate a fair value range that is, in fact, materially different from the actual intrinsic value of the stock.

In contrast to market risk, which most often is a nonmaterial and temporary issue, misestimating the fair value of a stock represents a material risk to capital, whether our valuation range is too low or too high. If we estimate a valuation range that is too low, we are likely to end up not allocating enough capital to the investment or using inappropriately light leverage. This means that we will have missed the opportunity to generate as much return on this investment as we may have. If we estimate a valuation range that is too high, we are likely to end up allocating too much capital to the investment or using inappropriately high leverage. In the best case, we allocate too much capital to an idea that generates low returns when we might have allocated it to a higher-return investment. In the worst case, we suffer a loss of capital when the market price falls and we realize that our original estimates were overly optimistic.

One of the best ways to protect against valuation risk is to invest in only the most compelling, most clearly mispriced securities. A friend who worked for years advising companies on mergers and acquisitions has a wonderful way of visualizing valuation risk that I have found particularly helpful.[1] In his conception, a company's stock price can be represented by layers. At the bottom layer is the value of the company's net assets if they were all sold today. The next layer assumes that, for instance, the company will cease to exist as a going concern after 10 years and will sell its net assets then. The next layer assumes that, for instance, the company exists perpetually as a going concern, but its free cash flow to owner(s) (FCFO) doesn't grow again. On and on, each layer represents a more aggressive assumption about the growth of its cash flows until we are assuming, for instance, that the company's FCFO will grow at an average of 50 percent per year for the next 15 years and then 6 percent for every year after that in perpetuity. We can visualize this in the following graphic:

Value of cash flows growing at 50 percent per year for 15 years and then at 6 percent per year after that—$52 per share.

Value of cash flows growing at 20 percent per year for 15 years and then at 6 percent per year after that—$27/share.

↓

Value of cash flows not growing but continuing on into perpetuity—$9 per share.

Value of cash flows not growing and lasting 20 years—$7 per share.

Market value of hard assets—$2 to $4 per share.

Let's assume that the present market value of the shares is $16 per share. This share price assumes a growth in FCFO of 8 percent per year for the next 5 years and 5 percent per year in perpetuity after that—roughly equal to what we consider our most likely operational performance scenario. We see the possibility of faster growth but realize that this faster growth is unlikely—the valuation layer associated with this faster growth is the $18 to $20 level. We also see the possibility of a slowdown, and the valuation layer associated with this worst-case growth rate is the $11 to $13 level.

Now let's assume that because of some market shock, the price of the shares falls to the $10 range. At the same time, let's assume that the likely economic scenario, even after the stock price fall, is still the same as before—most likely around $16 per share; the best case is $20 per share, and the worst case is $11 per share. Let's also say that you can sell a put option, struck at $10, for $1 per share—giving you an effective buy price of $9 per share.

In this instance, the valuation risk is indeed small as long as we are correct about the relative levels of our valuation layers. Certainly, in this type of scenario, it is easier to commit capital to your investment idea than it would be, say, to sell puts struck at $16 for $0.75 per share!

Thinking of stock prices in this way, it is clear that when the market price of a stock is within a valuation layer that implies unrealistic economic assumptions, you will more than likely be able to use a combination of stocks and options to tilt the balance of risk and reward in your own favor—the very definition of intelligent option investing.

Intelligent Option Investing

In my experience, most stocks are mostly fairly priced most of the time. There may be scenarios at one tail or the other that might be inappropriately priced by the option market (and, by extension, by the stock market), but by and large, it is difficult to find profoundly mispriced assets—an asset whose market price is significantly different from its most likely valuation layer.

Opportunities tend to be most compelling when the short-term picture is the most uncertain. Short-term uncertainties make investing boldly a psychologically difficult process, but indeed, it is those times that make the difference between a successful investor and an investor who nurtures many regrets.

In the end, an intelligent option investor is not one who has a much better knowledge of some sector, industry, or even company. It is not the investor who takes the biggest risks in the hope of realizing the biggest return. It is not the investor who attempts always to be the investing "hero" and make the most complex, theoretically beautiful, laboriously researched argument to justify an investment. Rather, the intelligent option investor is the one who has a sound, repeatable process for estimating the value of stocks, an understanding of the pitfalls that can limit an investor's potential, and a firm understanding of the tools that can be used to invest. It is the investor who understands the limits to his or her own expertise but who also understands that market risk does not equal valuation risk and has the courage to act boldly when the two deviate the most.

In short, the intelligent option investor is *you.*

Appendix A

CHOOSE YOUR BATTLES WISELY

I discuss specific option investment strategies in great detail in Part III of this book. However, after reading Chapters 2 and 3, you should have a good understanding of how options are priced, so it is a good time to see in what circumstances the Black-Scholes-Merton model (BSM) works best and where it works worst. An intelligent investor looks to avoid the conditions where the BSM works best like the plague and seek out the conditions where it works worst because those cases offer the best opportunities to tilt the risk-reward balance in the investor's favor.

Jargon introduced in this appendix includes

Front month
Fungible
Idiosyncratic assets

Where the BSM Works Best

The following are the situations in which the BSM works best and are the conditions you should most avoid:

1. Short investment time horizons
2. Fungible investment assets

Short Investment Time Horizons

When the scholars developing the BSM were researching financial markets for the purpose of developing their model, the longest-tenor options had expirations only a few months distant. Most market participants tended to trade in the *front-month* contracts (i.e., the contracts that will expire first), as is still mainly the case. Indeed, thinking back to our preceding discussion about price randomness, over short time horizons, it is very difficult to prove that asset price movements are not random.

As such, the BSM is almost custom designed to handle short time horizons well.

Perhaps not unsurprisingly, agents[1] are happy to encourage clients to trade options with short tenors because

1. It gives them more opportunities per year to receive fees and commissions from their clients.
2. They are mainly interested in reliably generating income on the basis of the bid-ask spread, and bid-ask spreads differ on the basis of liquidity, not time to expiration.
3. Shorter time frames offer fewer chances for unexpected price movements in the underlying that the market makers have a hard time hedging.

In essence, a good option market maker is akin to a used car salesman. He knows that he can buy at a low price and sell at a high one, so his main interest is in getting as many customers to transact as possible. With this perspective, the market maker is happy to use the BSM, which seems to give reasonable enough option valuations over the time period about which he most cares.

In the case of short-term option valuations, the theory describes reality accurately enough, and structural forces (such as wide bid-ask spreads) make it hard to exploit mispricings if and when they occur. To see an example of this, let's take a look at what the BSM assumes is a reasonable range of prices for a company with assumed 20 percent volatility over a period of 30 days.

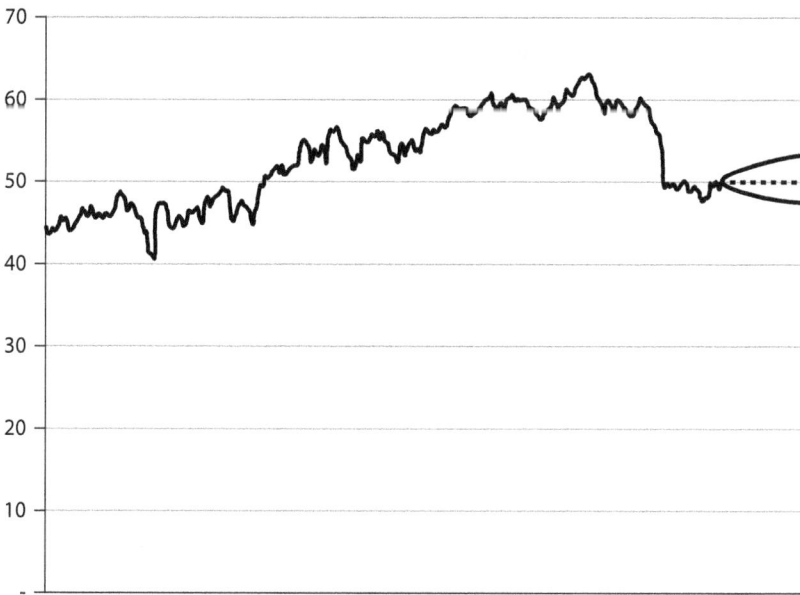

The range of prices implied over the next 30 days goes from around $47 per share to around $53 per share. If we translate what the BSM considers the reasonable range into percentage terms, it works out to a loss or gain of around 6 percent. Just thinking about this in terms of one's personal experience for a moment, this is actually not a bad guess for a range for a large-capitalization firm (the forward volatility assumption of 20 percent is consistent with a large-cap firm's "typical" implied volatility). I certainly would have no confidence in trying to guess the upper and lower stock price boundaries any better than the BSM on such a short time frame.

It is funny, then, that most investors insist on speculating in options on a short-term basis—usually at tenors of a month or shorter. Again, these seem like the kinds of bets you might get betting on red at a roulette wheel in Vegas. Sure, it makes one feel like James Bond the 50 percent of the time that the marble falls on red, but anyone who is the least bit thoughtful would, after a time, step back and wonder how far ahead he or she is getting by playing such a game.[2]

It is important to realize that the fact that options are usually efficiently priced in the short term does not prevent us from transacting in short-tenor options. In fact, some strategies discussed in Part III are actually more attractive when an investor uses shorter-tenor options or combines short- and long-tenor options into a single strategy.

Hopefully, the distinction between avoiding short-tenor option strategies and making long-term investments in short-tenor options is clear after reading through Part III.

Fungible Underlying Assets

Again, returning for a moment to the foundation of the BSM, the scholars built their mathematical models by studying short-term agricultural commodity markets. A commodity is, by definition, a *fungible* or *interchangeable* asset; one bushel of corn of a certain quality rating is completely indistinguishable from any other bushel of corn of the same quality rating.

Stocks, on the other hand, are *idiosyncratic assets*. They are intangible markers of value for incredibly complex systems called companies, no two of which is exactly alike (e.g., GM and Ford—the pair that illustrates the idea of "paired" investments in many people's minds—are both American car companies, but as operating entities, they have some significant differences. For example, GM has a much larger presence in China and has a different capital and governance structure since going bankrupt than Ford, which avoided bankruptcy during the mortgage crisis).

The academics who built the BSM were not hesitant to apply a model that would value idiosyncratic assets such as stocks because they had assumed from the start that financial markets are efficient—meaning that every idiosyncratic feature for a given stock was already fully "priced in" by the market. This allowed them to overlook the complexity of individual companies and treat them as interchangeable, homogeneous entities.

The BSM, then, did not value idiosyncratic, multidimensional companies; rather, it valued single-dimensional entities that the scholars assumed had already been "standardized" or commoditized in some sense by the communal wisdom of the markets. You will see in the next section that the broad, implicit assumption by option market participants that markets are efficient actually brings about the greatest opportunity to derive low-risk profits for intelligent investors. The point I make here is simply how difficult it is to invest in options on commodities or in fact any asset that you cannot analyze using fundamental valuation techniques.

For investors who simply cannot resist making commodity investments, I offer the following case study: I personally believe that climate change will make it harder for the world to feed its burgeoning population. Among exchange-traded funds (ETFs), futures, and options, it is very easy these days to express an investment opinion on such a belief, and I have done just that—put my money where my mouth is. While I have made such investments, I must admit that I have absolutely no basis for my valuation of the agricultural commodities in question and have no way to know if I have received my bullish exposure to these commodities at a reasonable or unreasonable price.

Such speculative investments satisfy some psychological need, but they are not investments in the strict "intelligent investor" sense because it is very hard to rationally calculate a fair value for the asset. Should these types of investments not be made, then? A strict adherent to rational investment principles might say, "No, they should not be." However, considering the irrational ways people find to spend money, it would seem that we have been somehow hardwired to do things in a way that an economist would not consider totally rational. Rather than fight that primitive urge, I prefer to give into it—but only with very small parts of my portfolio. This strategy is akin to taking only $50 to the casino floor and promising that once that money is gone, you won't spend any more.

You may have a gut feeling about the price of oil, the level of interest rates, the price of cotton, or whatever. Do yourself a favor, and if you chose to make a financial bet on the basis of your hunch, do as I do and make it a small one. While a small investment means different things to different people, a good way to judge is to imagine the capital being completely gone. If you have heart palpitations at that thought, keep cutting the prospective investment in half until you feel better.

Where the BSM Works Worst

Now that we know where not to look for intelligent option investments, let's look at conditions in which the BSM works worst—these are the best places for us to tilt the balance of risk and return in our favor.

1. Grossly mispriced assets
2. Bimodal outcomes
3. Long investment time horizons

Grossly Mispriced Assets

The main assumption of the BSM is that there are no grossly mispriced assets. I believe that this contention is wrong on the basis of behavioral and structural factors that are covered briefly in Part II of this book but would require another book to fully cover.

Just imagine, though, that, for some reason, a stock is dramatically undervalued. For right now, I will not discuss why this situation could come about, but let's say that rather than being worth $50 per share, a company is worth, best case, closer to $110 per share and, worst case, $70 per share. Let's further say that we had some sort of a hazy crystal ball that would give us a very high degree of certainty that these best- and worst-case values represent the real future range of values.

Here is what a diagram of that situation would look like:

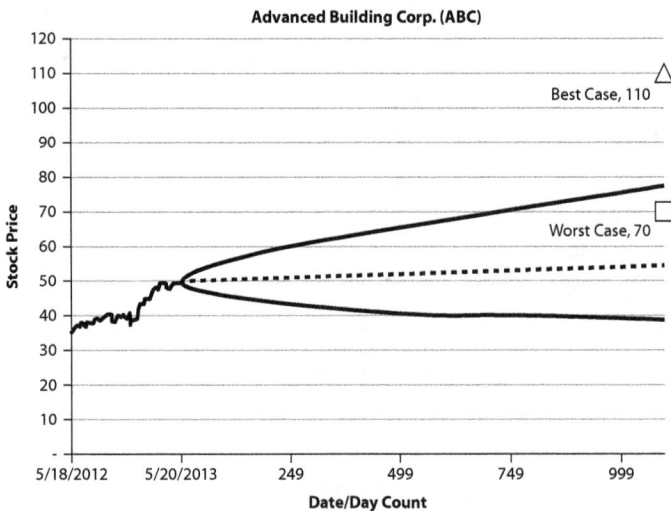

Now look at the following diagrams of a put and a call option and, based on what you know about the way the BSM prices options, think about the answers to the following questions.

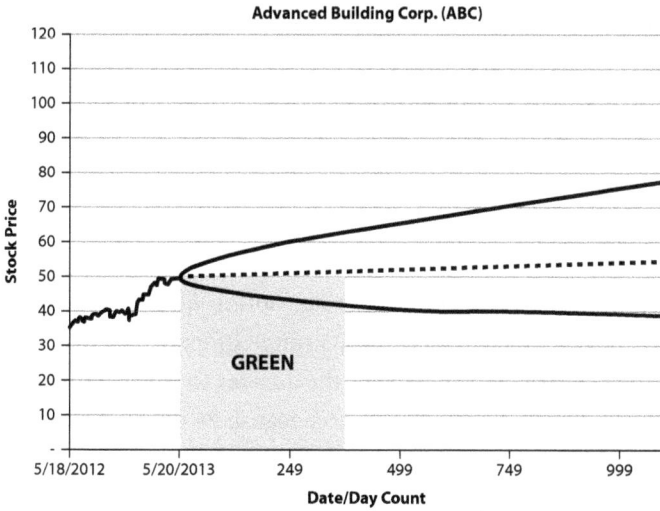

Put option

If someone were worried about this stock's downside potential below $50, what would likely be the price that investor would pay to buy this put option?

a. Almost nothing
b. A little
c. A good bit

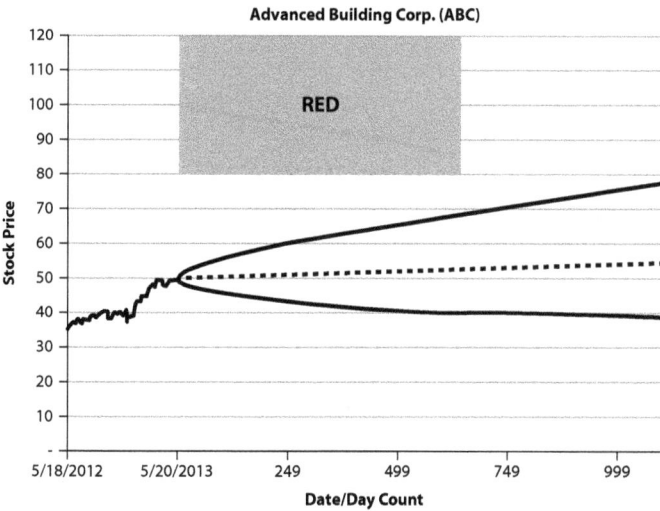

Call option

If someone wanted to make extra income by selling calls to accept exposure to the stock's upside, what price would they likely charge for someone wanting to buy this call option?

- a. Almost nothing
- b. A little
- c. A good bit

Obviously, the correct answer to the put option question is c. This option would be pretty expensive because its range of exposure overlaps with so much of the BSM cone. Conversely, the answer to the call option question is a. This option would be really cheap because its range of exposure is well above the BSM cone.

Remember, though, that we have our crystal ball, and we know that this stock will likely be somewhere between $70 and $110 per share in a few years. With this confidence, wouldn't it make sense to take the opposite side of both the preceding trades? Doing so would look like this:

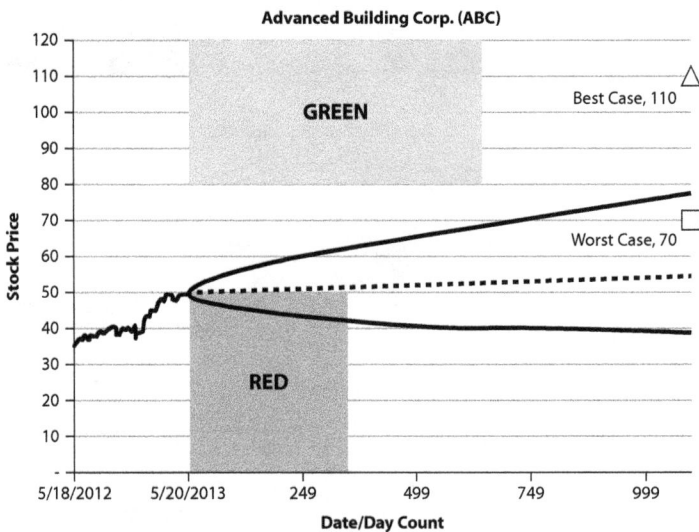

In this investment, which I explain in detail in Chapter 11, we are receiving a good bit of money by selling an expensive put and paying very little money to buy a cheap call. It may happen that the money we receive for selling the put actually may be greater than the money we pay for the call, so we actually get paid a net fee when we make this transaction!

We can sell the put confidently because we know that our worst-case valuation is $70 per share; as long as we are confident in our valuation—a topic covered in Part II of this book—we need not worry about the price declining. We do not mind spending money on the call because we think that the chance is very good that at expiration or before the call will be worth much, much more than we paid for it.

Truly, the realization that the BSM is pricing options on inefficiently priced stocks as if they were efficiently priced is the most profound and compelling source of profits for intelligent investors. Furthermore, finding grossly mispriced stocks and exploiting the mispricing using options represents the most compelling method for tilting the risk-reward equation in our direction.

The wonderful thing about investing is that it does not require you to swing at all the pitches. Individual investors have a great advantage in that they may swing at only the pitches they know they can hit. The process of intelligent investing is simply one of finding the right pitches, and intelligent option investing simply uses an extremely powerful bat to hit that sweet pitch.

Bimodal Outcomes

Some companies are speculative by nature—for instance, a drug company doing cancer research. The company has nothing but some intangible assets (the ideas of the scientists working there) and a great deal of costs (the salaries going to those scientists, the payments going to patent attorneys, and the considerable costs of paying for clinical trials). If the research proves fruitful, the company's value is great—let's say $500 per share. If the clinical trials show low efficacy or dangerous side effects, however, the company's worth goes to virtually nil. What's more, it may take years before it is clear which of these alternatives is true.

Given what you know about the BSM, does this seem like the kind of situation conducive to accurate option pricing? This example certainly does not sound like the pricing scenario of a short-term agricultural commodity, after all. If this hypothetical drug company's stock price was sitting at $50 per share, what is the value of the upper range the option market might be pricing in? Let's assume that this stock is trading with a forward volatility of 100 percent per year (on the day I am writing this, there are only four stocks with options trading at a price that implies a forward volatility of greater than 100 percent). What price range does this 100 percent per year volatility imply, and can we design an option structure that would allow us to profit from a big move in either direction? Here is a diagram of this situation:

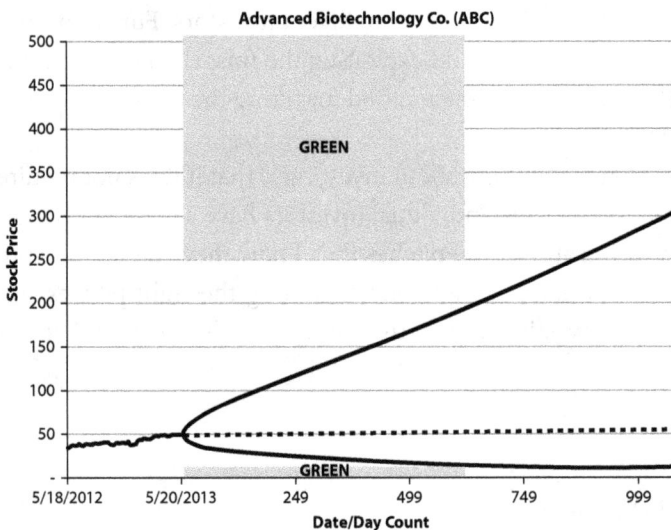

Indeed, even boosting volatility assumptions to a very high level, it seems that we can still afford to gain exposure to both the upside and downside of this stock at a very reasonable price. You can see from the preceding diagram that both regions of exposure on the put side and the call side are outside the BSM cone, meaning that they will be relatively cheap. The options market is trying to boost the price of the options enough so that the calls and puts are fairly priced, but for various reasons (including behavioral biases), most of the time it fails miserably.

Long Investment Time Horizons

This is simply a corollary to the rule that the BSM is generally good at pricing short-time-horizon investments. The BSM is built on the premise that stocks will only rise by as much as the risk-free rate. If you ask a finance professor or a market maker, he or she will be able to give you an elegant and logically consistent reason why this must be so.

However, as you saw in Chapter 3, this situation has never been so—the return on stocks is sometimes negative but often much more positive than risk-free bonds. If we average the returns out, stocks still generate returns that are heads and shoulders above bonds.

Over short time horizons, the difference simply isn't material. For instance, let's say that we assume that a given stock should generate around 10 percent compound annual returns over the next three to five years compared with a 5 percent assumption for the risk-free rate. If we are looking at very short time horizons—such as 60 days—and assume that our stock will grow at exactly that 10 percent rate over that short time, then we should compare our expectations with those of the option market. Here is the diagram we would get:

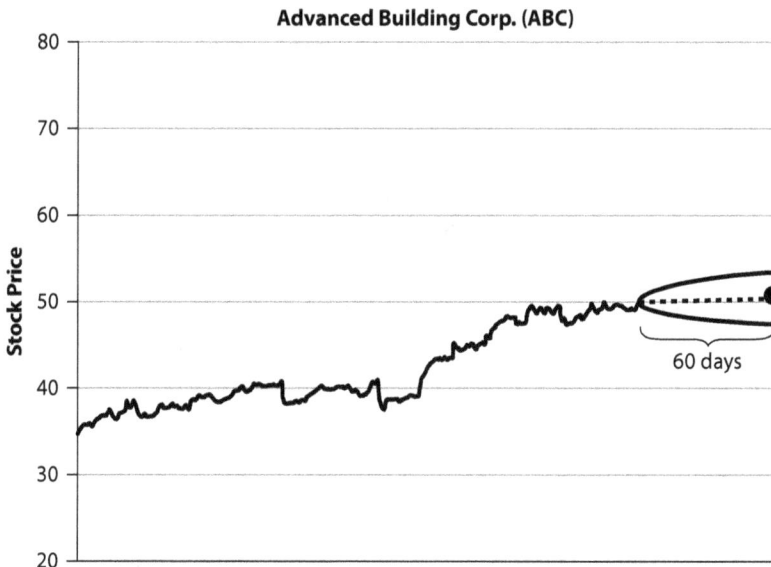

Advanced Building Corp. (ABC)

Clearly, there is not much of a difference between the BSM expected value (shown by the dotted line) and the dot representing a 10 percent upward drift in the stock. However, if we extend this analysis out for three years, look what happens:

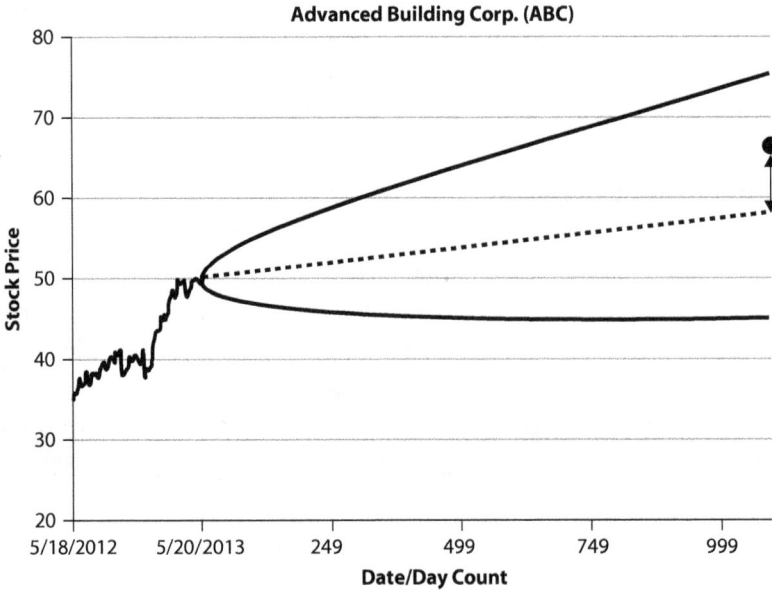

Advanced Building Corp. (ABC)

With the longer time horizon, our assumed stock price is significantly higher than what the BSM calculates as its expected price. If we take "assumed future stock price" to mean the price at which we think there is an equal chance that the true stock price will be above or below that mark, we can see that the difference, marked by the double-headed arrow in the preceding diagram, is the advantage we have over the option market.[3] This advantage again means that downside exposure will be overvalued and upside exposure will be undervalued.

How, you may ask, can this discrepancy persist? Shouldn't someone figure out that these options are priced wrong and take advantage of an arbitrage opportunity? The two reasons why these types of opportunities tend to persist are

1. Most people active in the option market are trading on a very short-term basis. Long-term equity anticipated securities (LEAPS)—options with tenors of a year or more—do exist, but

generally the volumes are light because the people in the option markets generally are not willing to wait longer than 60 days for their "investment" to work out. Because the time to expiration for most option contracts is so short, the difference between the BSM's expected price based on a 5 percent risk-free rate and an expected price based on a 10 percent equity return is small, so no one realizes that it's there (as seen on the first diagram).

2. The market makers are generally able to hedge out what little exposure they have to the price appreciation of LEAPS. They don't care about the price of the underlying security, only about the size of the bid-ask spread, and they always price the bid-ask spread on LEAPS in as advantageous a way as they can. Also, the career of an equity option trader on the desk of a broker-dealer can change a great deal in a single year. As discussed in Part II, market makers are not incentivized in such a way that they would ever care what happened over the life of a LEAPS.

Congratulations. After reading Part I of this book and this appendix, you have a better understanding of the implications of option investing for fundamental investors than most people working on Wall Street. There are many more nuances to options that I discuss in Part III of this book—especially regarding leverage and the sensitivity of options to input changes—but for now, simply understanding how the BSM works puts you at a great advantage over other market participants.

Appendix B

THE MANY FACES OF LEVERAGE

An intelligent option investor must understand investing leverage in order to make sense of option investing strategies. Investing leverage is, however, not the only form of leverage, and to have a well-rounded and well-educated view of investing leverage, you should understand the other forms as well. In addition, when assessing the value of companies, it is important to understand leverage because leverage often is the root cause of rapid changes in profitability during times of changing consumer demand such as inflection points in the business cycle.

Operational Leverage

Operational leverage is the acceptance of fixed operating costs in order to make a higher per-unit profit, such as when a company decides to build a factory rather than contracting for its products to be made by a third party. When a company spends cash to build a factory, that expenditure is not treated as an immediate cost on the income statement. Rather, the cost of the new factory is spread over future periods as the noncash expense known as *depreciation*.[1]

Let us take a look at two companies, both of which produce the same items, but one of which outsources production to a third party (Unlevered Co.) and the other of which has built a factory to manufacture its products

(Levered Co.). In reality, there are methods used by companies to front-load depreciation expenses in order to minimize taxable income for new projects, but let's assume that Levered Co. is using what is called *straight-line depreciation* so that the charge is identical each quarter.

	Unlevered Co.	Levered Co.
Revenues	100.0	100.0
Fixed depreciation expense	0.0	−65.0
Variable operating expenses	−85.0	−15.0
Operating profit	15.0	20.0
Pretax profit	15.0	20.0
Tax	−4.5	−6.0
Net profit	10.5	14.0

As you can see here, Levered Co.'s profits are a bit better than those of Unlevered Co. because the former is not paying a supplier and can produce the items at a lower cost. Note also that both companies have variable costs. For Unlevered Co., these variable costs include the costs of the items it has produced by the third party plus whatever salaries it has to pay to salespeople and administrative staff; for Levered Co., variable costs include the costs of raw materials plus the cost of any salaries paid to production, sales, and administrative staff. This is our base case—representing midcycle economic conditions (i.e., not boom or not bust).

Now let's look at the two companies during a trough in the business cycle—or bust conditions.

	Unlevered Co.	Levered Co.
Revenues	70.0	70.0
Fixed depreciation expense	0.0	−65.0
Variable operating expenses	−59.5	−10.5
Operating profit	10.5	−5.5
Pretax profit	10.5	−5.5
Tax	−3.2	+1.6
Net profit	7.3	−3.9

Costs at Unlevered Co. decrease proportionally to the decrease in revenues, so the operating profit margin is the same in its case. However, for Levered Co., even though the variable costs decrease proportionally to the decrease in revenues, the cost of depreciation stays fixed, causing a loss that is only slightly ameliorated through a small tax benefit.

Thus, obviously, in business-cycle trough conditions, profitability is hurt through the assumption of operational leverage. Let's take a look at what happens to both companies in peak conditions.[2]

	Unlevered Co.	Levered Co.
Revenues	130.0	130.0
Fixed depreciation expense	0.0	−65.0
Variable operating expenses	−110.5	−19.5
Operating profit	19.5	45.5
Pretax profit	19.5	45.5
Tax	−5.9	−13.6
Net profit	13.6	31.9

Obviously, having the operational leverage during peak times is a wonderful thing. After the fixed-cost hurdle of depreciation is cleared, each extra widget produced allows the company to generate profits that are governed solely by variable costs. Unlevered Co. is in a better position when there is a downturn, but its profitability falls behind Levered Co.'s more and more the better economic conditions are.

When thinking about the valuation of companies, we must remember what a large effect operational leverage can have on operations. Financial markets usually underestimate the effects of operational leverage both when the business cycle is at its peak and when it is at its trough. At the peak, analysts are wont to extrapolate high margins out forever and ignore the possibility that the sword of leverage swings both ways. At the trough, analysts are overly pessimistic and forget that a small improvement in demand can have a very large impact on financial results.

Operational leverage is neither good nor bad—it is merely a strategic business choice that has different implications during different parts of the business cycle and under different revenue conditions. An intelligent investor understands this fact and is happy to invest when the rest of the market has forgotten it.

Financial Leverage

Financial leverage involves the acceptance of fixed financial costs such as a loan or a lease contract to fund a business. Considering the expense of building factories, usually operational and financial leverage occur simultaneously, but to understand financial leverage itself, let's look at two companies that, other than the amount of debt on their balance sheets, are exactly the same in terms of revenues and profit margin. Our base case shows that the unlevered company will generate a higher absolute profit because it does not have the fixed financing costs.

	Unlevered Co.	Levered Co.
Revenues	100.0	100.0
Operating expenses	−80.0	−80.0
Operating profit	20.0	20.0
Interest expense	0.0	−15.0
Pretax profit	20.0	5.0
Tax	−6.0	−1.5
Net profit	14.0	3.5

Now let's increase revenues for both companies by 50 percent and see what happens.

	Unlevered Co.	Levered Co.
Revenues	150.0	150.0
Operating expenses	−120.0	−120.0
Operating profit	30.0	30.0
Interest expense	0.0	−15.0
Pretax profit	30.0	15.0
Tax	−9.0	−4.5
Net profit	21.0	11.5

The absolute profit is still higher for the unlevered company, but the percentage change from the first case to the second shows a big difference. The unlevered company's profits increased by 50 percent (from 14.0 to 21.0) with a 50 percent rise in revenues. However, the levered company's profits increased by a whopping 229 percent (from 3.5 to 11.5) with the same 50 percent rise in revenues.

Here we see an example of a defining characteristic of financial and investment leverage; that is, these sorts of leverage affect percentage calculations, but in absolute terms, unlevered transactions always generate more for a fixed level of exposure. We explore this concept in great detail when we discuss investment leverage in Chapter 8.

To see the dangerous side of leverage's double-edged sword, let's look at a case where revenues drop 50 percent from the original baseline.

	Unlevered Co.	Levered Co.
Revenues	50.0	50.0
Operating expenses	−40.0	−40.0
Operating profit	10.0	10.0
Interest expense	0.0	−15.0
Pretax profit	10.0	−5.0
Tax	−3.0	+1.5
Net profit	7.0	−3.5

Here we see that even with the tax benefit for the levered company, it is still running at a loss because of the fixed financial costs, whereas the unlevered company is still realizing a gain. In a worst-case scenario, fixed financial costs can exceed the cash coming into the business, leading to debt default and, depending on the situation, bankruptcy.

Thinking about the best and worst cases from an investment perspective for a moment, you can see why some equity investors actually prefer a highly levered firm: the higher the leverage, the greater is the incremental profit for equity holders when times are good. For a levered company that is in transition from bad to good—whether due to an upturn in economic conditions during a business cycle or a company-specific issue such as the introduction of a new product line boosting a flagging legacy business— a small improvement in business conditions creates a big improvement in profits available to shareholders. The flip side is that when business conditions turn downward—a transition from good to bad—a levered company's fall from profitability to loss is sudden, and its stock price fall can be even worse. The fact is that just in the case of operational leverage, financial leverage is not good or bad—it is simply a strategic business choice that has different implications in different situations.

Appendix C

PUT-CALL PARITY

Before the Black-Scholes-Merton model (BSM), there was no way to directly calculate the value of an option, but there was a way to triangulate put and call prices as long as one had three pieces of data:

1. The stock's price
2. The risk-free rate
3. The price of a call option to figure the fair price of the put, and vice versa

In other words, if you know the price of either the put or a call, as long as you know the stock price and the risk-free rate, you can work out the price of the other option. These four prices are all related by a specific rule termed *put-call parity*.

Put-call parity is only applicable to European options, so it is not terribly important to stock option investors most of the time. The one time it becomes useful is when thinking about whether to exercise early in order to receive a stock dividend—and that discussion is a bit more technical. I'll delve into those technical details in a moment, but first, let's look at the big picture. Using the intelligent option investor's graphic format employed in this book, the big picture is laughably trivial.

Direct your attention to the following diagrams. What is the difference between the two?

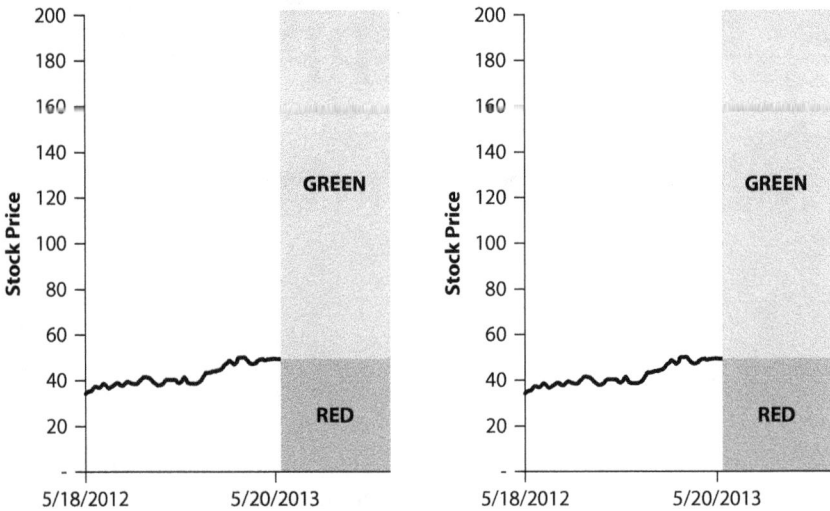

If you say, "Nothing," you are practically right but technically wrong. The image on the left is actually the risk-reward profile of a purchased call option struck at $50 paired with a sold put option struck at $50. The image on the right is the risk-reward profile of a stock trading at $50 per share.

This simple comparison is the essence of put-call parity. The *parity* part of put-call parity just means that accepting downside exposure by selling a put while gaining upside exposure by buying a call is basically the same thing as accepting downside exposure and gaining upside exposure by buying a stock.

What did I say? It is laughably trivial. Now let's delve into the details of how the put-call parity relationship can be used to help decide whether to exercise a call option or not (or whether the call option you sold is likely to be exercised or not).

Dividend Arbitrage and Put-Call Parity

Any time you see the word *arbitrage*, the first thing that should jump to mind is "small differences." Arbitrage is the science of observing small differences between two prices that should be the same (e.g., the price of IBM traded on the New York Stock Exchange and the price of IBM traded in Philadelphia) but are not. An arbitrageur, once he or she spots the small difference, sells the more expensive thing and buys the less expensive one and makes a profit without accepting any risk.

Because we are going to investigate dividend arbitrage, even a big-picture guy like me has to get down in the weeds because the differences we are going to try to spot are small ones. The weeds into which we are wading are mathematical ones, I'm afraid, but never fear—we'll use nothing more than a little algebra. We'll use these variables in our discussion:

K = strike price
C_K = call option struck at K
P_K = put option struck at K
Int = interest on a risk-free instrument
Div = dividend payment
S = stock price

Because we are talking about arbitrage, it makes sense that we are going to look at two things, the value of which should be the same. We are going to take a detailed look at the preceding image, which means that we are going to compare a position composed of options with a position composed of stock.

Let's say that the stock at which we were looking to build a position is trading at $50 per share and that options on this stock expire in exactly one year. Further, let's say that this stock is expected to yield $0.25 in dividends and that the company will pay these dividends the same day that the options expire.

Let's compare the two positions in the same way as we did in the preceding big-picture image. As we saw in that image, a long call and a short put are the same as a stock. Mathematically, we would express this as follows:

$$C_K - P_K = S_K$$

Although this is simple and we agreed that it's about right, it is not technically so.

The preceding equation is not technically right because we know that a stock is an unlevered instrument and that options are levered ones. In the preceding equation, we can see that the left side of the equation is levered (because it contains only options, and options are levered instruments), and the right side is unlevered. Obviously, then, the two cannot be exactly the same.

We can fix this problem by delevering the left side of the preceding equation. Any time we sell a put option, we have to place cash in a margin account with our broker. Recall that a short put that is fully margined is an unlevered instrument, so margining the short put should delever the entire option position. Let's add a margin account to the left side and put $K in it:

$$C_K - P_K + K = S$$

This equation simply says that if you sell a put struck at K and put $K worth of margin behind it while buying a call option, you'll have the same risk, return, and leverage profile as if you bought a stock—just as in our big-picture diagram.

But this is not quite right if one is dealing with small differences. First, let's say that you talk your broker into funding the margin account using a risk-free bond fund that will pay some fixed amount of interest over the next year. To fund the margin account, you tell your broker you will buy enough of the bond account that one year from now, when the put expires, the margin account's value will be exactly the same as the strike price. In this way, even by placing an amount less than the strike price in your margin account originally, you will be able to fulfill the commitment to buy the stock at the strike price if the put expires in the money (ITM). The amount that will be placed in margin originally will be the strike price less the amount of interest you will receive from the risk-free bond. In mathematical terms, the preceding equation becomes

$$C_K - P_K + (K - \text{Int}) = S$$

Now all is right with the world. For a non-dividend-paying stock, this fully expresses the technical definition of put-call parity.

However, because we are talking about dividend arbitrage, we have to think about how to adjust our equation to include dividends. We know that a call option on a dividend-paying stock is worth less because the dividend acts as a "negative drift" term in the BSM. When a dividend is paid, theory says that the stock price should drop by the amount of the dividend. Because a drop in price is bad for the holder of a call option, the price of a call option is cheaper by the amount of the expected dividend.

Thus, for a dividend-paying stock, to establish an option-based position that has exactly the same characteristics as a stock portfolio, we have to keep the expected amount of the dividend in our margin account.[1] This money placed into the option position will make up for the dividend that will be paid to the stock holder. Here is how this would look in our equation:

$$C_K - P_K + (K - \text{Int}) + \text{Div} = S$$

With the dividend payment included, our equation is complete.

Now it is time for some algebra. Let's rearrange the preceding equation to see what the call option should be worth:

$$C_K = P_K + \text{Int} - \text{Div} + (S - K)$$

Taking a look at this, do you notice last term $(S - K)$? A stock's price minus the strike price of a call is the intrinsic value. And we know that the value of a call option consists of intrinsic value and time value. This means that

$$C_K = \underbrace{P_K + \text{Int} - \text{Div}}_{\text{Time value}} + \underbrace{(S - K)}_{\text{Intrinsic value}}$$

So now let's say that time passes and at the end of the year, the stock is trading at $70—deep ITM for our $50-strike call option. On the day before expiration, the time value will be very close to zero as long as the option is deep ITM. Building on the preceding equation, we can put the rule about the time value of a deep ITM option in the following mathematical equation:

$$P_K + \text{Int} - \text{Div} \approx 0$$

If the time value ever falls below 0, the value of the call would trade for less than the intrinsic value. Of course, no one would want to hold an option that has negative time value. In mathematical terms, that scenario would look like this:

$$P_K + \text{Int} - \text{Div} < 0$$

From this equation, it follows that if

$$P_K + \text{Int} < \text{Div}$$

your call option has a negative implied time value, and you should sell the option in order to collect the dividend.

This is what is meant by *dividend arbitrage*. But it is hard to get the flavor for this without seeing a real-life example of it. The following table shows the closing prices for Oracle's stock and options on January 9, 2014, when they closed at $37.72. The options had an expiration of 373 days in the future—as close as I could find to one year—the one-year risk-free rate was 0.14 percent, and the company was expected to pay $0.24 worth of dividends before the options expired.

Calls				Puts		
Bid	Ask	Delta	Strike	Bid	Ask	Delta
19.55	19.85	0.94	18	0.08	0.13	−0.02
17.60	17.80	0.94	20	0.13	0.15	−0.03
14.65	14.85	0.92	23	0.25	0.28	−0.05
12.75	12.95	0.91	25	0.36	0.39	−0.07
10.00	10.25	0.86	28	0.66	0.69	−0.12
8.30	8.60	0.81	30	0.97	1.00	−0.17
6.70	6.95	0.76	32	1.40	1.43	−0.23
4.70	4.80	0.65	35	2.33	2.37	−0.34
3.55	3.65	0.56	37	3.15	3.25	−0.43
2.22	2.26	0.42	40	4.80	4.90	−0.57
1.55	1.59	0.33	42	6.15	6.25	−0.65
0.87	0.90	0.22	45	8.25	8.65	−0.75
0.31	0.34	0.10	50	12.65	13.05	−0.87

In the theoretical option portfolio, we are short a put, so its value to us is the amount we would have to pay if we tried to flatten the position by buying it back—the ask price. Conversely, we are long a call, so its value to us is the price we could sell it for—the bid price.

Let's use these data to figure out which calls we might want to exercise early if a dividend payment was coming up.

Strike	Call	Put (a)	Interest[2] (b)	Put + Interest (a + b)	Dividend	P + I − D	Notes
18	19.55	0.13	0.03	0.16	0.24	(0.08)	$P + I < D$, arbitrage
20	17.60	0.15	0.03	0.18	0.24	(0.06)	$P + I < D$, arbitrage
23	14.65	0.28	0.03	0.31	0.24	0.07	No arbitrage
25	12.75	0.39	0.04	0.43	0.24	0.19	No arbitrage
28	10.00	0.69	0.04	0.73	0.24	0.49	No arbitrage
30	8.30	1.00	0.04	1.04	0.24	0.80	No arbitrage
32	6.70	1.43	0.05	1.48	0.24	1.24	No arbitrage
35	4.70	2.37	0.05	2.42	0.24	2.18	No arbitrage
37	3.55	3.25	0.05	3.30	0.24	3.06	No arbitrage
40	2.22	4.90	0.06	4.96	0.24	4.72	No arbitrage
42	1.55	6.25	0.06	6.31	0.24	6.07	No arbitrage
45	0.87	8.65	0.06	8.71	0.24	8.47	No arbitrage
50	0.31	13.05	0.07	13.12	0.24	12.88	No arbitrage

There are only two strikes that might be arbitraged for the dividends—the two furthest ITM call options. In order to realize the arbitrage opportunity, you would wait until the day before the ex-dividend date, exercise the stock option, receive the dividend, and, if you didn't want to keep holding the stock, sell it and realize the profit.

NOTES

Introduction

1. *Options, Futures, and Other Derivatives* by John C. Hull (New York: Prentice Hall, Eighth Edition, February 12, 2011), is considered the Bible of the academic study of options.
2. *Option Volatility and Pricing* by Sheldon Natenberg (New York: McGraw-Hill, Updated and Expanded Edition, August 1, 1994), is considered the Bible of professional option traders.
3. The Greeks are measures of option sensitivity used by traders to manage risk in portfolios of options. They are named after the Greek symbols used in the Black-Scholes-Merton option pricing model.
4. "To invest successfully over a lifetime does not require a stratospheric IQ, unusual business insights, or inside information. What's needed is a sound intellectual framework for making decisions and the ability to keep emotions from corroding that framework." Preface to *The Intelligent Investor* by Benjamin Graham (New York: Collins Business, Revised Edition, February 21, 2006).

Chapter 1

1. In other words, if all option contracts were specific and customized, every time you wanted to trade an option contract as an individual investor, you would have to first find a counterparty to take the other side of the trade and then do due diligence on the counterparty to make sure that he or she would be able to fulfill his or her side of the bargain. It is hard to imagine small individual investors being very interested in the logistical headaches that this process would entail!

2. One more bit of essential but confusing jargon when investing in options is related to exercise. There are actually two styles of exercise; one can be exercised at any time before expiration—these are termed *American style*—and the other can only be exercised at expiration— termed *European style*. Confusingly, these styles have nothing to do about the home country of a given stock or even on what exchange they are traded. American-style exercise is normal for all single-stock options, whereas European-style exercise is normal for index futures. Because this book deals almost solely with single-stock options (i.e., options on IBM or GOOG, etc.), I will not make a big deal out of this distinction. There is one case related to dividend-paying stocks where American-style exercise is beneficial. This is discussed in Appendix C. Most times, exercise style is not a terribly important thing.
3. Just like going to Atlantic City, even though the nominal odds for rou- lette are 50:50, you end up losing money in the long run because you have to pay—the house at Atlantic City or the broker on Wall Street— just to play the game.

Chapter 3

1. We adjusted and annualized the prices of actual option contracts so that they would correspond to the probability levels we mentioned earlier. It would be almost impossible to find a stock trading at exactly $50 and with the option market predicting exactly the range of future price that we have shown in the diagrams. This table is provided simply to give you an idea of what one might pay for call options of different moneyness in the open market.
2. Eighty-four percent because the bottom line marks the price at which there is only a 16 percent chance that the stock will go any lower. If there is a 16 percent chance that the stock will be lower than $40 in one year's time, this must mean that there is an 84 percent chance that the stock will be higher than $40 in one year's time. We write "a little better than 84 percent chance" because you'll notice that the stock price corresponding to the bottom line of the cone is around $42—a little higher than the strike price. The $40 mark might corre- spond to a chance of, let's say, 13 percent that the stock will be lower;

this would, in turn, imply an 87 percent chance of being higher than $40 in a year.

3. *Tenor* is just a specialty word used for options and bonds to mean the remaining time before expiration/maturity. We will see later that option tenors usually range from one month to one year and that special long-term options have tenors of several years.

4. We're not doing any advanced math to figure this out. We're just eyeballing the area of the exposure range within the cone in this diagram and recalling that the area within the cone of the $60 strike, one-year option was about the same.

5. In other words, in this style of trading, people are anchoring on recent implied volatilities—rather than on recent statistical volatilities—to predict future implied volatilities.

6. Note that even though this option is now ITM, we did not pay for any intrinsic value when we bought the option. As such, we are shading the entire range of exposure in green.

Chapter 4

1. The "capital" we have discussed so far is strategic capital. There is another form of tactical capital that is vital to companies, termed *working capital.* Working capital consists of the short-term assets essential for running a business (e.g., inventory and accounts receivables) less the short-term liabilities accrued during the course of running the business (e.g., accounts payable). Working capital is tactical in the sense that it is needed for day-to-day operation of the business. A company may have the most wonderful productive assets in the world, but if it does not have the money to buy the inventory of raw materials that will allow it to produce its widgets, it will not be able to generate revenues because it will not be able to produce anything.

2. The *law of large numbers* is actually a law of statistics, but when most people in the investing world use this phrase, it is the colloquial version to which they are referring.

3. Apple Computer, for instance, was a specialized maker of computers mainly used by designers and artists in the late 1990s. Through some

inspired leadership and a large capital infusion from Microsoft to keep it afloat in its darkest days, Apple Computer changed its name to just Apple and began producing handheld music devices, smartphones, and other media appliances (including computers). By the late 1990s, Apple was facing severe structural constraints. The market in which it competed—the market for personal computers—had been commoditized, and prices did nothing but go down. It was clinging to a niche market of a few educational institutions and creative professionals—not a very robust or quickly growing market. However, the company was able to reinvent itself as a media technology company and media content provider using its investments and know-how in personal computing as a base. Doing so, Apple jumped from a mature company into a virtual startup and once again became a supply-constrained company in a very short period of time. This is a rare twist, but not unheard of.

4. Don't waste your time remembering this formula unless you already know it. You can always look up the exact equation when you need to use it. Just remember, "A dollar today is worth more than a dollar tomorrow."

5. If you are curious about the CAPM or any of the other related academic methods for determining discount rates, you have no further to go than your local library or various sources online. The CAPM is one of the pillars of modern finance, and there are plenty of resources to learn about it. In the end, though, the "proper" discount rate you will calculate will not be far off from these values. There are plenty of more important things on which to concentrate in a valuation, so my suggestion is to spend time on those and save learning about the CAPM.

Chapter 5

1. Note that, even though it may feel like it from a shareholder perspective, the period during which a company is making poor investments and generating substructural profit growth will only last for a limited time. Sooner or later, an activist investor or another company will acquire all or part of the capital stock of the underperforming company and run the enterprise in a more rational way.

2. For the structural stage, I usually only use one scenario. When I started in the business of valuation, I used 6 percent growth of cash flows in perpetuity. Recently, convinced by PIMCO's argument that we are entering an extended "new normal" period, I tend to use 5 percent instead.

3. For instance, a company may have only six very large and important customers, each of which it picked up in subsequent years. If it loses one of those customers, rather than +35 percent revenue growth over the next year, the revenue may decline by 20 percent. Or even if the company does not lose a customer, if it does not gain another, its revenue growth may be trivial—3 percent, let's say.

4. Please see the online materials for the specific formulas used for OCP and FCFO.

5. A person with a 100-share stake in Exxon—an investment worth just under $10,000—has a proportional stake of 0.000006 percent in the company. No wonder investors usually do not have a strong sense of being an owner of the companies in which they are invested.

6. In a counterexample, IBM's management should be commended for selling off the dying, undifferentiated PC business to Lenovo and realigning the tech giant as primarily a provider of software and services.

7. Networking behemoth Cisco Systems' (CSCO) purchase of Pure Digital (a company that made Flip video cameras) springs immediately to mind.

Chapter 6

1. The fact that a consensus of opinion is reached is an interesting social behavioral bias called *herding*. This bias, one that I will not go into great detail about here, is the tendency for people to be influenced by the actions or opinions of others when making a decision as a member of a group.

2. Paul Slovic, "Behavioral Problems of Adhering to a Decision Policy," paper presented at the Institute for Quantitative Research in Finance, Napa, CA, May 1, 1973.

3. This research report was quoted and summarized on the following site: http://www.valuewalk.com/2013/07/hedge-fund-alpha-negative/.

4. The original academic paper discussing prospect theory was published in *Econometrica*, Volume 47, Number 2, in March 1979 under the title: "Prospect Theory: An Analysis of Decision Under Risk."

5. Over the years, the paradigm for broker-dealers has changed, so some of what is written here is a bit dated. Broker-dealers have one part of its business dedicated to increasing customer "flow" as is described here. Over the last 20 years or so, however, they have additionally begun to capitalize what amounts to in-house hedge funds, called "proprietary trading desks" or "prop traders." While the prop traders are working on behalf of corporations that were historically known as broker-dealers (e.g., Goldman Sachs, Morgan Stanley), they are in fact buy-side institutions. In the interest of clarity in this chapter, I treat broker-dealers as purely sell-side entities even though they in fact have elements of both buy- and sell-sides.

Chapter 7

1. Round-tripping means buying a security and selling it later.
2. This bit of shorthand just means a bid volatility of 22.0 and an ask volatility of 22.5.

Chapter 8

1. This is one of the reasons why I called delta the most useful of the Greeks.
2. When I pulled these data, I pulled the 189-day options, so my chance of this stock hitting that high a price in this short time period is slim, but the point I am making here about percentage versus absolute returns still holds true.
3. A tool to calculate all the downside and upside leverage figures shown in this chapter is available on the intelligent option investor website.
4. "Buffett's Alpha," Andrea Frazzini, David Kabiller, and Lasse H. Pedersen, 2012, National Bureau of Economic Research, NBER Working Paper No. 19681.

Chapter 9

1. *Yale Alumni Magazine*, "The Fraud Detective," September/October 2013 Issue, http://www.yalealumnimagazine.com/articles/3737.

Chapter 10

1. This is, in fact, the crux of why U.S. taxpayers all got the opportunity to own a piece of AIG. One of the subsidiaries of AIG made commitments to carry out transactions that, with the collapse of the mortgage bubble, it had no ability to do. In this case, it was not a broker or exchange that had to bear the exposure to AIG's failure—the contracts AIG were trading were over-the-counter and thus not regulated by an exchange—it was the financial system at large and U.S. taxpayers in particular.
2. The fact that this strategy is unlevered means that percentage returns provide an accurate representation of the absolute wealth generated with the strategy. As we saw earlier, levered investments can show very high percentage returns, whereas absolute returns are not as great. This is not the case for short puts.
3. *Writing* an option means selling an option.
4. This is especially true for people investing in covered calls—a strategy I will discuss in Chapter 11 and that has the same risk-return profile as the short-put strategy.
5. Of course, there are other reasons for increased volatility during earnings seasons, and some of the volatility reflects issues that are material to valuation. In my opinion, though, the vast majority of information given at these times is helpful for understanding only a few months' worth of prospective business results and, as such, should not cause a material change in an intelligent investor's perception of long-run company value.
6. I am speaking here about the most attractive calls from a mathematical perspective, not a valuation one. I have not valued IBM and am most definitely not making an investment recommendation here. I used IBM because it is a liquid option with a good

many OTM strikes, not because I believe it's a bearish investment opportunity.

7. $100,000 × 5% = $5,000; $5,000/$196.80 per share = 25.4 shares.

Chapter 11

1. This is due to a statistical property known as *dispersion*. Dispersion—the fact that prices on many things do not usually move in lockstep with one another—is the root of all diversification strategies.

2. This assumes that crises are only temporary. Of course, structural or secular downturns are a different matter, and the whole process of investing must be done in a different way. In particular, conceptions of sensible terminal growth rates become vital during these times.

Chapter 12

1. I am indebted to Brent Farler for this image, which I think is really brilliant.

Appendix A

1. Refer to the discussion of investing agents and principals in Chapter 6.

2. It is only the nominal odds that are 50:50 anyway. The player always has to pay the house (and if you're James Bond, you must tip the dealer a cool million dollars), just as an investor must pay the broker. As such, the net odds are always against the owner of capital.

3. Remember that the dotted line in the BSM cone shows that 50:50 "expected" value. Because our expected value dot is much higher, this means that we are assigning a higher probability of that price occurring than is the option market as a whole.

Appendix B

1. The idea behind this process is to match the timing of the costs of equipment with revenues from the items produced with that equipment. This is a key principle of accountancy called *matching*.
2. The problem is that troughs, by definition, follow peaks. Usually, just like the timing of large acquisitions, companies decide to spend huge amounts to build new production capacity at just about the same time that economic conditions peak, and the factories come online just as the economy is starting to sputter and fail.

Appendix C

1. A penny saved is a penny earned. We can think of the option being cheaper by the amount of the dividend, so we will place the amount that we save on the call option in savings.
2. This is calculated using the following equation:

$$\text{Interest} = \text{strike} \times r \times \text{percent of 1 year}$$

In the case of the $18 strike, interest = $18 \times 0.14\% \times (373 \text{ days}/365 \text{ days per year}) = \$0.03$.

INDEX

A

Absolute dollar value of returns, 172–173
Accuracy, confidence vs., 119–121
Acquisitions (*see* Mergers and acquisitions)
Activist investors, 110
Against the Gods (Peter Bernstein), 9
Agents:
  buy-side, 132–136
  defined, 131
  investment strategies of, 137–138
  principals vs., 131–132
  sell-side, 136–137
AIG, 301n1
Allocation:
  and leverage in portfolios, 174–183
  and liquidity risk, 256
  and portfolio management with short-call spreads, 228–229
Alpha, 134
American-style options, 296n2 (Chapter 1)
Analysis paralysis, 120
Anchoring, 60, 97
Announcements:
  and creating BSM cones, 156, 157
  market conditions following, 68–69, 72–73
  tenor and trading in expectation of, 192
AOL, 103
Apple Computer, 101, 250–251, 297–298n3

Arbitrage:
  defined, 288–289
  dividend, 223, 288–293
Ask price, 147
Asset allocation, liquidity risk and, 256
Assets:
  defined, 78–79
  fungible, 272–273
  in golden rule of valuation, 77
  hidden, 110, 111
  idiosyncratic, 272
  interchangeable, 272–273
  mispriced, 274–277
  operating, 110
  price vs. value of, 79–80
  underlying, 33–34, 272–273
Assets under management (AUM), 132
Assignment:
  with covered calls, 247–248
  defined, 222–223
Assumptions:
  BSM model, 32–33, 40–47, 78, 150
  dividend yield, 67
  with forward volatility number, 156–157
  time-to-expiration, 64–67
  volatility, 60–64
At-the-money (ATM) options:
  BSM cone for, 53
  collars, 259
  covered calls, 242–243, 245, 246
  defined, 13, 16, 17
  long calls, 189
  long diagonals, 235–237

ABOUT THE AUTHOR

Erik Kobayashi-Solomon, a veteran from the investment banking and hedge fund world, is the founder and principal of IOI, LLC a financial consultancy for individual and institutional investors. In addition to publishing an institutional investor-focused subscription product, Erik runs option and investment "boot camps" and consults on risk control, option strategies, and stock valuations for individual and institutional investors.

Before starting IOI, Erik worked for Morningstar in its stock research department for over six years. At Morningstar, he first managed a team of semiconductor industry analysts before becoming the coeditor and driving force of Morningstar's *OptionInvestor* newsletter and serving as the company's Market Strategist.

In addition to coauthoring a guide to fundamental investing and option strategies used in the Morningstar Investor Training Options Course and popular weekly articles about using options as a tool for investment portfolios, Erik was the host of several popular webinars such as "Covered Calls A to Z" and "Hedging 101." His video lecture about avoiding behavioral and structural pitfalls called "Making Better Investment Decisions" was so popular that he was invited to be the featured speaker at several investment conferences throughout the United States. In addition, he represented Morningstar on television and radio, was interviewed by magazines and newspapers from Dallas to Tokyo to New Delhi, and was a frequent guest contributor to other Morningstar/Ibbotson publications.

Erik started his career in the world of finance at Morgan Stanley Japan, where he ultimately headed Morgan's listed derivatives operations in Tokyo. After returning to the United States, Erik founded a small hedge fund based on his original research in the field of Behavioral Finance and later became the Risk Manager for a larger investment fund. There, he designed option hedges for the fund's $800 million global equity portfolio and advised the portfolio manager on quantitative investment strategies and Japanese stock market investments.

Erik, the son of a NASA scientist father and a concert violinist mother, graduated *Magna Cum Laude* and *Phi Beta Kappa* from the University of Texas at Austin, where he majored in Asian Studies and Japanese. After working in Japan for several years as a teacher, translator, and television actor, he won a full-ride scholarship to study business at the number one ranked school for international business in the United States—Thunderbird—in Glendale, Arizona. There, he worked as a research assistant to Dr. Anant Sundaram (Finance, presently at Dartmouth) from whom he gained a love for finance and economics, Dr. Graeme Rankine (Accounting) who introduced him to Behavioral Finance, and Dr. Charles Neilson (Marketing) who taught him the importance of strategic thinking. Erik graduated *Summa Cum Laude* and was selected as the outstanding student of his graduating class.

Erik lives in Chicago, Illinois with his family and enjoys long distance running and reading. In his spare time, he volunteers at the local Japanese school to teach children Kendo—the Japanese art of swordsmanship.

www.ingramcontent.com/pod-product-compliance
Lightning Source LLC
Chambersburg PA
CBHW050454190326
41458CB00005B/1276